BRAND OF THE TARTAN

BRAND OF THE TARTAN

The  Story

by Virginia Huck

"The 3M Story"

is the history of a successful corporation, but it is more than
that. It is a tribute to the people who made such success possible, the employees of 3M, past and present, and its many
stockholders. The tremendous growth of Minnesota Mining
and Manufacturing Company is due to the ingenuity of
these men and women, their faith, industriousness, and
above all, their ability to work together down through the
years. Only a few of them can be mentioned by name in a
volume of this size, but the story reflects great credit on all
of them.

VIRGINIA HUCK

FOREWORD

The record of the Minnesota Mining and Manufacturing Company covers roughly 50 years, the first half of the present century. It thus coincides with the period of our economic history that began with the closing of the frontier.

The men who founded the company were not aware that they were pioneers of a new era. Indeed, they were under the impression that they were in the swing of the old tradition. They launched their venture on a misconception. They believed that they were the owners of a raw material of industrial value which they had only to exploit with wisdom and vigor to reap a reward similar to that which had come to so many Americans before them. They were mistaken, and in the story of the very great success made by these men and their successors is one of the most impressive examples in the industrial history of America of the contribution of free enterprise, backed by venturesome capital and imaginative management, to the power and wealth of the United States, and to the happiness and welfare of vast numbers of individuals.

Here was a company of entrepreneurs who thought they were embarking on a mining venture, who discovered that they had nothing of value to mine, and who thereupon became one of the great manufacturing enterprises of America. They began with an asset which turned out to be a liability. Their true assets were very different; they were the qualities of initiative and courage and insight which have served America so well in so many ways through its history.

The men who made the Minnesota Mining and Manufacturing Company great have almost literally created new wealth, new products, new jobs out of nothing except ideas, determination, and capital.

These men were motivated by a hope of profit and distinction. They risked money and invested their energies and talents. They were rewarded beyond their early hopes and expectations, and in their own enrichment, they have enriched the whole nation. But for them, or others like them, products that now add to the efficiency, convenience, and enjoyment of life would not exist. But for them, the thousands of jobs which this organization provides would not exist.

This book is the history of an American corporation, but it is also a good deal more than that. It is an unusually clear-cut case history in the practical operation of the American free-enterprise system.

CONTENTS

ILLUSTRATIONS

BRAND OF THE TARTAN

THE CORUNDUM PROPOSITION

MINING VENTURES were as common as pine trees in northern Minnesota following the discovery of iron ore in the rugged, densely forested land, yet every enterprise stirred fresh excitement and speculation. Wherever frontier settlers gathered, the conversation inevitably turned to prospecting and mining. Food for conversation was plentiful at the thimble bees, over the bunco tables, and in the saloons and logging camps along the shores of Lake Superior. Spurred by the success of the rich Vermilion and Mesabi iron mines, a multitude of self-styled explorers, bona fide geologists, and adventurous businessmen joined the search for iron, copper, silver, or any riches the land might yield. Each had a dream that he would find his fortune in the rich wilderness country. The slightest trace of a valuable mineral sent men scurrying to file Articles of Incorporation, and each new discovery sent hopes soaring and rumors flying.

Shortly after the turn of the century, one strange, new mining enterprise caused even greater than usual interest throughout the North Shore country. Up and down Lake Superior and inland as far as Tower to the northwest, and Virginia, Eveleth, and Hibbing to the west, word traveled that a valuable, nearly unknown mineral had been found in the rugged, rocky buttes bordering Lake Superior northeast of Two Harbors. It was reputedly as valuable as silver or gold, and soon news followed that five prominent North Shore men were selling stock in a company organized to exploit the new mineral. To buy or not to buy became a much discussed question.

Today, North Shore old-timers remember that strange, new mining enterprise simply as "the corundum proposition," for corundum was the name given the mineral discovery by its finders. Officially, the little North Shore venture that caused such a stir was known as Minnesota Mining and Manufacturing Company or, more familiarly, as just the "3M Company."

Legend has it that Minnesota Mining and Manufacturing Company was organized in Two Harbors, Minnesota; that the company mined corundum on the shores of Lake Superior, made sandpaper in an old garage in Two Harbors, and once mined copper as well as corundum. Many fabulous stories have circulated during the fifty-four years since the 3M Company was born. As usual, the legends bear only a slight resemblance to the truth, but in this case, the truth is more romantic than fiction. This book tells the fascinating and unique history of a company that was founded not only on a shoestring but a mistake, failed as a mining enterprise, brought its founders little but grief and yet, through the ingenuity, perseverance, diligence, and just plain luck of many men, grew into a $230,000,000 corporation.[1]

The 3M Company did begin in Two Harbors. That much is correct, and our story begins at the turn of the century in this thriving frontier village.

The conservative leading citizens of Two Harbors didn't want a boom, but, whether they liked it or not, the little frontier village was booming that spring when the corundum proposition was first in the news. No matter how much timber was cleared to make room for new houses and roads, there never seemed to be enough space for the ever-growing population. Since the founding of the village after discovery of iron ore in northern Minnesota, the population had grown from a handful of pioneers to more than 3,000 people and was still growing. Prospectors visited the village daily, buying up mineral rights and selling shares in oil, timber, gold, and iron ore ventures located in all parts of the United States. Railroads were adding new rolling stock and pushing their lines out of Two Harbors to the north and west to provide transportation to new iron ore developments.

The years just passed had been exceptionally progressive ones for Two Harbors. During 1899-1900, a long-hoped-for electric light plant had been installed. A stage had replaced the dogs and sled of mail carrier John Beargrease who carried the mail through the wilderness from Two Harbors to Grand Marais. In that year, too, folks shouted over long-distance telephones for the first time and joked that maybe writing a letter would be simpler. Electric street lamps replaced gas lamps at street corners, and the Two Harbors *Iron News* commented on their dimness, "For the next month or two when folks go stumbling home through the dark, they will wonder what 'them things' are good for anyway."

The new electric lights, the long-distance telephones, and the ever-expanding iron mining industry gave Two Harbors' residents plenty to talk about when they gathered to exchange the day's news. But no matter how interesting other events were, the conversation always settled on prospecting and mining. Was there iron ore around Two Harbors? How rich *were* the great Mesabi and Vermilion mines? Was there really copper in northern Minnesota? Or silver? A streak of copper had been found during the digging of a basement for a new Two Harbors' home. There must be more around! The general hope was that the rugged, forested land would yield more than iron ore in order to provide northern Minnesota with a more diversified economy.

In the cold spring of 1901, it looked as though this hope might be fulfilled. Rumors circulated that a new and valuable mineral had been found in the rocky bluffs near the shores of Lake Superior northeast of Two Harbors. North Shore residents, used to stories about new iron, copper, gold, and silver deposits, were intrigued. Ed Lewis, the Duluth prospector who claimed the discovery, called the mineral "corundum." Few knew what corundum was or what it was good for, but, if the stories were true, the strange-sounding mineral would bring new fortune to the North Shore. The rumor heard most often was that the Eastern grinding wheel manufacturers needed all the corundum that could be mined.

The rumors were close to the truth. If the mineral were really corundum,* the purest of natural abrasives, it would be in high demand by an increasingly industrial America. Its hardness, next to the diamond, made it at that time one of the most valuable abrasives for scouring, polishing, and sharpening metal, glass, and wood. The demand in the United States for the two most popular abrasives, corundum and emery, had doubled from 1897 to 1901 and was still growing. Only one commercially profitable mine of the rarely found mineral was operating in North America in northern Ontario, Canada. A ready market seemed assured for North Shore corundum.

Interest in the proposition increased sharply in April, 1901, when a company called the Minnesota Abrasive Company** was organized to mine corundum. Stock in the new enterprise was offered to the public at $10 a share.

*Corundum, composed of native alumina, was first discovered in India in the 18th Century, and was named "kurandam." Its finely colored, transparent varieties include such gems as the ruby and sapphire. In its impure and massive forms it is known as emery.
**The incorporators were The Honorable Charles Arnett Towne, U.S. Senator, Duluth; prospectors Ed Lewis and his brother Tom, both of Duluth; Alfred McCollum and Axel Wickstrom, two Duluth citizens who owned land on which "corundum" was discovered. The Minnesota Abrasive Company incorporated April 16, 1901.

But like so many mining enterprises of that day, the Minnesota Abrasive Company ran out of funds almost before it started. People were curious about corundum, but not interested to the extent of risking their money in so little known a mineral. North Shore old-timers have vague recollections of a small mining operation at Split Rock on Lake Superior where corundum was crushed, poured down the bluff in chutes into waiting boats, and shipped East. Unsuccessful efforts were made to sell the mineral to grinding wheel manufacturers.

But even though the Minnesota Abrasive Company dropped out of the news, interest in North Shore corundum didn't die. Two Harbors, Duluth, and other towns kept an eye open for new developments and speculated on the value of corundum. Speculation grew when a two-line item appeared August 23, 1901, in the Two Harbors *Iron News* "locals" saying, "H.S. Bryan, H.W. Cable and Job Dodge went down the lake* Wednesday to investigate a mineral proposition." Henry Bryan, Chief of Motive Power of the Duluth and Iron Range Railroad, and H.W. Cable, meat market proprietor, were among the village's most prominent citizens. Interest was fanned, too, by a Duluth *News Tribune* editorial which informed readers that the North Shore country offered not only wonderful prospects for investment in iron, copper, and timber, but in corundum as well.[2]

*In 1902, "down the lake" meant traveling in a northeasterly direction; "up the lake," southwest along the shore. Today it is just the reverse.

DOCTOR, LAWYER, MERCHANT, CHIEF

ON JULY 15, 1902, the Two Harbors weekly newspaper, *Iron News,* reported the founding of a second company to exploit corundum. Its founders, all North Shore citizens, were a doctor, a lawyer, a merchant, and two railroad executives. These men called their enterprise the "Minnesota Mining and Manufacturing Company."*

The *Iron News* explained that the five incorporators would also be the company's officers and directors: Henry S. Bryan, Chief of Motive Power of the Duluth and Iron Range Railroad, president; Dr. J. Danley Budd, Two Harbors general physician and chief surgeon for the D. & I.R.R., first vice-president; Hermon Cable, general manager and second vice-president; William A. McGonagle, assistant to the president of the Duluth, Missabe and Northern Railroad, treasurer; and John Dwan, Two Harbors attorney, secretary.

*This name has caused considerable confusion throughout the company's history. The founders' intention was only to mine "corundum." No manufacturing was planned then. In 1905, the company began to manufacture sandpaper and shortly thereafter mining operations were abandoned. Not until 1930 did the company's title again become an accurate description of its operations. In that year a quarry was purchased and quartz mined. Often, too, the company is associated with Minnesota iron mining because of its title, especially since 3M employees refer to their company as "The Mining." At all times, the firm has promoted the official abbreviation, "The 3M Company."

In the year following incorporation, these North Shore entrepreneurs learned painfully that getting a mine into production wasn't like running a meat market, a law office, or even a railroad. But in the beginning the five founders innocently made big plans.

Initial intentions were to quarry the North Shore corundum and sell it in bulk to grinding wheel manufacturers, but 3M's Articles of Incorporation covered every possible phase of the abrasive business:

"The general nature of the business...shall be to engage in... Mining, Quarrying, Crushing, Analyzing, Smelting, Shipping and Marketing abrasives and all kinds of minerals and Metals and the Manufacturing of abrasives of all kinds and other mineral products."

The first working capital was furnished by the five founders. Each purchased 1,000 shares out of the $500,000 capital stock at the set par value of $1 a share, and agreed to try to sell 25,000 shares to the public. An agreement was made to issue Henry Bryan 100,000 shares in exchange for a warranty deed to the corundum property which he owned, and a similar agreement was made with McGonagle, who owned land adjacent to Bryan's.[1]

The hope was to get 3M corundum on the market by the summer of 1903. General manager Cable energetically set about to make this possible. During the winter months of 1902-03, he shuttled back and forth between the corundum property and Two Harbors, making preliminary plans for mining, evaluating the timber, and laying out campsites. The rugged, rocky buttes which 3M believed contained corundum lined the shore of Lake Superior near the mouth of the beautiful river which the French fur trader Curot had recorded generations before in his diaries as "au Baptéme," the Baptism River. In summer the forest-covered buttes were accessible by boat from a deep, sand-bottomed bay. In winter when the bay was frozen, the corundum property could be reached only by going through dense, virgin forest of majestic pine, birch, and cedar. Hermon Cable's trips to the property were watched with interest in December, 1902, through the locals of the *Iron News*:

"Dec. 5, 1902: H.W. Cable went to Little Marais yesterday to look after the interests of the Minnesota Mining & Manufacturing Company. With his woods uniform he made quite a stunning appearance. And two weeks later, "That wide cut through the snow drifts from the woods to the shore at Little Marais is not the opening of a new logging road, but the trail of Alderman Cable's stroll down the beach at the corundum mine." This was a friendly reference to the unusual bulk of Alderman Cable."

While Cable was working on production plans, the 3M Company was called on to make its first major business decision. Scarcely before the ink had dried on the newly issued 3M stock certificates, President Charles Towne of the Minnesota Abrasive Company wrote 3M President Bryan, asking: "Would 3M be interested in purchasing controlling interest in the Minnesota Abrasive Company?" Towne's company was unable to raise money to continue operations.

At a board meeting on December 5, 1902, 3M decided to table this proposition. This was only a delaying action until 3M could more carefully consider such a transaction. Undoubtedly the purchase of the Minnesota Abrasive Company holdings would enhance 3M's chances for success since it would eliminate competition. But the company couldn't pay cash for Minnesota Abrasive's stock; it would have to be a stock-trading transaction. Finally, in January, 1903, 3M took Towne up on his offer. A total of 60,018 shares of Minnesota Abrasive were exchanged for 54,302 shares of 3M stock, and 3M paid the other company's debts by issuing 2,948 shares to its debtors.

3M's purchase of controlling interest in the Minnesota Abrasive Company attracted a great deal of attention, not only on the North Shore, but in Eastern financial circles as well, raising the old questions all over again about the value of Minnesota corundum. New York City's *Financial Review* commented:

The annual meeting of the Minnesota Abrasive Company in Duluth, Minnesota, which practically means the reorganization of the company, has been rendered exceptionally interesting for the reason that action was taken to elect a successor to Hon. Charles A. Towne, the former president of the company. Mr. H.S. Bryan, the new executive is well known in Two Harbors, Minnesota, hc being president of the Minnesola Mining and Manufacturing Company, and it is conceded that he possesses the needed qualifications for success, even at the head of such a large company as the one referred to, owning as it does, extensive quarries on the North Shore of Lake Superior.[2]

To those who were worried about the prospects of the corundum mines, the following Duluth *News Tribune* report was somewhat encouraging:

"The annual meeting of the Minnesota Abrasive Company is in progress and what amounts to a reorganization will result. H.S. Bryan of Two Harbors has been elected president in place of former U.S. Senator Charles A. Towne. The latter continues as a stockholder, as do the Lewis Bros. who were the early promoters of the enterprise."

The new board of directors is composed of W.A. McGonagle, Duluth; and H.W. Cable, H.S. Bryan, John Dwan, and Dr. J.D. Budd of Two Harbors. The new officers are as follows: President, H.S. Bryan; Vice President, H.W. Cable; Treasurer, W.A. McGonagle; Secretary, John Dwan.

The Minnesota Abrasive Company owns extensive deposits or quarries of corundum on the North Shore of Lake Superior a few miles below Two Harbors. It is claimed that its utility as an abrasive has been thoroughly demonstrated and plans are now in progress for developing the property and getting the product on the market. It is reported that the newly organized concern has important matters under consideration that may be announced in the next few weeks.[3]

Like so many others who organized mining ventures in the early 1900's, the founders of 3M apparently incorporated first and investigated later. Shares in 3M were sold, mining plans laid, and the Minnesota Abrasive Company deal made before anyone really knew whether North Shore "corundum" would sell. Not until March, 1903, after many had invested in the company, was there any investigation of the marketability of the mineral. In that month, Hermon Cable was authorized to go to Chicago and Detroit "to have the mineral made into grinding wheels and other abrasive products and tested for its abrasive strength and quality and to determine its merchantable value." Further, general manager Cable had instructions, if possible, to "obtain a market for such corundum and investigate the cost of manufacture and comparative value of the different abrasives now on the market."[4]

In spite of closed navigation out of Two Harbors, impassable trails to the corundum property, and snow covering the corundum deposits, Cable managed to blast out substantial samples of corundum for test purposes. With $250 of the company's limited funds in the pocket of his black, Sunday suit, he departed for Chicago and Detroit to see the grinding wheel manufacturers. The week Cable was gone was an anxious one. What would the tests of the corundum show? Would Cable find buyers for their product as they had so profusely promised investors?

Cable returned in time for the regular meeting of the board of directors on April 7, held in the 3M headquarters above Dwan's law office at 113 Poplar Street. President Bryan let Cable report immediately.

Cable shuffled through a handful of scribbled pencil notes on the desk in front of him, drew a luxurious puff from his cigar...."Gentlemen, as you know, I have been to both Chicago and Detroit to have our corundum tested. A couple of factories in these cities were good enough to make up and test sample grinding wheels for me. One of the wheels–four inches by two feet–will be sent to Two Harbors so the boys at the roundhouse can test it."

What was the report on the corundum? The question was on all the directors' minds. Cable was enthusiastic–even reassuring. "The tests show the corundum to be fairly satisfactory; and, in my opinion, we should go ahead immediately with our plans to get the corundum on the market."

Cable's enthusiasm, as always, was contagious. The four directors sitting around the curved oak desk apparently paid little attention to his exact words, and heard only his recommendation to go ahead with mining operations. Had they known more about abrasives, the words "fairly satisfactory" would have been a warning signal that all was not well with their corundum scheme. An effective abrasive for grinding wheel manufacture must be more than "fairly satisfactory." The directors apparently weren't worried over the fact that Cable hadn't brought back any orders for corundum. After all, it was a little early; they hadn't gotten any of the corundum out of the ground yet. In fact, after Cable's reassuring report, the founders felt again as they had a year before, that Minnesota Mining and Manufacturing Company was an undertaking which might make them wealthy and bring new prominence to Two Harbors. The fact that 3M had made very little progress gnawed a little at their peace of mind. But each rationalized the situation with the thought that a great deal could be accomplished in the weeks before a report had to be made to stockholders at the first annual meeting on May 5, 1903.

Unfortunately, little more was accomplished before May 5. The board of directors could only report what the stockholders already knew: There were now 64 stockholders representing 162,450 shares, most of which had been issued in payment for corundum property and services, and did not represent cash stock sales. Alger Smith & Company of

Detroit had purchased $1,050 worth of timber from 3M's property. Controlling interest in the Minnesota Abrasive Company had been acquired through exchange of stock. Hermon Cable had taken the corundum to Chicago and Detroit to be tested and had recommended going ahead with mining operations. Nothing more could be reported for that first year. No mining operations had been started. No orders had been obtained for corundum. There was little cash in the treasury.* Obviously, more had to be done if the corundum proposition were to be a success.

From the beginning, costs had exceeded estimates, and available cash had melted away like ice in Lake Superior on a sunny spring day. Minnesota speculators who usually were eager to buy in on a new discovery weren't anxious to invest in something they knew as little about as corundum. The handful who invested in 3M during 1902-03 were mostly close relatives and friends of the founders. For the most part, they had purchased only small blocks of from 2 to 50 shares. Only a few had bought as many as 100, 200, or 500. One exception was a St. Paul railroad officer named Edgar Ober who later was to play a prominent role in the history of 3M. He bought 5,000 shares. But Twin Cities and Eastern capital, while interested in the new corundum development, invested little money at this stage.

The lack of progress in the first year made one thing plain. General manager Cable, no matter how hard he worked, couldn't handle the job of getting corundum on the market by himself as planned. It would take more active cooperation from all the founders.

Emotions of 3M's directors were mixed after the annual meeting of 1903. Dr. Budd wondered just what he was get-

---

*The limited cash position was indicated only by a note in the minutes that "Whereas the available funds of this corporation may at times be insufficient to meet the demands of the business and to pay in cash any salaries...payment may be in capital stock at par value without giving notice to the stockholders."

ting into with this corundum scheme. It had been strictly a speculative venture for him at the beginning. Now it looked as though he would be very much involved with the active management of the company.

Maybe it wouldn't be too bad. He was used to a busy schedule. Two Harbors was continually amazed at the rugged pace kept by the 55-year-old physician. All day long the hardy doctor worked in his 50-bed hospital, and at any time of day or night he would hitch up his two fine mares and take his buggy over nearly impassable trails to get to the sick and injured. As county coroner, Dr. Budd was frequently called to examine the body of a murdered lumberjack found in the woods or a transient railroad worker killed in a saloon. He was an ardent sportsman and spent many an hour fishing in the Stewart, Knife, and Gooseberry Rivers and stalking white-tailed deer through the snowy woods.

Dr. Budd had learned a great deal about practicing medicine under the hardship conditions of pioneer life since coming to Two Harbors in 1889; he was an expert hunter and fisherman. But he knew little or nothing about corundum. He could only take his friends' word for it that there was a great potential market for it. As Dr. Budd pondered over the future for 3M, he thought perhaps he should have kept his spare money for the Budd hospital. But he was as susceptible as any man to the thrill of investing in a "sure thing," and it was too late now to back out. He decided to help all he could even if it meant giving up other activities.

To Michigan-born, 41-year-old John Dwan, Minnesota Mining and Manufacturing Company was one more adventure into the realm of business speculation. Since starting a Two Harbors law practice in 1891 after graduation from the University of Michigan, the shrewd young lawyer had put a finger in almost every investment pie in the North Shore area as well as many oil, timber, and mining ventures in other parts of the United States. From the beginning, his interest in 3M was high. He had visions of Two Harbors becoming not only the nation's leading shipping center for iron ore, but for corundum as well. Since the company's incorporation, he had worked long hours drawing up papers, writing letters to friends on the corundum proposition, and keeping meticulous records of 3M's affairs.

No one could understand how Dwan found time to work on affairs of 3M. In 1903 he represented 14 insurance companies, practiced law, and served as village attorney for $300 a year. He was a volunteer fireman at $2 a fire, served on the library board with Henry Bryan, and was a charter member of the Two Harbors Commercial Club.

Dwan, too, had invested in 3M as a speculative venture, but he didn't mind the extra work. He looked forward to the challenge of making the company a paying proposition.

Big, chubby Hermon Cable was used to responsibility, too. He had worked hard all his life, especially since starting a meat market in Two Harbors in 1891. From the beginning, Two Harborites had been impressed with Canadian-born Cable's business ability.

Cable's prosperity in the meat market moved Editor James Coggswell of the *Iron News* to comment, "The secret of Cable's success is due to the fact that he attends strictly to business, studies the requirements of his customers and meets them, and, last but not least, is an all-around good fellow and citizen."[5]

Cable continued to prosper, but he had greater ambitions than running a meat market. He was one of the chief promoters of Minnesota Mining and Manufacturing Company, and it soon became his major interest. During its first year of operation he had devoted almost all of his time to the much-talked-about "corundum proposition." After the first annual meeting, he promised the other directors he would redouble his efforts in the coming months.

Henry S. Bryan, at 67, was reaching an age where he was reluctant to assume more work than he already had on his hands at the Duluth and Iron Range Railroad. Like Dr. Budd, he wondered if he were taking on more than he could handle with the new 3M Company.

In the past, all his spare time had been spent in building and boosting Two Harbors. He had served as village president, on the library and school boards, and on Commercial Club committees. He had helped fight for new waterworks, an electric light station, and a public park on the shores of Lake Superior. He had aged considerably in the past few months. His thick, wavy hair was almost pure white now. He felt it was time to give up some activities and decided he'd better make sure the other officers of 3M didn't expect too much from him. In spite of the fact that he had owned the corundum land, Bryan intended 3M to be only an investment for him, not an active responsibility.

William A. McGonagle was dubious, too, about his ability to devote more time to 3M. He was now vice-president of the Duluth, Missabe and Northern Railroad and the position consumed most of his time. The fact that he lived in Duluth was also a handicap. Not that he wouldn't like to devote more time to 3M. The new venture was a challenging one, and McGonagle hated to pass up an opportunity to help get the corundum mine going. He had helped put over many a challenging pioneer project of the North Shore since his early twenties.

In 1882, at the age of 21, he had supervised the crew that laid the first rails for the Duluth & Iron Range Railroad from Agate Bay (Two Harbors) to the Minnesota Iron Company mines at Soudan and Tower, Minnesota. The line was completed in July, 1884; and that November,

---

*The famous "Three-Spot" is now on display on the railroad station lawn in Two Harbors. McGonagle made the dedication speech when the locomotive was put on permanent display there.

McGonagle and others manned the company tug and towed the first locomotive* for the new line up Lake Superior from Duluth to Agate Bay, an extremely dangerous trip due to a strong nor'easter which was raging over the lake. McGonagle and the other men stood on the deck of the *Ella G. Stone* with axes in hand, ready to chop the scow loose should it threaten to go under and sink the tug.[6] This was only one of many adventures.

McGonagle was 42 now, and one of the North Shore's most successful men. More than 20 years in railroading had given him valuable experience for managing Minnesota Mining and Manufacturing affairs. He knew he was needed by 3M; while he had little time to spare, he promised the other directors after that first annual meeting that he would devote all possible hours to making the corundum proposition pay.

Had these men the power to see into the future, they might not have been so ready to stay with 3M. A scientist named Acheson and their own inexperience in the abrasive field were to turn their dreams for the 3M Company into a nightmare of failure. Out of the five, only Dwan was to reap anything but a harvest of financial worry, overwork, and discouragement from the efforts to turn North Shore "corundum" into profit. Fortunately, they weren't clairvoyant; and, unaware of the failures ahead, they set a pattern of pluck and persistence which was to pay rich dividends to those who followed them in 3M.

Edward Goodrich Acheson was a restless, brilliant inventor who dreamed of replacing natural abrasives such as corundum, flint, emery, and garnet with an artificial abrasive. If this could be done, he reasoned, manufacturers would no longer have to depend on nature's limited supply of abrasive minerals. In 1891 he experimented and made a discovery which revolutionized the field of abrasives and changed the future for 3M and many other abrasive companies. His discovery was carborundum, an artificial abrasive of carbon and silicon made in an electric furnace, which soon began to supplant natural abrasives for many industrial abrading jobs in America's factories and shops. Acheson organized his own company and began making carborundum in quantity. He soon lost control of the Carborundum Company, but those who took it over went into full-scale production of silicon carbide at Niagara Falls, New York. By 1903, when 3M was struggling to get a foothold, consumption of artificial abrasives was increasing by leaps and bounds and the use of natural corundum and emery was decreasing.

There is nothing in 3M records to indicate that the directors were aware of the revolution being brought about by Acheson's invention. They believed there was a ready market for their mineral, and in blind enthusiasm made their plans to open a mine on the North Shore.

Even more amazing, they were unaware that they were building their entire business on a mistake. Even if Acheson had not invented an artificial abrasive, 3M's "corundum" would never have sold. North Shore "corundum" was not corundum at all, but a low grade anorthosite, unfit for effective abrasive work. No one discovered this for several years. In their ignorance, Bryan, McGonagle, Budd, Dwan, and Cable laid the foundation for a corporation destined to become a multimillion-dollar business, one of the largest sandpaper manufacturers in the world, and one of the Carborundum Company's chief competitors. Such is the strange beginning of Minnesota Mining and Manufacturing Company!

EARLY CRISIS

PRODUCTION by fall was the goal set after the annual meeting in May, 1903. Unaware of coming obstacles, Bryan, Budd, McGonagle, Dwan, and Cable enthusiastically cooperated to make this possible. In June they hired the steamer *America** to take them to the corundum property where they laid final plans for mining operations. Only Cable had been there before. June 12 was an ideal day for the trip on Lake Superior, a balmy, blue-sky day which erased memories of the winter's sleet, snow, fog, and treacherous nor'easters. With such good weather, work at the property was accomplished in less than a day.

When the *America* reached the beautiful bay which gave access to the 3M corundum buttes, the 3M founders "then and there on the 12th day of June A.D., 1903...christened said bay 'Pickwick Bay.'" Later, they renamed it "Crystal

*The *America* was one of the Booth Fisheries' fleet of Great Lakes boats which played an important role in the dramatic development of Northern Minnesota. The hundred-passenger boat plied Lake Superior from 1898 to 1928, hauling supplies, business passengers, and sightseers to Grand Marais, Isle Royale, 3M's "corundum" mines, etc. She sank near Isle Royale after striking a rock on a foggy day in 1928, and can still be seen on the bottom of the lake.

Bay" to describe its deep, clear waters. This is the name it still bears. On shore, the men followed trails chopped by Cable through the thick forest and chose the best spot for quarrying operations. They decided a gravity-type, aerial tramway would be best to convey the quarried corundum down the butte to a crusher on the beach. A site was chosen on the beach for the six-story crusher building, a shipping dock, and housing for employees. Realizing that expenses for equipment would far exceed available cash, it was agreed that 15,000 shares of stock should be sold to cover the cost of machinery, installations, and buildings.

From this point on, progress was painfully slow.

All summer, Hermon Cable neglected his duties as village alderman, his own business, and his family for 3M. He spent long hours pouring over equipment catalogues and blueprints. He shuttled between Two Harbors and Crystal Bay, directing the clearing of the land, the hauling of supplies, and the hiring of help. At night he was too exhausted to do anything but fall into bed, and usually he found it more convenient to camp on the shore of Crystal Bay than to make the long trip back to Two Harbors by boat or stage.

Crushers, screening machines, and an engine were ordered in June from Allis Chalmers of Milwaukee; an aerial tramline from A. Leschen & Sons Rope Company of St. Louis. In August, a Two Harbors carpenter, George Spurbeck, was awarded the contract for construction of the building to house the crusher. This gave the Two Harbors *Iron News* another opportunity to assure the townspeople that "the material [corundum] is there and its worth has been proven. The market is adequate for all that can be produced were there a number of plants. Probably no plant of this kind in the country has like facilities for bringing their products to the shipping point. The result of this undertaking will be watched with interest by the whole state of

Prospective stockholders inspecting the 3M Company's North Shore "corundum" in 1903. The promoters offered a free boat trip from Two Harbors to its Crystal Bay property to anyone interested in buying shares. The steamer *America* was chartered for such tours.

Artist's sketch of original 3M plant at Crystal Bay.

Henry S. Bryan, one of 3M's founders, and its first president. Executive on Duluth and Iron Range Railroad in 1902, when 3M was organized. Two Harbors resident.

William A. McGonagle, prominent North Shore pioneer and one of 3M's founders. At the time 3M was organized, he lived in Duluth and was an executive on the Duluth Missabe and Northern Railroad.

Hermon W. Cable, one of 3M founders. Two Harbors meat market proprietor when 3M was organized.

Dr. J. Danley Budd, Two Harbors physician and 3M founder.

John Dwan, one of 3M founders, and its first secretary. Prominent Two Harbors attorney, and North Shore pioneer.

Minnesota, it adding to another of our many great industries."[1]

It was August before the crushing machinery arrived at the Duluth railroad terminal, and another week passed before Cable could hire a scow to transport it to Crystal Bay. The housing for the machinery wasn't completed until October. It was late in October before Leschen & Sons sent a man from St. Louis to install the aerial tramway; and, when they did, fresh trouble began. Apparently their expert wasn't an expert, and Cable had to redo the entire installation of the conveyor system.

All work at Crystal Bay was handicapped because 3M had no dock, but there were no funds to build one. Good help was difficult to find, and working conditions were anything but pleasant in the wilderness country. This was especially the case when the cold bitter rains of fall came. Storms on Lake Superior made existence at Crystal Bay rugged. Typical of these storms is the one reported in the *Iron News:*

"General Manager Cable of 3M came up from Crystal Bay Wednesday. He reports they were kept mighty busy all night during the storm removing the material on the shore to a place of safety. The waves would strike the 40' bluff and dash way on top, sending a flood of water down into the ravine, which with the water from above, transformed the dry run into a raging torrent. A little lumber which was washed away was recovered the next day.[2]"

So 3M didn't get into production by fall as planned. The only thing produced was expense, and 3M began suffering from a shortage of working capital that was to become chronic. The financial situation was so acute by October that a special directors' meeting was called at which treasurer McGonagle tallied expenses as follows:

Crushers, screeners, engine	$7,100.00
Tramway	2,703.00
Lumber carriers @ $7.50	37.50

| Crusher building | 4,677.75 |
| Office furniture and supplies | 255.00 |

He read on: Man and wife to run the boarding house—$50 a month; salaries for an 8-man crew at Crystal Bay; officers' salaries; rent at 113 Poplar Street; lights, telephone, transportation[3]....It seemed as though McGonagle would never stop reading. Each man was thinking the same thing. 3M stock would not sell until the company sold some corundum. No sales could be made until some corundum was mined. No corundum could be mined without additional funds to complete the Crystal Bay plant. The only way to break this vicious circle was to get a loan. After a worried discussion, the directors agreed to try to borrow $5,000 from the Bank of Two Harbors.

The bank apparently had no doubts about lending money to Minnesota Mining and Manufacturing Company. The founders were successful businessmen in their own right, and their signatures were good. A loan of $5,000 at seven percent was advanced in October, 1903, payable in three months on demand. 3M used part of this money to complete earlier arrangements for a sales agent and to establish its first branch office and warehouse in Chicago in order to be nearer industrial customers. The money also paid for company stationery, gunny sacks in which to ship corundum, fire extinguishers, insurance for the Crystal Bay boilers and other equipment, and a multitude of daily expenses. Unfortunately, the borrowed funds didn't last long. In December, with the Crystal Bay plant still not in production, 3M approached the bank for another $5,000. Again they unhesitatingly loaned the money.

Finally, in the worst part of a North Shore winter—January 1904—Hermon Cable, almost exhausted from months of back-breaking work and financial strain, sent a welcome message to the other officers via the Grand

Marais-Two Harbors stage: "The corundum crusher made a trial run January 21. Everything seemed satisfactory."

Now the only worry, besides repaying a $10,000 loan, was to find a way to get the mineral from Crystal Bay to Two Harbors so orders could be filled if 3M got any that winter. Editor Coggswell of the *Iron News* cheerfully suggested:

"Now that navigation is closed, it will probably be necessary to transport the product from the crusher by team, and there is a possibility of some party having a few teams securing a good contract for several months' work."[4]

3M officers weren't so cheerful about it. Hauling the crushed corundum out by team was the only way, but where would they find someone willing to haul a wagonload of hundred-pound sacks over nearly impassable trails in below-zero weather? They feared it wouldn't be easy. One driver promised to do it but failed to show up. Others wanted $20 a ton, which was about all 3M could sell it for. In desperation Dr. Budd hitched up his two mares one day in February and, with Hermon Cable, made a trip to Crystal Bay to bring back a load of corundum to Two Harbors. According to the local paper, he "enjoyed a stiff northwest breeze all the way."

At last 3M was ready for business. The Crystal Bay plant was operating at full capacity. A warehouse and sales agency had been opened in Chicago with John S. Webb as sales agent. A young stenographer named Hattie Swailes,* who had once worked as cashier in Cable's meat market, was hired for general clerical work in the 3M office at 113 Poplar Street. Hermon's son, John, agreed to do the Crystal Bay janitor work for $10 a month.

3M made its first sale the second week of March 1904. One ton of corundum was sold for $20 by John Webb to L.A. Whitney, President of the Champion Corundum Wheel Company. The directors became more optimistic than they

---

*3M's first woman employee.

had been in many months and attended the second annual meeting in May 1904 in high spirits. Hermon Cable reported he had 4,400 pounds of crushed mineral ready for sale, and stockholders were assured that it was only a matter of time before sales would be streaming in.

As it turned out, this was the last as well as the first sale of bulk corundum the company was to make; but, to the directors, the future looked bright. With no funds in the treasury and only one sale on the books, they voted themselves substantial yearly salaries: $3,000 a year for the president; $2,100 for the treasurer; $2,400 for Dwan as secretary and counsel; $3,600 for Cable as general manager; and $1,200 for assistant general manager, Dr. Budd. All officers and directors were re-elected for another year.

The Two Harbors *Iron News* reported after the 1904 annual meeting:

"A very interesting 3M meeting was held...and attended by...prominent stockholders from Chicago, St. Paul, and Duluth; and the expressions of satisfaction given out by the nonresident stockholders as to the condition of the company's affairs and the efficiency of its management were very hearty.[5]"

Reality soon closed in on 3M, however. Before two months had passed, it was clearly evident that 3M was failing. No more sales were made. Expenses continued to mount. Hurriedly the board directed sales agent Webb to find cheaper quarters in Chicago, which he did at 65 Canal Street South. All salaries were abolished, except for general manager Cable's which was reduced to $150 a month. Webb's contract was revoked and his salary for July and August paid in stock. The sale of more treasury stock was authorized, but this was a futile gesture; for once again 3M was caught in the familiar vicious circle—no sales of corundum, no return to stockholders, no sale of shares.

As the summer of 1904 progressed, the situation became steadily worse. In August, William McGonagle suggested that 3M make its own abrasive wheels if wheel manufacturers wouldn't buy the corundum. A committee was appointed to investigate a factory site and determine the cost of equipping a factory for the manufacture of abrasives. Duluth was considered the best location, but nothing came of the idea at this time.

The founders of Minnesota Mining and Manufacturing Company, all of them successful in their own work, felt acute embarrassment over the continued failure of their corundum enterprise. Tempers grew short, and even the usually cheerful Cable became harried and silent. For the first time since his arrival in Two Harbors, hard work wasn't paying off. Almost completely discouraged, he made a trip to Chicago to close the office, ship back supplies, and dispose of the corundum stored in the warehouse. The company had to borrow money from Henry Bryan to finance the trip. While in Chicago, Cable discontinued Webb's salary and put him on a commission basis. He made up his mind to resign as soon as he got back to Two Harbors. He did just that at the November 1, 1904 board meeting, with Miss Swailes following suit.

At the meeting, the board tabled the resignations and considered ways of getting out of debt. Allis Chalmers was pressing for payment of a $1,038 promissory note. A total of $347.25 in salaries was due the Crystal Bay employees; $987.25 was due a Duluth lumber firm. No funds at all were available for future operations, as noted tersely in the minutes of the November 11, 1904 board meeting:

"The secretary is hereby instructed to suspend the treasurer's surety bond, inasmuch as there are no funds in the treasury of such company making such bond necessary, and it is not probable that such moneys will be in the hands of said treasurer for some months."

The board adjourned that meeting without knowing which way to turn. It convened again the next day and the brief entry in the minutes reflects the futility of the discussion that evening:

"A quorum being present, the board proceeded to consider many matters of interest to the company and particularly the providing of funds to meet present indebtedness and to provide operating expenses for getting out a supply of crushed corundum for the winter market. No definite conclusions having been reached, the board adjourned."

The board of directors met every week during the cold November of 1904, seeking a solution. The founders were determined not to give up. Fortunately their employees felt the same way. Every one offered some personal sacrifice to keep the company going. Hermon Cable offered to work for nothing. Miss Swailes agreed to work half days only for $25 a month. Sales manager Whitney offered to take a 10 instead of a 20 percent commission. Bryan, McGonagle, Budd, and Dwan paid employees' salaries out of their own pockets. Dwan secured an extension on the Allis Chalmers note. In order to raise cash, each director offered to sell some stock at a loss if buyers could be found. Dwan was authorized to offer buyers one bonus share for every two shares purchased. The board agreed to offer 6,000 shares on the "bonus plan," and Dwan traveled to Ely, Duluth, St. Paul, Minneapolis, and other Minnesota towns attempting to sell 3M stock.

But these efforts were not enough. Expenses continued to mount, creditors kept demanding money, the personal funds of the directors were almost exhausted, and the corundum still did not sell.

By the end of 1904, 3M stock had dropped to the all time low on the barroom exchange—two shares for a shot, and cheap whiskey at that.

RICH MAN, POOR MAN

IN A SMALL LOOP RESTAURANT in St. Paul in early January 1905, 3M stockholder Edgar B. Ober let his morning coffee grow cold as he read a letter from his friend John Dwan of Two Harbors. Dwan's message was not news to him. He already knew that Minnesota Mining and Manufacturing Company was in serious financial trouble, but seeing it in official form from 3M secretary Dwan made him realize there was no time to lose if 3M were to be rescued from insolvency.

Ober, the general freight agent for the Chicago, St. Paul, Minneapolis & Omaha Railway, had been actively interested in 3M ever since his investment of $5,000 in early 1903.* He had been thinking about its financial problems for some time and was convinced that the company could not sell bulk corundum.

The way to get a financial return on Crystal Bay corundum, in his opinion, was to manufacture sandpaper and abrasive wheels. The drawback to this plan was that it would take even more money to open a factory than 3M now

*It is not known how Ober first became interested in 3M. He was a friend of William McGonagle through railroad connections, and, as both were members of the Gitchi Gammi Club of Duluth, it is possible they met there.

needed to pay its bills. The immediate amount of cash needed for debts was around $14,000. Another $25,000 would be needed to get an abrasive factory started. His own ability to invest...heavy responsibilities. His only hope was to interest someone with capital in taking over 3M with him, someone who could furnish money while he furnished time. According to Dwan, 3M stockholders would sell 60 percent of the issued stock to anyone who would pay the debts of the company and furnish working capital until 3M could be put on a paying basis.

Ober had someone in mind with capital enough to buy the stock–one of St. Paul's most active civic leaders, a man with means who was interested in new places to invest his money. Now if he could be persuaded to furnish 3M the money....

Forgetting about breakfast, Edgar Ober paid his check and went out into the snowy, sub-zero day. His destination was the plumbing supply firm of Crane and Ordway on Fifth and Rosabel Streets.

Lucius Pond Ordway, Vice-president of Crane and Ordway, puffed thoughtfully on his pipe as his friend Ober outlined his plan and occasionally scratched a few figures on a piece of note paper to illustrate a point.

"I know it doesn't look like a good investment on the face of it, Lucius, but I think there's a big future for the company if they make sandpaper. Just look at all the factories springing up all over the country. They'll need sandpaper. There's all the corundum at Crystal Bay we'll ever need. You furnish the money to clean up their debts. We'll get control of the stock and start a factory in Duluth or Superior. I'll manage the company. You won't have to worry about any of the details."

"How much does the company owe, did you say?"

"About $14,000: $10,000 to the Bank of Two Harbors, the rest for salaries, machinery, and running expenses."

"How do you know we can get 60 percent of the stock?" Ordway asked.

"Dwan says most of the stockholders have already agreed to that arrangement. The few that haven't been heard from wouldn't make any difference. Bryan, McGonagle, Budd, Dwan, and Cable own the controlling interest, and they've made up their minds it's the only way to save the company."

Ober was a most persuasive man. Lucius Ordway found himself becoming interested in spite of the company's pattern of failure. While Ober sat patiently at his desk, he read Dwan's letter and made some notes.

He finally leaned back in his chair and said, "All right, Ed, I'll do it. You make up the agreement for me and handle the other details. Remember, I want nothing to do with running the company. I've got my hands full here in St. Paul."

Ober was elated. If there was one thing he liked, it was a tough nut to crack, and 3M was certainly a tough one. Maybe with Ordway's help he could turn his $5,000 investment into a profit able one.

It took several weeks to work out details of the proposed agreement. It was in March 1905 that Ober sent a letter to Dwan and the other directors:

March 23, 1905

MESSRS. DWAN & CABLE

GENTLEMEN:

Am now prepared to make you and the other stockholders of the Minn. Mining & Mfg. Co. a proposition.

Assuming that we can make proper contact with the party we have in mind [H.W. Boynton, a sandpaper expert] so as to insure us of his services for not less than five years, it is the belief that a profitable business can be developed [manufacturing sandpaper].

I do not feel warranted in the outlay necessary to clean up the debts of the Co. and expend the large amount necessary to properly equip a plant and give it the necessary working capital...unless the stockholders are willing to make a heavy shrink in their holdings. The present status of the Co. and its *known* assets do not warrant it.

Contingent on proper titles of property listed on your records now as Minn. Abrasive Co. and Minn. Mining & Mfg. Co. real estate being shown and further the delivery of the 285 shares of Abrasive stock and the delivery to me of 60% of the outstanding stock of Minn. Mining & Mfg. Co. (222,846 shares) I will agree and give proper bond to protect you and other stockholders.

First—To pay the indebtedness of the M.M. & M. Co. not exceeding $13,250. Make five year contract...with party we have in mind, give him out of this stock delivered to me, 5% (11,142 shares) delivery. Will further agree to loan the Co. sufficient money (believed to be $25,000) to properly equip a rented plant at Duluth or Superior for manufacture of articles of which we talked. Will also agree to supply from time to time as needed sufficient working capital for proper conduct of its business...this money in both cases to be loaned at rate of not more that six percent per Annum.

Further will agree to retain control of the stock and the Co. and not to issue a share of stock beyond its present issue; namely, 222,846 shares without consent of yourselves.

If it is not possible to get the Bryan and McGonagle holdings on this basis, will buy them at 15¢ per share with the understanding that their holdings, namely 23,904 and 22,154 shares of M.M.& M. Co. and five shares each of Minn. Abrasive Co. be delivered me with proper transfer of escrow stock with full ownership and voting power for release of escrow stock, and to be delivered at time of delivery to me of 60% of the released escrow or treasury stock.

Will further agree to conduct the business on a strictly...square basis and give each shareholder the same pro rata rights and returns as given myself and associate...

Am prepared to carry out this proposition...at any time between now and April 23, 1905.

Respectfully,

E.B. Ober

The deal between Ober, Ordway, and 3M was completed by May 1905, the date of the third annual meeting. The stock sale gave the two St. Paul men control of the company and caused a stir all through Minnesota, for Lucius P. Ordway and Edgar B. Ober were well-known in Northwest business circles.

Business associates of Lucius Ordway were a bit surprised that the shrewd young executive would get mixed up with so obscure and unsuccessful a company as Minnesota Mining and Manufacturing Company, but then he had many irons in the fire. Ever since his arrival in St. Paul at the age of 21, Ordway had been a leader in civic and business affairs of the city.

Ordway had come to St. Paul in 1883 after graduation from Brown University. His marriage to Miss Jessie Gilman at the home of her father, the Hon. John M. Gilman, was "one of the most brilliant weddings of the week."[1] His first business connection was with the plumbing and steam supply firm of Wilson & Rogers, then with Rogers alone in 1884. In 1893, he became associated with Crane Plumbing Supply House, doing business as Crane and Ordway. At the time Ober approached him about 3M, Ordway was vice-president and general manager of the firm and worth close to a million dollars. Outside of Crane and Ordway, his major holdings were in St. Paul real estate and commercial buildings.

One of Ordway's deepest civic interests was the promotion of the City of St. Paul. He helped new businesses settle in the city and later was instrumental in getting the St. Paul Hotel built. An ardent sportsman, he helped found the White Bear Yacht Club in 1897, won its first regatta, and became its first Commodore. Yachting was his first love, but he was also enthusiastic about automobiling and curling.

Tall, thin Edgar Ober was also well-known in St. Paul. He had come to Minnesota with his parents three years before Ordway, and after finishing high school worked his way up from clerk to general freight agent for the Chicago, St. Paul, Minneapolis, and Omaha Railroad. In 1905 he was 39, still a bachelor, and much in demand for St. Paul's most fashionable parties. But Ober preferred work to social activities; his railroad job did not satisfy him and his ambitions led him into the deal with 3M.

The combination of Ober and Ordway put a new light on 3M affairs. Optimism over the company's future returned. Again the press cheerfully prophesied success for 3M. The Duluth *News Tribune* said

"E.B. Ober, L.P. Ordway, and D.D. Smith of St. Paul have secured control of 3M...and under the new management the company proposes to spend $100,000.00 in the establishment of a plant in Duluth for the manufacture of sandpaper, emery wheels and other abrasive products."

The stockholders expect to see a large and successful plant for the manufacture of abrasive products established in this city. Extensive experiments with the Crystal Bay rock have been made in Chicago...and it is claimed that they have been highly successful.

One of the stockholders says that it is generally understood that the Armours are behind the new proposed enterprise.[2]"

Some inaccuracies of the *News Tribune* story prompted Minnesota Mining to issue a statement which the Two Harbors *Iron News* published two days later under the headline,

"MINNESOTA MINING AND MANUFACTURING COMPANY HAS BRIGHT FUTURE"

Here is what 3M wanted to make known:

"The annual meeting of the stockholders of Minnesota Mining and Manufacturing Company was held...May 2, 1905. The following are directors chosen to manage the affairs of the company for the ensuing year: E.B. Ober, L.P. Ordway, H.W. Cable, D.D. Smith, John Dwan.

...The Board of Directors met and organized by the selection of the following officers: E.B. Ober, president; L.P. Ordway, first vice president; H.W. Cable, second vice president; D.D. Smith, treasurer; John Dwan, secretary.

The former president, H.S. Bryan, of this place, and the former treasurer, W.A. McGonagle of Duluth, retire from the board of directors and from the company, all their stock having been purchased by other stockholders...Dr. Budd, a former director, retires from the Board, but retains his interest in the company, and still remains an active factor in the company's future wellbeing.

The article appearing in the May 3 Duluth *News Tribune* was in many respects incorrect and in others misleading, and especially in its intimation that Armour and Company were supposed to be back of present arrangements. There is not a vestige of truth in that statement.

All of the company's affairs are in a most healthy condition and no reorganization of the company as was intimated in the *News Tribune* article was attempted or desired and none has been effected other than the changes in the board and officers as above set forth.

All who are interested in the company...will be pleased to know that its future prospects are most gratifying and that it will be a most active factor in the Head of the Lakes region and in the business world.[3]"

The Two Harbors *Iron News* editorially commented in the same issue:

"No event of greater importance to Lake County has occurred in years than the reorganization and financing of Minnesota Mining & Manufacturing. It assures the profitable development of one of the great resources of the eastern part of the country where the company possesses an almost inexhaustible supply of corundum.

While none of the stockholders are claiming the honor of rescuing the corporation from the perilous possibilities towards which it was drifting, it is said that credit is due to the determination and energy of Messrs. John Dwan and H.W. Cable. They have hustled untiringly for some time and are entitled to that sense of security which follows an entrance on easy street."

Editor Coggswell's opinion that Dwan and Cable were about to travel easy street seemed to be the general consensus. Actually, some of its real trouble was about to begin. Ober, Ordway, and even H.W. Boynton, who had spent years with another sandpaper manufacturer before becoming 3M's general manager in 1905, were unaware that Crystal Bay "corundum" was virtually worthless. For years they were to travel the same road of failure that founders Bryan, McGonagle, Budd, Dwan, and Cable had been traveling since 1902.

FRESH START, OLD TROUBLE

IN JUNE, 1905, Two Harbors reluctantly watched Minnesota Mining and Manufacturing Company move to Duluth and make arrangements to convert the old Imperial flour mill into a sandpaper factory. Civic-minded John Dwan would have preferred that 3M locate its factory on Agate Bay in Two Harbors, but there was no dockage available for private enterprise on the bay.

The abandoned flour mill seemed ideal for 3M's sandpaper factory. The large, six-story building was located on the water front on Rice Point, making it easily accessible for Lake Superior boats. A railroad siding ran by the mill on the land side. There was plenty of room for both machinery and storage, and there was extra space in two connecting warehouses. Using the money furnished by Lucius Ordway, 3M began the task of converting the mill into an abrasive factory. While Cable managed the Crystal Bay plant, Boynton supervised Duluth operations. President Ober kept track of things by mail and on week-end trips to Duluth. Secretary Dwan went back and forth between Duluth and Two Harbors taking care of the necessary legal and secretarial work of 3M.

While the conversion work was going on, Boynton proudly announced to the newspapers that 3M expected to be in operation by September 1. "We'll turn out 800 to 1,000 reams of sandpaper a day, or an estimated annual production worth $750,000 to $800,000," he told a reporter on the Duluth *News Tribune*. "People scarcely realize the enormity of the demand for ordinary sandpaper. They'll be surprised to learn that one shoe manufactory in St. Louis alone consumes $50,000 worth annually," said Boynton.

Like others before him, Boynton was too exuberant. 3M didn't get into production in 1905. Expenses mounted at an alarming rate, draining the capital Ordway furnished as fast as he could sign checks. More than $50,000 worth of machinery had to be designed and made to order. The mill needed a multitude of repairs. Other expenses ran into thousands of dollars for office supplies, glue, paper for sandpaper, working funds for the new Boston and Chicago sales offices, freight charges for hauling corundum from Crystal Bay, and so forth. By the end of six months, Ordway had advanced not only the promised $25,000 but $75,000 more and still the plant was not in production.

The elements added their bit to Minnesota Mining's troubles. On November 28, 1905, one of the most devastating storms in the history of the Great Lakes struck Lake Superior, leaving in its wake the heaviest toll of damage to ships and shore property ever experienced on the North Shore.* 3M took a substantial loss along with the others. At Crystal Bay, the newly built dock and a warehouse full of corundum were washed into Lake Superior, and other buildings were damaged. As 3M was not aware that Crystal Bay "corundum" was practically valueless, the loss seemed like the proverbial backbreaking straw.

*In this storm, the now famous ore boat *Mataafa* was dashed against the concrete piers of the ship canal in the harbor of Duluth, within sight of shore. The crew froze to death on the storm-swept deck while those on shore watched helplessly.

But finally, in January 1906, the factory wheels began to turn in the old Imperial Mill and the first batch of sandpaper was produced. The second attempt to make Crystal Bay "corundum" pay off was underway!

Abrasive paper in one form or another had been used for centuries when 3M entered the sandpaper manufacturing business that stormy winter of 1905-06, but it had been produced on a commercial basis for only fifty years. Centuries ago the Chinese used huge, gummy plant leaves covered with sea sand for abrasive work, and sailors used sand to polish the decks of ships. Then someone got the idea that crushed mineral such as quartz and flint could be dropped on a piece of sticky paper for use as an abrasive and "sandpaper" was born. Although no sand was used, the term sandpaper was never changed.

The development of abrasives up to the 19th century was slow and tradition-bound. Up to 1855, sandpaper users made their own sheets of abrasive paper, a single sheet at a time, by hand-smearing glue on rope paper and dropping crushed quartz or ground glass on it. An era of progress finally began in 1855 when Baeder-Adamson, founded by Charles Baeder for the manufacture of glue in 1828, started to make flint and emery paper and cloth on a fairly extensive scale. Another step forward came in 1880 when the mineral garnet was substituted for flint and quickly proved superior for the sanding of hard wood. Furniture and shoe manufacturers especially found garnet more economical and efficient than flint. At about the same time, Acheson's silicon carbide was revolutionizing the abrasive field, although its full impact had not yet been felt when 3M began to make sandpaper.

Between 1855 and 1906 sandpaper-making machines had gradually been developed also. Machinery was designed by each individual company, not by outside manufacturers. Blueprints were carefully guarded because the design of the machinery had a great bearing on the quality of the sand-paper. In these same years, sanding machines using abrasive discs gradually evolved from homemade appliances. A disc of sandpaper glued to the faceplate of a wood-turning lathe probably represented the first power sander. A disc about three feet in diameter, set up with glue and ground glass, used to bevel or groove boxes in a box factory is believed to be the origin of the disc grinder. A sheet of sandpaper fastened to a wood drum was the start of the sanding drum used in the lumber and furniture industries.

The origin of a roll-feed type of sanding drum is credited to a coffinmaker who was looking for a more economical method than hand-sanding the sides of wood coffins.

All of these inventions and improvements had developed in the 50 years just prior to 3M's entry into the sandpaper business. At this time, the major production of sandpaper manufacturers consisted of emery, flint, and garnet paper and cloth, and abrasive discs for use in America's furniture, shoe, and other factories.

Few realized it, but in the early 1900's the abrasive industry was on the brink of a period of growth to be paralleled percentagewise only by the mushrooming automotive industry. New, undreamed-of markets for all kinds of abrasives were created by the inventions of the incredibly productive 19th century, especially in the automobile industry. It was impossible to foresee at a time when only a few thousand horseless carriages had been made, that the automobile industry would be one of the major contributing factors to the growth of the abrasive industry.

January 1906, was a momentous month for 3M. The first orders for sandpaper finally started trickling in both by mail and from the branch offices. They were small ones, to be sure, but sales nevertheless. The first sandpaper sale recorded on 3M books was to the South Bend Toy Company in the amount of two dollars. The Fort Madison Chair

Company became 3M's second customer with a four-dollar order.

The potential market for abrasives was as varied and wide as industry itself, for sandpaper was, and is, an almost indispensable item in the manufacture of everything for man's needs from cradle to grave. The Kenosh Crib Company was another of 3M's first customers; so was the National Casket Company. Furniture makers, sash-and-door companies, and hardware stores made up the bulk of early customers.

Among these were International Harvester Company; Kelly How Thomson; Elgin National Watch Company; Bain Wagon Company; Chicago, St. Paul, Minneapolis & Omaha Railway; Chicago, Burlington & Quincy Railroad; Crane Company; Deere and Company; Farwell Ozmun Kirk Company; and the Janney Semple Hill Company.

By summer, more new customers were added: The Excelsior Bobbin Spool Company; Sure Hatch Incubator Company; Montgomery Ward & Company; Looschen Piano Case Company; White Hickory Wagon Manufacturing Company; and the Rockford Chair and Furniture Company.

The first month's sales totaled only $291 but grew to an average of $2,500 a month by May. But unfortunately, expenses were running an average of $9,000 a month, and this forced Lucius Ordway to continue advancing money to keep 3M going. Edgar Ober, who could scarcely afford it at the time, also loaned the company money.

So in the summer of 1906, almost before 3M had taken its first stumbling step in the business world, a new financial crisis was reached which created, for the first time, some ill feeling among the directors.

Lucius Ordway had poured more than $100,000 into 3M by June and felt that he could risk no more of his capital. Some of the other directors thought Ordway was reneging to a degree on his agreement, which read in part, "Ordway will also agree to supply from time to time as needed sufficient working capital to properly conduct its business and to operate the Crystal Bay plant."[2]

Ordway thought 3M should get a loan from other sources without his help. Budd, Dwan, and Cable wanted Ordway to continue to furnish funds. As for president Ober, he was in an awkward position in view of his long friendship with Ordway. After a conference with him, it was Ober's unpleasant job to tell 3M that Ordway would no longer continue in his role of angel. He did so reluctantly in a letter July 3, 1906. Excerpts from this letter and the correspondence which followed reflect the strain and hardship of 3M's three-year existence:

"OBER TO DWAN AND CABLE:

Have just ascertained today through Mr. Ordway that the bond suggestion cannot be put through. Unless something can be done at once by stockholders other than Mr. Ordway, we will not be able to pull through. Can you persuade the banks to loan us $10,000, on the company note endorsed by Dr. Budd, Cable, yourself and myself. If you can get the money on four months' time, we may pull thru o.k.

Please give this immediate attention as we sh'd have this money this week."

Dwan replied on July 5, asking Ober to talk things over once more with Ordway. Ober answered on July 9, 1906.

"OBER TO DWAN:

I have again interviewed Mr. Ordway. I regret to say that there is nothing further that Mr. Ordway can do in this matter, and something must be done by you three. If you will send me a company note endorsed by you three for the amount mentioned, we will try and have it put through one of the St. Paul banks. In addition to you three, I will also endorse the paper.

I think you appreciate that I have made every possible effort to avoid this conclusion."

Three days later Dwan dispatched a lengthy reply, hurriedly penciled on brown scratch paper:

DWAN TO OBER:

My return last P.M. from Twin Cities found your favor of 9th inst. awaiting me. I had hoped against hope for a different result. I am now making desperate efforts to meet your requirements and will advise you definitely very soon as to what can be done. Meantime, it is vitally important to us that we know just how precisely what is to be done with the amount mentioned and just how it is expected that this amount if obtained, will save the company. How can you figure that it would not be simply pouring the coin into a knot hole? Can the *company*, on its reasonable business expectations meet such a note at maturity.

If I were in the position you and Mr. O. are in to say what shall be paid, what deferred etc. I could figure better than now the hazard incident to the proposed endorsement. I find now as before that larger capital is more easily interested on proper basis than smaller capital. Hundreds of thousands are really more available than a few thousands.

July 13, 1906

OBER TO DWAN:

It is impossible for me to advise you definitely in regard to the various points mentioned in your letter.

The money will be used to pay bills that are due this month. I am of course unable to speak for Mr. Ordway, but in view of the fact that he as well as myself, have assumed obligations that are far in excess of what we ask you and other directors to look after, I hardly think it necessary to get a definite assurance from him.

It is very important that this matter be put through at once, and I hope to hear from you not later than Sunday.

July 13, 1906

DWAN TO OBER:

In re financial consideration of 3M Co.

You state in your last letter that Mr. Ordway can do nothing further in the matter and that means ruin to the Company and great loss to each and every stockholder unless something radical is done. It is not fair or just to stockholders to keep them longer in the dark and thus tie their hands. It is time they were advised of conditions.

You stated that the reason Mr. Ordway could do no more to help is that he says he can stand a *certain* loss without jeopardizing his other business interests, but that beyond that he cannot afford to go. Just what loss is he willing to take in consideration of his being relieved from further liability for Company debts and also from further liability to finance the Company under his agreement made with stockholders at the time of reorganization in 1905?

If satisfactory arrangements of this kind cannot be made, stockholders must be notified of existing conditions. Much more money is needed and if Mr. Ordway can't furnish it, someone else must, but no one will do so unless proper inducement is made. We made the necessary *inducement* a little more than a year ago—we went the limit and made good. For another party to assume the burden at this time, the proposition must be made alluring. Can that proposition be made at once for submission to proper party?

July 14, 1906

OBER TO DWAN:

Am afraid I did not make myself clear when advising you as to Mr. Ordway's position. He has no intention of voluntarily taking any loss; what I meant to convey was that he did not wish to assume any responsibility beyond the amount he had already gone good for. I hardly think any other stockholder would criticize him for such action, particularly as he has gone way beyond what he agreed to do.

Further I have myself assumed responsibility for a large amount ($40,000 on notes). Are stockholders in a financial position to stand a 20¢ assessment, or such other amount as is deemed advisable to assess? This matter must be given immediate attention.

July 17, 1906

DWAN TO OBER:

I can see several ways out of this financial crisis but evidently, we do not view the situation through the same spectacles. Our trade conditions are certainly improving very rapidly and many of our bills receivable are payable this week. In fact, there are approximately $10,000 worth of accounts (good accounts) due our Co. this week including those over due. A little rustling in of accounts due us and a little financial diplomacy in procuring extensions of bills payable will I think, result in tiding over present difficulties.

I note in your last letter the following: "I hardly think that you, or any other stockholder, would criticize him (Mr. Ordway) for such action, particularly as he has gone way beyond what he agreed to do. Further I have myself assumed responsibility for a large sum."

I have no desire to split hairs, Mr. Ober, but really, when we stockholders gave up 60% of our stock, was it not for purposes of having the Co. financed? I sincerely wish Mr. Ober, that I were in financial condition to do all that you or any one interested in the Co. seems to think necessary for I am fully convinced that we have encountered the "Turn of the Tide" and that it is only a very short time until all will be smooth sailing.

Trusting that no difficulty will be encountered in getting the extensions that are made necessary just at this time, I remain...

July 20, 1906

OBER TO DWAN

I am sure you know that I am making every possible effort to arrange matters referred to without getting into any difficulties. I do not know at this writing what the outcome will be, but have hope to fix it so that we can get over the present difficulties which I agree with you, once overcome, will make the future comparatively easy.

Concerning working capital would say that there is of course limits to the amount and the original figures which I have on file are a little less than 1/2 the amount that has already been put in. However, as previously stated, this has no bearing on the situation, it is not a question of post-mortem, but one of immediate action, and I understand from your letter that it will be useless to call a meeting of the stockholders, and that yourself, Mr. Cable and Dr. Budd are not in position to assume any financial responsibility.

Don't understand please that I am taking you or the others to task in any way for not assuming direct financial responsibility. It is simply a question of determining what you can do, and I understand that nothing can be done by you or the others mentioned, or stockholders. If matters cannot be shaped up properly, a meeting of the directors will be called promptly.

Letter undated

DR. BUDD TO OBER:

John Dwan came over to my office and asked me to sign a note for $10,000 to raise money for the 3M Co., there to be three others on the note with me including himself. As it would be absolutely impossible for me to meet such a note when it became due in the event of our having to pay it, I replied that I could not do it as I had no available funds and could not run the risk of having my hospital taken from me to satisfy my endorsement.

A year ago I with the directors and stockholders promised to give sixty per cent of all my holdings to any one who would pay the debts of the company which was only about $13,000 and furnish money as a loan at not over six percent to equip and run a plant till it was on a paying basis.

You accepted our offer and the transfer of sixty per cent of all the stock of the company was made to you and your associate as such bonus practically before we knew the name of your associate.

There was no limit named as to the amount you were to advance in equipment or running expenses of the two plants. Nor time set when such money was to be paid back to you and as you had a majority of stock and a majority of directors, everything connected with such matters was entirely in your own hands and I not being any longer a director had no say or vote with handling of financial affairs.

If I had the ability to help raise the $10,000 [you wish] I could have no say as to how it would be used or when returned. I am not able to do that; it might mean my absolute financial ruin.

I am led to believe that the affairs of the company are in the most promising condition as to sales and quality of goods and the time not very far off when the income will take care of expenses and soon thereafter to reducing the loan. In view of which the stockholders who have given so large a bonus should not be called on to help those who have reaped the benefit and will surely receive their money advanced with good interest. *The 3M Co. will not go under.*

Following this flurry of correspondence, Ordway called a special meeting of the board of directors at the Minnesota Club, St. Paul, for Saturday morning, August 4, to discuss the financing of the company through the crisis. All the directors were present, and, after President Ober reminded them of the seriousness of the financial situation, Lucius Ordway took the floor. If Dwan, Cable, and the others expected him to offer a solution to the problems of 3M, they were disappointed.

"I've furnished all the cash and credit for 3M that I'm able to," Ordway told them. "Much as I regret it, you'll have to find someone to relieve me of some of the existing liabilities of the company."

There was nothing anyone could say. Lucius Ordway had advanced thousands of dollars more than he had planned, without any real expectation of early repayment of the loans. While business was picking up, there was little reason to believe that the volume would be sufficient in the near future to pay off 3M's debts and take care of operating expenses.

Ordway continued, "I'm willing to take a substantial loss if someone else can be found who'll take my place in furnishing money and credit for the company's operations. I'll surrender my stock for treasury funds if a buyer can be found."

There was discouragement that morning, and some bitterness. Everyone had the feeling that this time, if 3M had the money, they could make a go of it. The meeting ended with John Dwan and Hermon Cable, who had already worked for years trying to raise money, promising to continue their search for new capital. Ordway gave them thirty days in which to do it.

In the meantime, the books of the company show, Ordway loaned the company from time to time $15,000 to carry 3M through August, September, and October. How he was persuaded to continue furnishing capital remains a mystery. Those who know how persuasive Edgar Ober could be, feel that it was undoubtedly he who talked Ordway into continuing the loans.

But even with continued lifts from Ordway, the money troubles of the young abrasive firm were far from settled, and it became apparent that a special meeting of the stockholders was necessary.

It was called for November 24, 1906, at the St. Louis Hotel, Duluth, and a thorough airing of company affairs took place. By this time, Ordway had loaned the company $200,000 and was still anxious to be relieved of some of this burden.

At the stockholders' meeting, president Ober reported that "the business of the company is rapidly increasing and the firm is in a most prosperous condition, and the only thing needed is additional money to carry on the business properly and to preserve properly the company's credit. If," explained Ober, "we could increase the capital stock to a total of 300,000 shares, disposing of an additional 77,654 shares, this would provide ample money to carry on the company's business and relieve Mr. Ordway of the pressure."

The suggestion was a good one except that 3M still could show no return on moneys invested, and all the stockholders were more than familiar with previous unsuccessful efforts to sell treasury stock. No definite decision was reached on this proposition. Ober promised to wire Ordway for a thirty-day extension on raising more capital by selling Ordway's stock for treasury funds. The stockholders agreed that if Dwan and Cable failed in this effort, they would then authorize the sale of 77,654 shares to finance the company through immediate future operations.

Dwan and Cable failed to find buyers for the Ordway stock. No record exists as to what actually took place, but from the books it is evident that once again Ordway changed his mind and continued in the role of benefactor. One thing is certain. At that stage, neither Lucius Ordway nor anyone else had the slightest idea that in a short time not only would 3M pay its debts, but eventually the outstanding shares of stock would be worth millions. Ordway's only thought in the fall of 1906 was to get his money out of 3M before he was forced to take a total loss on his investment.

Another mystery to many who know the history of the company is why L.P. Ordway didn't take over the company instead of continuing to lend it money. Those who were close to Ordway at the time explain that the St. Paul financier was so busy with important business and civic affairs in St. Paul, and particularly with his own firm of Crane and Ordway, that he had no time to bother with a struggling sandpaper factory 170 miles away. And if he had had the time, the chances are he still wouldn't have taken 3M over, for 3M required a great deal of close supervision and Ordway thoroughly disliked routine, detail work.

Except by a vague supervision by mail, Ordway left the management of 3M to Ober and general manager Boynton. Boynton had his own philosophy on how to make 3M a success, and the board of directors had to rely on him because they knew nothing about the manufacture of sandpaper. From 23 years' experience in the making and selling of abrasives, Boynton knew that those who used abrasives in industry were slow to accept either a new product or a new company. 3M's competitors were comparatively few but well-entrenched in 1906.* They had three distinct advantages. They were established with the trade. They were in control of the supply of domestic garnet, which was superior to imported garnet. With the exception of one, all were located nearer than 3M to the large manufacturers who consumed the most sandpaper. Tradition-bound manufacturers became used to one company's products and were reluctant to change. Boynton's plan was to sell them the kind of sandpaper they were already using–garnet, emery paper and cloth–to establish confidence in 3M, and then gradually to convert the customer to Crystal Bay corundum products.

This plan was not easy to execute. 3M found it nearly impossible to get good garnet, the supply of which was held by Eastern concerns who had no inclination to sell it to a new competitor. Even so, Boynton's formula might have worked if everything had been as he supposed. But as Crystal Bay "corundum" was not corundum, and Acheson's silicon carbide was replacing natural abrasives at a rapid rate, his plan was doomed.

Miles of "corundum" paper were manufactured by Boynton before he realized, to his great consternation, that good sandpaper could not be made with Crystal Bay mineral. According to all common-sense rules, this should have stopped 3M from making any more abrasive paper with this mineral, but it didn't. Instead, it was decided to explore a famous North Shore landmark, Carlton Peak, near Tofte, Minnesota, for a "higher grade corundum" to "mix with the Crystal Bay corundum."[3] Hermon Cable made the long

*Baeder-Adamson Company, Philadelphia; The American Glue Company, Boston; Armour Sandpaper Works, Chicago; Herman Behr & Company, Inc., Brooklyn; H.H. Barton & Son Company, Philadelphia (owner of the Rogers garnet mine in Warren County, New York); Carborundum Company, Niagara Falls; The United States Sandpaper Company, Williamsport, Pennsylvania; and Wausau Abrasives Company, Wausau, Wisconsin, 3M's only Midwest competitor.

arduous trip to Carlton Peak on March 18, 1907, to explore the area. He reported he was unable to reach the mountain even on snowshoes because of the depth and softness of the snow. So the exploration didn't get underway until late spring 1907. A Tofte crew was hired to do the prospecting. For several months, day and night, they blasted tunnels into Carlton Peak seeking a "higher grade corundum." There was great excitement at one stage when a streak of copper was discovered, but it must have been a nonpaying vein, for nothing more about copper appears in the records. No corundum, however, was found; and, as with all the other early 3M ventures, the costs of this operation were very high and there was no return on the investment.

The fact that Crystal Bay mineral was valueless as an abrasive was kept secret for many years. If the company knew the exact nature of the deposit, there is nothing in the records to show it. Efforts to sell Crystal Bay sandpaper continued. As late as 1910, three years after the Carlton Peak explorations, an R.G. Dun credit report shows the worth of the company to have been still based on the value of the Crystal Bay mineral:

The real estate item [in the financial statement of the company] represents property on the North Shore of Lake Superior in Lake and Cook counties (600 acres) from which they secure their raw material, *value of which is regarded as being in a large measure contingent upon the success of the business. The mining property is said to include...liberal deposits of corundum.* Being very largely tied up in real estate it is difficult to define net worth, but the company is regarded subject to adequate financial backing, all obligations are reported promptly paid, and credit position appears good."[4]

Not until November 1913 did interested parties get a hint of the true situation when another credit report quoted a 3M foreman as admitting that the Crystal Bay mineral was a failure for sandpaper.

When Boynton realized the situation, the company was nearly five years old and all there was to show for the tremendous investment of time, money, and talent was a mountain of debts. As for the future, without the North Shore deposit to count on, 3M's mineral supply problem would be acute unless the Eastern concerns relaxed their control of domestic garnet.

It is remarkable that under the circumstances everyone concerned didn't give up and write the whole thing off as a bad experience. But the records do not give the slightest hint that anyone even thought of giving up. As in the past they stumbled on, trying to find constructive solutions to seemingly insoluble problems. Ober personally tackled the job of trying to buy domestic garnet and he succeeded in getting some. Dr. Budd, Cable, and Dwan continued to try to get capital by selling stock and were able to raise a few hundred dollars to augment Ordway's loans. In December 1906, at a special meeting of the directors, Ordway was elected president and Ober became vice-president. Ordway made some attempt as president to protect his heavy investment. No materials were to be ordered without his consent, and expense checks were to be countersigned by him. In view of the acute 1907 depression, the board of directors considered shutting down the factory and filling orders from inventory stock, but, instead, all parties were ordered to keep expenses to a minimum. Foreign prices were advanced 15 per cent, but 3M took whatever it could get for its sandpaper from domestic customers. This domestic price policy caused great concern among its competitors and eventually brought a request to cooperate on price standardization from Wausau Abrasives Company and the United States Sandpaper Company, two of the smaller competitors. On Boynton's recommendation, the company replied that "3M had built up its business by independent action and was able to maintain same and would continue to do so."[5] This was an action regretted later.

Duluth Business University, Duluth, Minnesota, along with others outside of 3M, was unaware of the shaky financial position and uncertain future of the little sandpaper company. They could judge it only by such glowing newspaper accounts as the feature in the 1906 Historical Edition of the Duluth *News Tribune,* which described 3M as the "largest manufacturer of sandpaper in the world." So in May, 1907, when 3M called for an assistant bookkeeper, they sent one of their most promising students, a young man who had completed only five months of the prescribed six-month course, but who they felt was quite ready to go out and do credit to the school. His name was William Lester McKnight. At the headmaster's request, the shy, red-haired youth of 20 set out for Imperial Mill on Rice Point to apply for the job of Assistant Bookkeeper of Minnesota Mining and Manufacturing Company. His assets were a most brief, business-school training, inherent determination, and high ambition; his only experience was in farming. No one who saw the quiet, serious boy apply for the job could have possibly predicted that in a very short time he would become the major influence in the success of Minnesota Mining and Manufacturing Company.

TWO FARM BOYS, TWO LEADERS

LIKE DOZENS of other adventurous young couples in the early 1880's, Scotsman Joseph McKnight and his wife, Cordelia, left the settled East to make their living from the windswept prairies of South Dakota. Lured by visions of rich returns from the deep, black soil, the McKnights homesteaded in 1881 in Brookings County on gently rolling farmland near the Minnesota border. In a little sod house, two and a half miles from the settlement of White (population 580), they endured the rigors of pioneer life to till the land and raise their family.

William Lester McKnight, born on November 11, 1887, was the youngest of three children. His childhood was like that of many boys in a pioneer community. He was raised in an atmosphere of family devotion, strict discipline, and the worship of God. Sunday was a time for rest and a trip to the Methodist church in White.

At six, William started school in a one-room country schoolhouse a mile or so down the road from the farm. At fourteen, his parents sent him to high school in White. Like other farm boys, he was expected to help with the chores after school and all summer long. McKnight hated the chores and at an early age reached a very important decision. He was *not* going to be a farmer like his father. He knew this would be a disappointment to his father, who loved the land as did his entire family, his seven brothers being farmers too. But the older William grew, the more he inwardly rebelled against cleaning the barn, feeding the pigs, and milking the cows. He hated the flies and bugs that swarmed everywhere on hot, summer days. Watching a field of wheat ripen to a rippling sea of gold, or seeing the corn grow "knee high by the Fourth of July," was not nearly so thrilling to him as to some of his farm friends. Going to school was much more to his liking. Not that he liked to study, but school took him away from the farm chores for at least part of the day.

Slender, red-haired, freckle-faced William McKnight was a quiet and inconspicuous pupil at White High School. He had no particular flare for any one subject but did passably in them all. He traveled to school by horse and buggy and arrived and left so punctually that the townspeople could set their watches when he passed by. He was more interested in playing catch with his cousin Wayne McKnight than in girls. Secretly his fellow students thought he didn't have much fun, studied too hard, and undoubtedly would become a professor like his grandfather when he got out of school.

Young McKnight really didn't know what he wanted to do after he finished high school. Perhaps he would become a bookkeeper like the man in the flour mill in White who sat on a high stool, working over a big, red leather ledger. Bookkeeping looked like a pleasant, clean occupation. The more he thought about it, the more McKnight concluded that sitting on a high stool keeping books would be better than sitting on a low stool milking cows. Maybe when he finished school, he could go to business college some where and take a course in bookkeeping...

But when McKnight left high school, he was forced to put any thoughts of business college behind him for a while. Farming in Brookings County was not so profitable as the pioneers had hoped it would be. There were no funds in the McKnight family for a hired hand.

Not one to drop an ambition, young McKnight day-dreamed about college as he helped his father plow and plant. His sister Edith was married now and living in Duluth. Maybe he could stay with her and go to school.

When he was eighteen, things were a little better at home and McKnight went to see his sister in Duluth and found the city had a thriving business college called the Duluth Business University. He talked to his sister and her husband, Calvin Doughty, about going to school and they agreed to give him room and board if he could raise the $60 tuition.

Doughty had a suggestion. Why not get a job in Duluth and work while going to school? "I saw a lot of activity out at the old Imperial Flour Mill yesterday. They tell me a new sandpaper factory's going to start up there and they'll need 40 or 50 men. Maybe you could get a job there and earn enough for tuition."

Taking his brother-in-law's advice, McKnight made the long trip out to the 3M plant in the elevator district on Rice Point and made his first contact with the company which he did not know was to become his lifetime employer.

When he asked for a job as a laborer, he was told to sit on a bench outside the office and wait for a red-headed man who was in charge of employment. Obediently he sat down with other job seekers. After a long wait, the man finally arrived, strode through the room without stopping and said, "No jobs today, boys." After this one attempt to get a job, McKnight temporarily gave up job hunting and college; he spent the remainder of his vacation in Duluth sightseeing.

But school was not forgotten. He returned home determined to save the money for tuition at Duluth Business University. In the fall of 1906, he borrowed a team of horses from his father so he could work for one of the crews threshing grain around Brookings. McKnight's job was to drive to the nearest creek, hand-pump water into a portable tank, drive back to the threshing outfit, and pump the water into the tender for the engine. For this labor and the use of the horses, he received $4 a day, and earned $280 by the end of the harvesting season. Then he stayed with his parents, who now lived in Brookings, until time for school in January 1907 when he enrolled in Duluth Business University for a six-month course, his goal since high school.

Life in Duluth was much more to young McKnight's liking. He stayed with his relatives on Orange Street in Duluth Heights and, when not in class, wandered around the city exploring the busy Head of the Lakes port. The little metropolis was as up to date as it knew how to be and there was much to see. School was even more pleasurable. Duluth Business University, which had an enrollment of 200, was located over Mrs. Webster's restaurant on West Superior Street, and five days a week McKnight attended classes in bookkeeping, penmanship, and business letter writing. He studied hard and ranked high in the class.

But McKnight never finished the six-month course. In May 1907, the new sandpaper factory, where he had once applied for a job as a laborer, requested a bookkeeper from the University. Professor William Gray, head of the bookkeeping department, called McKnight into his office. "The 3M Company over on Rice Point wants an assistant bookkeeper, William, and I think you're ready to take the job. Go over and see what they have to offer."

McKnight needed no coaxing, but as he later recalled, "I was the scaredest boy that ever lived when I applied for the job." The conscientious business student didn't feel qualified to take a business job as yet, even though Professor Gray assured him he could handle the work.

For the second time in two years, William McKnight climbed the narrow stairs to the dusty 3M office in search of a job. This time he was interviewed by a stern-faced man named A.I. Spooner, head bookkeeper and office manager. What little confidence he had mustered left him when Spooner abruptly opened the interview by demanding, "Let's see your handwriting." McKnight had merely supposed Spooner would want to know whether he could keep books and, in his surprise, became so nervous he could hardly write at all, though he normally wrote a neat, legible script.

After the interview, he was aware that Spooner was not very impressed. Brusquely informing him that he'd let him know about the job, Spooner dismissed the scared young applicant who quickly escaped from the stuffy office into the clear, fresh lake air of Duluth.

Discouraged, he returned to school. Then a few days later there was another call, this time for a timekeeper at the Oliver Mining Company in Iron Mountain, Michigan. Professor Gray again sent McKnight. At the office of the Oliver Mining Company in Duluth, he was interviewed by a sympathetic, elderly man who seemed to think that the young business student was just right for the job. McKnight accepted and went home to pack his belongings.

Looking back, McKnight feels that perhaps Fate stepped in at about this time. On returning to his sister's, he found a telegram saying his mother was ill and he was needed at home. After notifying the Oliver Mining Company that he couldn't take their job, he started packing for the trip to South Dakota. But before he could leave, he got word that his mother was better and that he needn't come home. For a moment it looked as though he now had no job, but, in the meantime, Minnesota Mining and Manufacturing Company had decided they wanted him to come to work. McKnight quickly accepted.

May 13, 1907, was a dull day in Duluth. For that matter, it was a dull day the country over. On the national scene, the Taft political boom to beat Roosevelt was gaining momentum, but there were no fireworks. In Duluth, everything was quiet after the settlement of a lengthy strike by the building laborers.[1] All in all, May 13, 1907, was a very ordinary day for almost everybody except William Lester McKnight. On that gray, rainy day he reported to work in Duluth for Minnesota Mining and Manufacturing Company. It was his first job in the business world and the kind he had dreamed about when milking cows in South Dakota. Business college had paid—he was assistant bookkeeper for the "largest sandpaper manufacturer in the world," according to the Duluth *News Tribune*. In reality, 3M was a small, near-bankrupt newcomer in the abrasive industry; but McKnight didn't know that and wouldn't have cared if he had. The important thing was that he had an income of his own at last. The salary of $11.55 a week (a $10 gold piece and $1.55 in silver change) was enough to pay his room and board, take a girl out once in a while, and perhaps even build a savings account.

Gradually 3M and McKnight got acquainted. He saw John Dwan hurrying in and out of the office on quick trips from Two Harbors. He met blustery, good-natured Hermon Cable and his young son, John, who spent most of their time at the Crystal Bay plant. Occasionally, when he worked overtime on Saturday, he saw President Edgar Ober conferring with Cable or Boynton. From his work, he learned something of the company's early history of near failure, its current financial distress, its North Shore property, and how sandpaper was made and sold. He soon learned, too, that 3M was far from being the largest sandpaper company in the world. But this in no way discouraged him. Soon the young bookkeeper found himself thinking about how the company could sell more sandpaper, cut costs, and even how 3M could make better sandpaper.

Hermon Cable began to notice the reliable and pleasant young man from South Dakota. On the few occasions they conversed, he noticed that McKnight had a quick mind, an ability to come straight to a point and, above all, depend-ability and loyalty to 3M. Soon McKnight was made 3M's first cost accountant and, two years later, when business picked up to an extent where an office manager was needed for the Chicago sales branch, was again promoted.

When McKnight became cost accountant in April 1909, Duluth Business University was again called to fill the vacancy of assistant bookkeeper. This time the school sent a gregarious 22-year-old named Archibald Granville Bush, who was also destined to play a major part in 3M's rise to leadership.

A.G. Bush was the opposite of McKnight both in appear-ance and personality. He was an athletic-appearing young man, 5'10", with straight blond hair, blue eyes, and a light complexion which always had the "just scrubbed" look of a small boy ready for church. He mixed will with people and liked to keep on the go; his energy seemed limitless, and he was usually impatient with slowness in others. He was hap-piest when juggling several projects at once.

While the personalities were different, the backgrounds and ambitions of the two young men were quite similar. Both had grown up on a farm and left it to attend Duluth Business University. Both started at Minnesota Mining and Manufacturing Company as assistant bookkeeper. Both were curious about the world, eager to broaden their hori-zons, willing to work hard, and ambitious. As is often the case with opposites, they became friends. Together they made the long climb to the top, cooperating successfully at every step to push the company to greater accomplishment.

First headquarters for the 3M Company in Two Harbors. Founder John Dwan owned the building and rented space in his law office on the second floor to Minnesota Mining and Manufacturing Company until 1905 when the company moved to Duluth.

The law office which served as 3M Company headquarters from 1902-1905. The board of directors met here for many years after the company moved from Two Harbors. John C. Dwan, current board member and son of founder John Dwan, sits at the desk used by his father and early 3M directors.

Original 3M plant for mining and crushing corundum at Crystal Bay. Rock-crushing machinery was housed in the building to the left. On the right, is the bunkhouse for 3M employees. During heavy storms on Lake Superior, waves often dashed against these buildings, and in 1905, part of the warehouse and the dock were swept away.

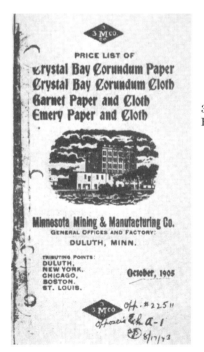

3M Company price list used in 1905 featuring Crystal Bay corundum paper.

Duluth plant, 1905, where 3M manufactured its first sandpaper. The six-story building and adjoining warehouses were originally used by the Imperial Flour Mill. Growth-minded 3M wanted plenty of room for "the proper conduct of business on a large scale." Corundum was shipped to this plant from Crystal Bay, and later, garnet and emery mineral from the East. This plant was used until 1910, when 3M moved to St. Paul.

Modern machinery for making coated abrasives in the early 1900's. Before the invention of such machines, in the late 1800's, sandpaper was coated by hand. This picture is of the Baeder-Adamson Company, Philadelphia, a company founded in 1828 and purchased by 3M in 1929.

Edgar B. Ober, 3M president 1905-1906, and from 1909 to 1929. He served without compensation his first eleven years as an officer, to help the company through early financial troubles. Mr. Ober was general freight agent for the Chicago, St. Paul, Minneapolis, and Omaha Railroad when he became 3M's second president; In 1916 he left his position with the railroad, when 3M was able to pay him a salary.

Lucius Pond Ordway, noted St. Paul civic leader and financier, and 3M's financial "angel." He loaned the company thousands of dollars to carry it through the lean early years. 3M president, 1906-1909.

Emma and Thomas T. Bush had moved from Texas to Minnesota in the winter of 1887, settling in a log cabin on a 240-acre grain farm in the rich, scenic Minnesota River Valley in Renville County, 123 miles west of the Twin Cities.

Archibald Granville was born March 5, 1887, the third of five children. It was soon apparent that Archie was going to be aggressive and extroverted, characteristics which were to contribute greatly to his success in the sales field for 3M when he grew up.

When old enough for school, he attended a three-room schoolhouse in East Granite Falls, walking or riding horseback the three miles into town. It was often below zero or blizzarding when he and his brother and sisters made the trip. Later, Archie went to school in Granite Falls proper. Like McKnight, Bush usually had to hurry home after school, for his father needed him to help with farm chores. Unlike McKnight, however, he didn't mind the chores too much; and, by the time he was out of school, he decided to stay on the farm with his father. While farming, he took an active part in church and community affairs. With an early eye for profits, he picked up an extra three or four dollars on Saturday nights managing a three-piece dance band in Maynard, a small town near Granite Falls and another few dollars on Sundays managing a ball team, although he had no serious interest in athletics.

Bush was happy with this busy schedule of farming, social activity, the dance band and ball team, except for one thing. He was bothered with hay fever, acutely so during the harvest season when he was needed most on the farm. It became worse and worse, and early in 1908 he realized he could never be comfortable on the farm. Reluctantly he made up his mind to move to some other section of the country where hay fever wouldn't bother him. The pollen-free air of Duluth, Minnesota, was recommended to him, and in

1908, at the age of 21, he moved to the port city to start a new life.

On his arrival in Duluth, Bush investigated the possibilities of entering the Duluth Business University to learn the rudiments of office work. Like McKnight, he found he didn't have enough money for the tuition, so he got a job as a construction laborer on the Superior ore docks to earn the money. From August to December 1908, he earned two dollars a day and saved enough for tuition and living expenses. In January 1909, he enrolled for the school's six-month course. Seldom content with a normal workload, Bush persuaded the school to let him go to both day and night classes, and in four months finished the six-month course in penmanship and bookkeeping.

When he was ready to look for work, Minnesota Mining needed a new assistant bookkeeper to replace McKnight, and Bush applied. Hermon Cable, now manager of the Duluth plant, hired him. On April 26, 1909, Bush reported for the job which served as his springboard to a lifetime of success with 3M, the same springboard on which William McKnight had stood a short time before.

The $11.55-a-week job was not to hold the ambitious Bush long, either. In August 1909, he became head bookkeeper in the Duluth office. In rapid succession, he became a salesman, sales manager, a director, a vice-president, and executive vice-president, and in 1949, chairman of the executive committee. His forceful direction of 3M sales programs is an inseparable part of the history of Minnesota Mining and Manufacturing Company.

CHAOS AND CHANGE

OPERATIONS of 3M were most haphazard from 1907 to 1909. The board of directors was potentially strong but too busy with other personal affairs and too scattered to function effectively. President Ordway made a greater effort to protect his heavy investment, but he had little time to be in Duluth. Management of Crane and Ordway, plans for the St. Paul Hotel, yachting, and numerous civic affairs filled his busy calendar. Consequently, he still left most decisions to vice-president Ober. Ober, busy with his duties in St. Paul as general freight agent for the railroad, left as many decisions as he could to H.W. Boynton, general manager of the Duluth plant and office. The Chicago sales office was a headache. Charles C. James, the company's sales agent, was autocratic in his dealings with the home office. Too often he ignored the Duluth office's instructions on credit matters. As a result, 3M was constantly caught with accounts due from companies which went bankrupt, especially during the 1907 depression.

Salesmen were a problem. 3M couldn't afford to hire the caliber of man they would have liked. The men worked on a commission basis, selling sandpaper along with other products. Occasionally, before 3M could get around to bonding a new salesman, he would quit without returning some of the company's funds. The amount was never large because 3M didn't have much money to give its salesmen for expenses. But even the $22 dollars which one salesman kept when he left 3M was a major loss in those days.

To complicate matters, John Dwan had to handle the legal and secretarial work of the company from Two Harbors, because his law practice and insurance business kept him from spending any appreciable time in Duluth. Had he been able to be in the Duluth office more of the time, he might have been able to prevent some of the internal dissension and watch costs more carefully.

Hermon Cable, who preferred outdoor work to office management, escaped the administrative problems by staying at Crystal Bay. Dr. Budd's practice kept him from taking a more active part in company business, and he really had little interest in 3M since its reorganization, except as an investment.

Not only were management problems out of hand, there was little agreement on sales and price policies. Ordway and Ober, both experienced businessmen, wanted 3M to maintain a profitable price schedule. Boynton, primarily a sandpaper maker, not an executive, wanted to cut prices. On November 4, 1907, he wrote Dwan in a complaining tone, "I thought I would write you a few lines to advise you how the new price proposission [sic] is working out. And I am frank to admit that I feel the stand that we have taken is a very bad one for the company. We are getting letters in every mail passing us up at the new price. I also have copies of letters from Boston branch to James advising that Armour and Company are quoting anywhere from 60 and 5% to 65 and 5% on flint goods. Such being the case I hardly see where we will make a killing at 60%. I am at a loss why L.P.O. [Ordway] takes this stand on prices at this particular stage of the game." Feeling as he did, Boynton often overrode Ordway's directions, and eventually 3M became known as a price cutter. This policy was to cause endless trouble until it was corrected years later.

Internal dissension was highly distasteful to Ordway and Ober; and Boynton's services were discontinued in 1908, and Spooner and James were released in 1909.

The problem was to find replacements for these men. The company could offer only a low wage plus stock in the company, and hope that an ambitious employee would do his best to help make 3M successful. Ordway and Ober could and did, however, make promotions from within the organization where possible. Cable was made general manager to replace Boynton.* Orson Hull was made plant manager, and Charles Alliss, an experienced sandpaper maker, was named second in command of the plant. McKnight was moved to the job of office manager in Chicago where someone was needed to watch costs, answer correspondence, and the like. A highly recommended salesman named John W. Pearse replaced James as sales manager in Chicago. Bush was hired as Duluth bookkeeper to take McKnight's place.

The board of directors hoped the new combination would work more efficiently and harmoniously, and it did. With internal harmony established, concentration could now be on manufacturing and sales where it belonged.

The nationally peaceful period from 1909 to 1914 was a time of price wars, internal chaos, and change for 3M, and also for the infant abrasive industry as a whole. 3M definitely had a footing in the industrial world by 1909, but a most precarious one. While sales totaled $192,000 in 1909, the slim profits had to be used for working capital and to reduce the debt of $198,000 still owed Ordway. The quality

---

*Hermon Cable didn't live to see the success of the company to which he had devoted all his personal fortune and energies. He died of Bright's disease at 47, on August 20, 1909. After his father's death, John Cable became office manager then secretary and treasurer of the company, and served as a director until his death in 1939.

of 3M sandpaper was far below that of competition. Improvement was imperative.

The board of directors took a long look at its sales and production picture and made recommendations for major changes. Ober again became president; and Ordway, vice-president. The company shifted its method of selling by mail and through commission men to a salaried organization. "Organization" was a grandiose description. There were only three salesmen on the payroll. The first salaried sales-man hired by sales manager Pearse was Robert H. Skillman who not only became a star salesman but later played an important part in the company's development apart from sales.*

The most drastic change was made in the location of the plant. By 1909, the company realized that the Duluth climate was unsuitable for the manufacture of sandpaper. There were no scientifically controlled drying ovens in those days, and the dampness of the waterfront hampered the drying of the festoons of sandpaper. Moreover, Ordway was anxious to have 3M operations closer to him, and it was decided to move the plant to St. Paul in 1910.

St. Paul, Minnesota, a picturesque city nestled in a valley on the banks of the Mississippi River southeast of its twin, Minneapolis, had a population of 214,000 when Minnesota Mining and Manufacturing Company located there. According to Historian Henry A. Castle, the hilly city with its narrow downtown streets was at that time "a great fur center of America, one of the largest manufacturers of grass twine and its derivative products, home of one of the largest law publishing houses in America [West Publishing Company], a commercial-art center, and a major manufacturing center for sashes and doors, paints and varnishes–a city where life is eager and abundant."[1]

*See Chapter 13.

The spring of 1910, when 3M opened its St. Paul plant, was an extraordinarily busy season for St. Paul Society, then definitely spelled with a capital "S." Particularly so for Ober, who married Agnes Elmer, the nineteen-year-old niece of Lucius Ordway, in March. The newlyweds settled in their Goodrich Avenue home just in time to join the spring social whirl with the Ordways. They attended the opera to hear Geraldine Farrar and the Minneapolis Symphony, to hear soloist Madame Schumann-Heink, and took part in many gay parties held in the fashionable Portland and Summit Avenue mansions. That spring, too, the new St. Paul Hotel, built through the efforts of Lucius Ordway and other St. Paul citizens, opened in a "blaze of glory" with many of Minnesota's notables present.[2]

During this time Ordway supervised the opening of the St. Paul plant. A year before, in answer to a plea from St. Paul's East Side, he had chosen a site for 3M's new home on Forest Avenue near Fauquier, bordering the Chicago, St. Paul, Minneapolis and Omaha trackage. This location, which was only a few minutes' trolley ride from downtown St. Paul, soon gave 3M a chronic headache. When room for expansion was needed, the management had to buy, move, or tear down houses, barns, sheds, and shops to provide space in which to build. This process is still necessary today whenever 3M needs to build adjacent to its other St. Paul buildings.

Although 3M was already in debt to Ordway more than $225,000 in 1910, he financed the construction of a three-story, brick building at a cost of $35,302. The building was barely adequate for 3M's needs, but it was all the firm could afford. Ordway had to wait six months for the first payment of $300 on the building, fifteen months for the next payment of $150, and another six months for the company to start reducing the debt regularly by $100 a month.

The move to St. Paul was to mark the beginning of a remarkable growth and expansion, but at first it looked as though 3M's bad luck had followed the company down from Duluth.

One warm evening in June 1910 when the new plant had been completed but the machinery not yet installed, Bush and Hull decided to take an inventory of the raw material–garnet, Crystal Bay corundum, flint–shipped from Duluth to St. Paul. To get an accurate count, they stacked the hundred-pound bags of crushed abrasive grain in the center of the empty first floor bay, eight bags deep. This was the first time it had been possible to take an accurate inventory of the company's supply of mineral, and Bush and Hull went home quite pleased that evening, unaware they were getting 3M into trouble.

After Bush and Hull had left, the new night watchman started his rounds. If anything went wrong, it was his duty to turn a crank which sounded an alarm in the American Delivery and Telegram central office. It was past midnight, and the building was quiet except for the sound of trains rumbling past the factory. The watchman checked the doors and windows; on the third floor first, then the second, and finally the first. He walked past the huge stacks of mineral piled in the center bay of the first floor, then back to his post, and settled down with the evening paper.

Suddenly the watchman was startled by a terrific crash. Springing to his feet, he was horrified to see through great clouds of dust that the factory floor had given way and the hundred-pound bags had crashed through to the basement. The frightened watchman didn't stop to turn the A.D. & T. crank or notify anyone. He fled the building without reporting the accident and didn't show up for a week.

On Monday morning when 3M workmen arrived to see about installing machinery and office furniture, they found the gaping hole in the middle of the floor and sacks of mineral spilled all over the basement. It was one more setback for a company that had cut its teeth on crises; one more mistake made through inexperience. The floor wasn't built to hold the weight of the mineral sacks, but no one was around to tell that to Bush and Hull.

Fortified by improved production facilities in St. Paul and a new sales force, 3M redoubled its efforts to push the sales volume up. Strong, established competitors blocked its progress wherever they could; and, before long, there was a rough-and-tumble fight within the industry to capture new customers and retain the old. In a fierce price war, 3M was often guilty of being the first to quote an extra discount, often selling below cost. Other companies followed suit. These price-cutting tactics hurt the whole industry.

3M, unable to buy the good domestic garnet controlled by Eastern abrasive manufacturers, had to use an inferior, pink Spanish garnet. To meet competition, the company dyed the glue in its garnet paper red to simulate the appearance of domestic garnet, but competition soon nipped this effort. Competitive salesmen dipped 3M garnet paper in hot water, the red dye dissolved instantly, and the customer knew he was being tricked.

3M replied to this exposé by telling the trade that the tiny black specks in domestic garnet were magnetic particles which ruined the sandpaper as an effective abrasive. Some of the 3M salesmen even carried tiny magnets with them to prove the point. A few customers who didn't know that good domestic garnet has black particles which have no effect on its qualities as an abrasive were impressed.

In spite of the chaos, business improved a little, but not enough to satisfy sales manager Pearse, the first really sales-minded person in the company. He realized that the poor quality of 3M sandpaper was the problem, but he didn't know what to do to improve it, and he got little help from the St. Paul factory or the office. Ober traveled to Chicago nearly every weekend to confer on quality and selling problems; but the truth was he didn't know either why 3M sandpaper was unsatisfactory to customers. Office-manager McKnight, who usually worked on Sundays, sat in on these conferences between Ober and Pearse. During the discussions about complaints, Ober would ask Pearse questions on the Chicago office operations and Pearse often referred the question to McKnight. As a result of these conferences, McKnight began to think more and more about the problem of quality. But he had no idea it would soon be his to solve.

Pearse became discouraged by 1911. He had been unable to get the yearly sales even as high as they were in 1907. He couldn't lick the problem of quality, and he felt the St. Paul factory wasn't sympathetic to his problems with dissatisfied customers. He probably didn't know it, but the fact was that they didn't know all the answers to the quality problem either. In those days, making sandpaper was a matter of "know-how," not science.

Any foreman would tell you it was a simple process. Take paper or cloth, smear on glue, and drop crushed abrasives on it. Dry the product, cut it up, and you have sandpaper. Wonderful machines for smearing on the glue and dropping the mineral on the paper or cloth had only recently taken the place of hand-spreading sheets of sandpaper, and the men who designed them were justifiably proud. H.W. Boynton had designed much of the 3M machinery. But in 1910, even experienced sandpaper makers like Boynton, Hull, or Alliss couldn't explain exactly why the sandpaper turned out as it should one day and was limp and mushy another. They couldn't explain why sometimes the mineral rubbed off the sandpaper too fast when customers used it, and why sometimes a sheet would last through several jobs just as it should. Variations as high as 1,000 percent in the usefulness of the sandpaper plagued all manufacturers. Tests were mostly a matter of the keenness of the workmen's vision. They assumed that if the sandpaper looked right, it must be right. Some workers used the "ear test," snapping a sheet next to their ear. If it was brittle and snapped, it was assumed to be all right. If it was mushy, something must have gone wrong in the maker.

Everyone had his own opinion as to why a batch was a failure. Some blamed the glue, some the paper, and some the weather. The mysterious thing about the whole process was that even if the glue came from the same company, barrel after barrel, the paper from the same supplier, and the grits from the same source, some sandpaper was satisfactory, some inferior. A great deal of 3M's paper turned out to be inferior.

Before Pearse resigned, he lined up several candidates for Ober to interview for the sales manager position, but Ober never got to Chicago to see them. Pearse finally left before anyone had been hired, and Ober now had to find someone himself. One of Ober's basic principles was that loyalty to 3M should be rewarded, and he decided that William McKnight should have the job. So he invited him to St. Paul to talk over the sales problems in preparation to taking over as sales manager.

McKnight was taken by complete surprise because he had had no sales experience, but Edgar Ober knew what he was doing. His appointment of McKnight as sales manager was the turning point in the nine-year struggle to get ahead. The young ex-bookkeeper was a novice in the sales end of the business, but he was to ferret out some of the answers to the quality problem, and under his direction, basic policies were formed which gradually swung the company to the profit side of the ledger where it has remained.

NEW SALES TECHNIQUES

THE CUSTOMARY sales technique in the abrasive industry when William McKnight became sales manager was for the salesman to call on the front office of a plant, show the purchasing agent a catalogue, and take his order. Industry leaders like Baeder-Adamson had been doing it that way for years. Twenty-four-year-old McKnight had a different concept of how a new and unknown company like 3M should sell abrasives.

McKnight reasoned that a salesman would have a better chance of displacing competitive sandpaper if he could get into the back shop, talk to the workmen who used the competitive products, and demonstrate the superiority of 3M abrasives right on the machines or at the workbench. It was a bold theory for young McKnight who had seldom been in any kind of a factory and knew practically nothing about the technical use of sandpaper. However, it seemed to him the only practical way to sell unknown garnet paper and cloth, flint and emery products in a competitive situation. To prove his theory, McKnight went to Rockford, Illinois and personally called on the plants in this furniture-manufacturing center. The furniture trade was one of the mainstays of 3M's business. Once a month he took the train to Rockford and called on as many of the city's 29 furniture plants as he could in one day. At first he rode the trolleys, but they were too slow, and he finally rented a horse and buggy at three dollars a day.

In Rockford, McKnight learned that the front office had little inclination to let a salesman into the back shop; and, if he did manage to get there, the workmen had little desire to be bothered by a sandpaper salesman, especially one from a relatively unknown concern like Minnesota Mining and Manufacturing Company. But McKnight had made up his mind that this was the way 3M should sell, and he was determined to prove that it was an effective way. On his calls, he was content only when he could talk to the man who used the sandpaper, find out his problems and complaints and what he needed in the way of abrasive products for a particular job. Before long, purchasing agents and shop foremen found their sales resistance weakening when approached by the soft-spoken 3M sales manager. Neither McKnight's appearance nor his manner suggested a typical salesman of the day. Often he gained a hearing where a more aggressive glad-hander might have had the door shut in his face. Fourteen orders out of fourteen calls was his goal, and amazingly often he reached it.

In the back shops, McKnight found to his chagrin that 3M products often didn't stand up to competition. This was a fact he had long known but hated to have proved. Before long, the problem of quality was absorbing most of his thoughts. Back in Chicago in his office, he would patiently write the factory in St. Paul reporting what he had found on his Rockford calls, pleading for better quality and uniformity. Sales managers before him had complained, too, but the difference was that McKnight's reports were backed by firsthand experience in the plants; he knew what the workmen needed and the basis for their complaints. Unfortunately, quality in sandpaper continued to be an elusive thing. The St. Paul factory didn't or couldn't respond to

McKnight's pleas. Far from defeating McKnight, however, the problem challenged him to the point where he spent even his spare time working on its solution. Except for an occasional Sunday off to watch the Chicago Cubs' Tinker, Evers, and Chance make history with their famous double play, McKnight could always be found in his office when he wasn't on the road for 3M. A Pullman became his second home as he traveled back and forth seeing buyers and conferring with Ober.

Along with the problem of quality control, McKnight inherited the industry price war. The chaos it caused made a deep impression on him. His feeling against price cutting grew stronger each time he faced a buyer who eyed him coldly and remarked, "Your competitor has offered me garnet paper at an additional five percent discount. If you can better this price, maybe I'll order from you." The "additional discount" usually meant the loss of a fair profit, or even selling below cost to get the order. Though inexperienced, McKnight could appreciate that there was no future for 3M or even the abrasive industry if such tactics were to continue. President Ober, Ordway, and Dwan agreed with him. They had tried unsuccessfully to get sales managers James and Pearse to refuse special discounts.

Out of McKnight's obsession for quality and his deep disapproval of special or confidential discounts grew a decision which was responsible for a large measure of 3M's success and growth. McKnight resolved that if he had anything to say about it, 3M would make such superior products that the customer would be willing to pay a decent price to get them. Moreover, 3M would stay out of highly competitive markets. He found no disagreement with these thoughts among the directors.

The avoidance of highly competitive markets was to be especially significant later when the company became diversified. The memory of that disruptive price war during

1909-1914 influenced McKnight in many a decision as to whether 3M should enter a new market. All through its history, 3M has preferred uncrowded fields for product development, and the records show it has been a financially prudent policy.

If 3M products were ever to become superior in quality, there must be, in McKnight's opinion, greater coordination between the factory and the salesmen. It was up to the salesmen to know how 3M abrasives were performing on the job and how they compared with competitive products. It was up to the factory to take the salesmen's recommendations seriously. Systematically, McKnight trained his salesmen to (1) get into the back shop; (2) determine the best type of abrasive for the job by talking with the workmen and demonstrating 3M products; (3) report the specific nature of complaints to the sales office and furnish the factory with samples of the unsatisfactory sandpaper. The establishment of this system of selling was a tremendous step forward for 3M.

Three salaried salesmen were under McKnight's direction as sales manager. This was too small a number to call into St. Paul for regular sales meetings, so McKnight trained his men personally by going on calls with them. There were a few commission salesmen, too, and mail orders amounted to eight or nine thousand dollars a year. Not only were salesmen handicapped by lack of quality in 3M products in those days but lack of funds for entertainment of customers. Neither could long-distance telephone calls be made without special clearance, and trips were planned to the last mile to avoid unnecessary cost.

McKnight's sales force used any method it could think of for finding new customers. Each man was furnished with a list of firms already buying from Minnesota Mining, but finding new customers was up to the individual salesman. "We looked for smokestacks, took names out of the telephone directory and from reference books like Dun and Bradstreet," reminisces one 3M man. First orders were hard enough to get because of strong competition; repeat orders were next to impossible because of poor-quality products. But there were always some manufacturers who would order if the price were low enough, and 3M struggled along.

After three years of persistent hammering at the quality problem, progress was barely perceptible, in Sales Manager McKnight's opinion. His feelings of dissatisfaction culminated after a particularly trying day at Piqua, Ohio. He had spent most of the day testing garnet-cloth endless belts at the Pioneer Pole & Shaft Company, a heavy user of garnet cloth in belt form for the sanding of buggy poles, whiffle-trees, and shafts made of hickory, one of the hardest of woods.

"I had about a dozen sample belts for trial at Pioneer Pole," relates McKnight. "To my disgust, one belt of garnet I demonstrated would be good and the next one terrible. There was no uniformity."

Back in his hotel room that night, after his call on Pioneer Pole & Shaft, McKnight composed a long letter to president Ober, venting his feelings about quality and uniformity. Carefully and with considerable force, he pointed out that there was no future for 3M if there couldn't be greater coordination between the sales force and the factory. He recommended that a general manager be appointed over sales and factory to accomplish this coordination by dividing his time between the field and the factory.

President Ober made a prompt decision when he read McKnight's letter. He agreed with his sales manager's suggestion that there be one boss for sales and production, and Ober knew who it should be. William L. McKnight had proven in his seven years with 3M that he could not only grasp and intelligently solve current problems but that he had the ability to look ahead and plan constructively for the future. From his experience in the field, he now knew both selling and manufacturing problems. The men who worked for him admired him and worked hard to please him. Who was there in Minnesota Mining better suited for general manager?

Ober knew of two men, however, who might not agree with him. He felt that Plant Superintendent Orson Hull and Office Manager John Cable would both want the job if it were created. Hull had been with 3M since 1905 and was a minor stockholder. Cable was a major stockholder, having inherited his father's stock. It was a ticklish situation which Ober would have liked to avoid, but he faced the issue and invited McKnight, Hill, and Cable to dinner at the Minnesota Club in St. Paul.

McKnight has never forgotten that evening. Everyone was ill at ease. Neither Hull, Cable, nor McKnight had been a guest at the club before. Each was trying to make a good impression on Ober. The latter, usually poised and calm, was also nervous, for he faced the possibility of alienating the loyalties of both Hull and Cable through the appointment of McKnight. It was a situation he couldn't sidestep, and during the dinner in the quiet private dining room, he outlined the new setup to the men.

"If the appointment of McKnight as general manager isn't satisfactory to you, gentlemen," said Ober firmly to Hull and Cable, "then I'll have to go outside the company to find a man, and this I'd rather not do." Hull and Cable realized that Ober had no intention of giving either of them the assignment and fortunately took McKnight's promotion with good grace. McKnight naturally was pleased. He liked the pleasant excitement of Chicago and hated to leave, but he was anxious to be at the St. Paul plant to put his ideas to a test.

While McKnight was serving as sales manager, A.G. Bush had persuaded president Ober that he could be useful in the Boston branch office as a combination bookkeeper, stenographer, and shipping clerk. Soon after his transfer, he not only was keeping books, answering mail, and shipping orders, but was also out on the road selling. He'd take an order in the afternoon, then come back to the office in the evening and ship it. His job in Boston was similar to McKnight's first assignment in the Chicago office.

At the time in the Boston area, 3M was calling mostly on wood-working plants and shoe factories and had only one full-time salesman. In 1912, the Boston office added a book-keeper, shipping clerk, another Boston salesman, and a New York State salesman. When the latter resigned, McKnight offered his territory to Bush who quickly accepted.

As a salesman, Bush was in his element because of his tremendous energy and liking for people. The problems he encountered were typical for all 3M salesmen. On one of his first calls, the customer (Standard Desk Company) thought 3M products so bad they wanted to return the whole previous order and get their money back. Bush had to talk the desk company into letting 3M replace the whole order, and then, recounts Bush, "pray fervently that the second order would be satisfactory." This sort of thing happened many times a week.

Gradually Bush realized that 3M competitors were, as he expresses it today, "standing by, waiting for 3M to fall." At the time McKnight was appointed general manager in 1914, Bush had gone nearly two weeks without an order. As he traveled back to his hotel after a discouraging tour of the Reading, Pennsylvania, territory, he wondered how to explain the lack of sales to his boss. When he reached the hotel, the desk clerk handed him a large white envelope from McKnight, and Bush's heart sank. He thought maybe he was being fired. Reluctantly he opened the envelope and pulled out its contents.

There was no notice of dismissal. Instead, there was a long letter from McKnight in which he told Bush about his recommendations to Ober for coordinating sales and production and his subsequent appointment to general manager. Then came the entirely unexpected question to Bush: "Would you," wrote McKnight, "consider being sales manager for 3M?" Bush's spirits soared. Nothing would please him more. It took him just three days to complete the necessary calls in the East and head for Chicago, where he began a successful and colorful career as sales manager for Minnesota Mining and Manufacturing Company.

Bush had less than three years' sales experience when he became sales manager, but the dynamic 27-year-old had the potential for making a success of the job. He was sales-minded, economy minded, and he had the ability to push his men to limits they often thought impossible. His idea was to pay his staff well and to expect hard work of them.

Most important to 3M, Bush was resourceful. This is a desirable characteristic for any sales manager but was a necessity in the face of 3M's strong, established competition. As a salesman, Bush had found new customers by tracking down smokestacks and he had innovated sample-carrying in the abrasive industry as a way to more efficient selling. As sales manager, he tried not only to develop new techniques but new touches for established routines. For example, he developed a relationship between 3M and its distributor houses that went far beyond the usual manufacturer-distributor arrangement.

Early in 1914 McKnight had arranged for two industrial distributors to carry 3M products–T.B. Rayl of Detroit, and E.A. Kinsey of Cincinnati. A good connection with a distributor house was one way of quickly building prestige, because the distributor already had standing with the trade. There was nothing new in this arrangement; every manufacturer who wanted to extend his business dropped his line in the lap of a distributor. But Bush added a new twist. Usually, the manufacturer let the distributor do all the selling. If the distributor carried ten products, his salesmen could devote approximately ten per cent of their time to each one. Bush felt that distributor salesmen could not do a good job of selling 3M abrasives unless they thoroughly understood the product and the needs of the workmen using the product, so he arranged for 3M salesmen to accompany the Rayl and Kinsey men on calls, and the two worked out the customer's needs together. 3M was one of the first manufacturers who gave this type of cooperation to a distributor salesman. It paid rich dividends for both 3M and the distributor. After such a training period, the distributor's salesman knew much more about 3M products than most of the other items in his catalogue and consequently sold more of them. Eventually, the distributor's salesman could handle big accounts, such as the large auto manufacturers, and serve the customer in the manner 3M desired. So successful was 3M's program of cooperation that within a year T.B. Rayl stopped carrying competitive sandpaper and handled 3M products exclusively.

The combined efforts of 3M and the distributor house resulted in the seeing of customers as often as once a week compared to the three times a year by competitive abrasive salesmen.

For years 3M's cooperation with Rayl and Kinsey gave them an edge over competitors who didn't bother to include such a program in their merchandising plans. Connections with the distributor houses were increased rapidly during and after World War I. Indianapolis Belting and Supply Company took on the 3M line in 1915; then W. Bingham and Company of Cleveland, wholesale hardware distributors. Others followed. By 1917 there were 15 large distributor houses augmenting the 3M sales force of five salaried men and two commissioned men who worked large territories out of Detroit, St. Paul, Chicago, Milwaukee, and Cincinnati. These connections quickly built prestige for Minnesota Mining and Manufacturing Company; a prestige, however, that would have been impossible to achieve had 3M not already established its own standards of high quality, stable prices, and a desire to serve the trade better through research.

Like McKnight, Bush gave the salesmen as much personal training as time would permit, but according to modern standards, it was scant indeed. One salesman (now a vice-president), who joined the company after World War I, recalls being assigned to a large territory the day he was hired. "It was sink or swim. Salesmen in those days didn't get the mollycoddling they do today. I remember when I was assigned to my territory, Bush came to town and we called on one customer together and that was it. He had another appointment, and I was completely on my own, looking for smokestacks in a strange territory."

For the most part, from 1914 until after World War I, Bush continued the sales policies set by McKnight. 3M men were instructed to get into the back shop and work with the men using the abrasives. Price cutting was forbidden. The salesmen were on the strictest of expense accounts. As an incentive, salesmen were paid extra compensation if sales costs were kept below a certain level. 3M believed in putting what meager working capital it had into making better sandpaper and hiring good salesmen. As a result, while its competitors were carrying ads in *Iron Age*, *Abrasive Industry*, other trade journals, and popular magazines such as *The Saturday Evening Post*, 3M was limited to direct mail advertising.

Bush's early years as sales manager were nearly as difficult as those of his predecessors, but he loved every minute of it. 3M now gave him approximately $200 a month, and later some profit sharing, which was munificent in comparison with his $11.55 a week starting salary as bookkeeper.

His new position and salary allowed him to think of marriage; and, in 1919, he married Miss Edyth Bassler of Chicago, a talented young actress and dancer, who gave up her professional stage career but transferred her interest in the stage to the Little Theater movement.[1]

More promotions came rapidly for Bush. He was elected a director of 3M and its treasurer in May 1921. In 1925, McKnight called him to St. Paul to be general manager in charge of all sales.* The force had grown to forty-eight by now—forty regulars, five commission men, and three foreign salesmen. Bush set standards for these men to match those that McKnight had set for laboratory and production workers, and vigorously trained his staff to meet them. Often he worked seven days a week. He planned sales campaigns, wrote sales letters, and called on customers both with his men and alone. He inspired and pushed his staff to meet sales quotas they often thought impossible. Under his direction, sales meetings were held regularly for the first time. At these conferences salesmen were given the opportunity of talking problems over with top management; they were taken through the 3M factory to acquaint them with production problems. Each salesman was asked to prepare and present sample sales arguments at the meetings where they were discussed in open forum. Emphasis at these conferences was always on coordination between sales, factory, and laboratory, and on service to customers as well as sales.

Through such intensive efforts, Bush built one of the most effective sales teams in the industry. His constant

*During 1918-19, when 3M was growing substantially, it divided its sales territories into two divisions, Eastern and Western. From 1919 to 1925, Bush was sales manager of the Western Division, and Robert H. Skillman, 3M's first salaried salesman was sales manager of the Eastern Division.

refusal to be satisfied with less than the best during decisive years is one of his most valuable contributions to the success of 3M.

OUT OF A STORM, A LABORATORY

IN THE SUMMER OF 1914, 3M was plunged without warning into a new crisis which threatened to destroy years of hard work. At one moment, everything was going along fairly satisfactorily. During the three years McKnight had been sales manager, monthly sales had reached an all-time high of $22,000, and quality was very slowly improving through persistent effort. The company was paying its bills on time, had paid for the St. Paul plant, and was gradually reducing its debt to Lucius Ordway. The next moment, a cloud-burst of new complaints drenched 3M. Garnet paper and cloth were returned in quantity by the furniture manufacturers, hardware companies, and, in fact, everyone who used garnet abrasives. Repeat orders became almost impossible to get. The complaint, always the same and always on garnet products, was, "The abrasive mineral drops off after a few minutes' operation." For a sandpaper manufacturer, no complaint could be more serious.

Factory Superintendent Hull knew of no reason that the garnet products should be defective. No matter how carefully he supervised and checked production, goods kept coming back with the same complaint. The factory and sales department became frantic, for the prestige so recently and painstakingly built up with the trade was rapidly dwindling. It was a discouraging beginning for McKnight in his new assignment as general manager and for Bush as sales manager. President Ober began to wonder if 3M hadn't been born under an unlucky star after all. To the men in the factory, the problem was like a specter haunting them as they made batch after batch of garnet paper, all ill-fated as before.

Long weeks went by before the factory found the trouble. No one remembers exactly who made the discovery, but it is recalled that one day a workman noticed an oily film on water standing in a scrub pail. The water contained garnet mineral which had been mopped up from the floor. He called Hull. Hull looked at the water and, sure enough, there was a film on it which appeared to be oil. This was puzzling because the uncrushed garnet in stock did not show evidence of oil contamination. But if the oil were coming from the *crushed* garnet in the pail of water, it might explain the trouble with 3M's garnet paper. Hull knew that glue wouldn't stick to any oily surface; and, if the garnet grits were contaminated with oil, they would pull out of the glue in the finished sandpaper after a few minutes' use, just as the customers had reported.

Hull immediately tested samples of crushed garnet from 3M's stock to see if it was oily. He found that the garnet, when crushed and graded to sandpaper-grit size and dropped into a glass of water, sank to the bottom slowly in the shape of an angleworm, and an oil film formed on top of the water. Samples of mineral known to be oil-free left no film and sank to the bottom of the glass evenly. Such testing left little doubt that the garnet was oily and unfit for sandpaper.

The big question was, how could oil have gotten into 3M's stock of uncrushed garnet? Had it happened before 3M got the garnet from Spain, or had it happened at the plant after

it was received? Would each new supply of garnet be contaminated in the same way?

Office Manager Cable started checking the source of 3M's
garnet supply. He wrote the supply house in New York, the
railroad companies, and everyone connected with the shipment before he found the answer. The story he unearthed
was that months before, a Spanish tramp steamer had
sailed for America carrying a cargo of olive oil. It was bal-
lasted with the sacks of Spanish garnet consigned to 3M.
Far out on the Atlantic the little ship had run into heavy
seas, and as it pitched and rolled, the casks of olive oil had
been tossed about. Apparently some had broken open, and
before the storm subsided, olive oil had seeped into the
sacks of garnet. As no one realized that any important damage had been done, the accident was not reported when the
ship docked; and, by the time the garnet reached St. Paul,
there was no outward evidence of oil contamination.

The company was faced with the problem of what to do
with the garnet now that they knew what was wrong. The
two hundred tons on hand at the St. Paul plant represented
a major share of 3M's working capital. Unsuccessful efforts
were made to recover damages from the steamship company
and the garnet mines in Spain. 3M had no insurance to
cover such a peculiar accident. They could not afford to
dump the garnet and order more. Somehow, the oil-
contaminated garnet had to be made usable. Hull tried boiling it in a solution of caustic soda after it was crushed, but
the process left an alkali deposit on the grains which made
them as unsatisfactory as oily garnet for sandpaper. Finally,
after months of experimenting, a method of making the garnet oil-free was found. Hull discovered that by spreading a
thin layer of crushed mineral over a hot plate and heating it
thoroughly, the oil could be roasted off. After this discovery,
all crushed garnet for 3M sandpaper was washed first, then
heated. This process insured the mineral staying in the

glue. Meanwhile, before the roasting process was discovered, 3M had to struggle along making poor-quality sandpaper and enduring complaints.

As is often the case, some good evolved from trouble. The olive oil incident persuaded McKnight more than ever of the need for greater control over raw materials and the quality and uniformity of the finished sandpaper. At his insistence, 3M's first laboratory was organized. Existing testing operations which had been carried on in various parts of the plant were consolidated in the new laboratory. This was a small, closetlike room which in no way fitted the modern conception of the word "laboratory" either in physical appearance or functions. McKnight's idea was to improve quality and uniformity of products by providing a central place for the systematic testing against predetermined standards of (1) raw materials; (2) coated abrasive products at successive stages of their manufacture; and (3) finished products. These definite, predetermined, quality standards were not in existence when the laboratory was organized but had to be gradually developed by the laboratory in collaboration with the factory to meet customer requirements.

To carry out this idea, a small corner of the ream storage room on the second floor of the plant was enclosed to house laboratory equipment. Into this small space (5' x 11') 3M installed a sink and glue bath for making sample glue mixtures for testing; a Perkins tensile-strength tester for checking the paper or cloth backing for the sandpaper; a rub-test machine; and a workbench where hand spread samples could be made. A big, black book for recording test data was kept on the bench, and pails, pipettes, and miscellaneous supplies were put under it. The walls of the laboratory were left rough and unpainted; the aisle between the equipment was so narrow that when McKnight or someone else from the office or plant wanted to come in, the laboratory worker had to step outside into the ream storage room. The laboratory wouldn't hold all the necessary equipment. There was no room for a wooden chopping block used to cut up sandpaper or for the treadle-operated tin shears for cutting sandpaper. These were placed just outside the door of the laboratory, in the ream storage room.

The cost of this little laboratory was just under $500. This was a considerable sum for 3M in 1916 but turned out to be a most profitable investment.

The laboratory operation didn't run too smoothly at first. There were personnel problems which slowed progress. The men supervising the manufacture of sandpaper for 3M thought that personal experience was all that was needed to control the steps of manufacture and to rate the quality of the finished product. The factory superintendent, for example, would run his thumbnail across the paper after the mineral had been applied but before the glue had set to determine whether the proper amount of each had been applied to produce a good quality sandpaper. The attempt to control quality through a so-called laboratory was regarded to a certain extent as an invasion of their prerogatives. This feeling created a problem at first. The sandpaper business was an extremely secretive one. Each sandpaper maker developed his own formulas and designed his own machinery. There was no public information available regarding the processes used. 3M's factory supervisors had irreplaceable experience in manufacturing sandpaper and designing machinery. Furthermore, they were extremely hard-working, loyal employees. It would have been almost impossible to replace them if they left 3M, and for this reason it was necessary to find a laboratory man who would recognize this personnel problem and not alienate their loyalty but, rather, prove to them gradually the value of the tests to be made. A man with the proper diplomacy to deal with the personalities involved was hard to find. Three young men were tried without success. Then in October 1916, a young high-school graduate named William Vievering was hired to make the tests in the laboratory. Vievering had had no chemistry or technical training, but he had the knack of getting along with people. Gradually, in collaboration with McKnight and Hull, tests already being used were improved, and a series of new tests were developed to check uniformity of manufacture and to attempt to rate the quality of the finished sandpaper.

For years, glue had been tested for viscosity by sucking up a pipette full of a sample and timing it as it ran out of the pipette. The time it took for the glue to run out gave some indication of its strength. Another common test to help determine the strength of the glue was the "jelly" test. A glassful of glue dissolved in a given amount of water was placed in an icebox to "set." The resistance of the jellied glue to thumb pressure gave a further indication of the strength of the glue. The laboratory developed new methods of accumulating, measuring, and recording these tests.

Another problem for the laboratory was to obtain uniformity of grit sizes for its sandpaper. At the time the laboratory was set up, these various grit sizes were obtained by passing the mineral through grading machines. Bolting cloth was used as the screening medium. Fine-grit sizes were obtained by sifting the crushed mineral over bolting cloth with a certain number of mesh openings per inch; coarse sizes with a different number of openings, and so on. The difficulty was that, regardless of the representation of the seller, the number of openings per inch often varied in different pieces of bolting cloth which were supposed to be the same. As a result, there were variations in the degree of coarseness of grit sizes on sandpaper instead of a uniform-size mineral coating. To overcome this, small hand-screens made with bolting clothing containing the right number of openings per inch for each grit were developed for testing purposes. Samples of graded mineral for use in coating sandpaper were run through the test screens to see if the grits were uniform in size.

Also, tests were developed to determine the amount of mineral applied to a given grit size of sandpaper during manufacture. These tests were made by cutting out a 4" by 6" sample of paper backing before it passed through the gluing rolls and then cutting another piece from the same section after the mineral and glue had been applied. The difference in weight between the uncoated and coated pieces determined the coating weight of the mineral and glue. In this manner, standard coating weight for each grit size of sandpaper was established and through these tests, coating weights were kept fairly uniform.

Finally when the sandpaper was coated and dried, a "rub test" was made on a machine conceived by McKnight and developed by 3M engineers. This test consisted of cutting out a 4" by 6" sample, weighing it, clamping it on a block and mechanically rubbing it under a given pressure a given number of times against another piece of the same grit size sandpaper. The sample would then be weighed to determine mineral loss. If the mineral loss did not exceed a predetermined amount, the sandpaper was considered up to standard.

After the olive oil incident, McKnight became more concerned than ever with the quality problem. In addition to establishing the laboratory, he saw to it that everyone in 3M who had anything to do with making the sandpaper was impressed with the need for high quality. Each batch, or "run," was coded, and the code numbers to label the runs had to be made up from the following combination of letters and numbers:

C O M P L A I N T S
1 2 3 4 5 6 7 8 9 0

The word "complaints" was a continual reminder to factory workers of what the company could expect of inferior sandpaper.

William Vievering remembers one day when McKnight became so fed up with customer complaints that he ordered the young laboratory worker to make a rub test of a sample from each of the 1,100 rolls of sandpaper in stock that had been manufactured before run-testing had become standard procedure. "The shipping room was a shambles before I got through," recalls Vievering. "The bulky rolls of sandpaper were wrapped for shipping, and I had to rip off the packing paper from each one in order to cut out a rub-test sample. But we knew when I got through whether the stuff was good enough to send out, and that's what McKnight wanted to be absolutely sure of."

3M's small, crude laboratory remained a one-man, one-room affair for several years, but it was the company's first real beginning in the field of research and quality control. It remained, however, to find the genius who would bring the laboratory to its full potential.

DEBT FREE AT LAST

3M MIGHT have remained small and debt-ridden indefinitely except for a new coated abrasive product branded "THREE-M-ITE" and a war called World War I. The combination of the two converted the company from an unprofitable to a debt-free, prosperous one.

Early in 1914 things were peaceful in the abrasive industry after the end of the price war in 1912. Sandpaper manufacturers were enjoying increased business, mostly due to the automotive industry, which had been growing with spectacular speed ever since its diaper years. The parade of new models chugging along America's dusty highways grew longer each day. Among them were now near-forgotten names and some still with us: Knox Waterless, Apperson, Searchmont, Locomobile, Haynes, Peerless, Winton, Long Distance, Stevens, Duryea, Franklin, Berg, Crestmobile, Stearns, Pierce Arrow, Packard, Cadillac, Oldsmobile, Plymouth, Studebaker, and Buick. All needed sandpaper at some stage of their manufacture. Workers used it to sand the wooden frames, metal parts, and the body finishes.

Mass production, so effective in Henry Ford's automobile factory, was being adopted in more and more factories before World War I. The speed and precision of mass-production methods created the need for a more durable, faster abrasive for sanding metal parts in order to keep assembly lines moving. To meet this need, sandpaper manufacturers were experimenting extensively with artificial minerals. For months, 3M had been working with an abrasive cloth made with aluminum oxide, an electric furnace product made by the Norton Wheel Company. Branded THREE-M-ITE abrasive cloth, it proved far superior to the natural mineral, emery, for cutting metal, and in June 1914, 3M put their product on the market. Almost simultaneously, the heir to the Austrian throne was assassinated by a Serbian fanatic and Europe plunged into war.

These two events, seemingly so unrelated, marked the beginning of 3M's first prosperity.

In the opinion of many, this new construction was the best metal working abrasive available to industry, though not the first artificial abrasive to be marketed. Industry was hungry for this aluminum oxide cloth to sand down metal parts; and, in less than three years, it became 3M's best-selling line. It was a product superior enough to be in demand; a product on which 3M could, for the first time, earn a fair profit; a product which put the company in the position advocated by McKnight when he was sales manager. Between 1914 and 1916, the company's gross sales, swelled by orders for the new product, more than doubled.

The automotive and machine tool industries were its chief consumers until America's entry into the war. Staggering quantities of sandpaper were needed to help turn out the automobiles rolling off the assembly line, and the machine tool industry also ordered the new abrasive in quantity.

At first, the automobile companies balked on the price differential between emery abrasive cloth and the new aluminum oxide construction. But after determined effort by Bush's sales force, Briggs Manufacturing Company of

Detroit started the new product on its way with an order for 20 reams. They wanted immediate delivery, and 3M didn't have 20 reams in stock as yet. Both Superintendent Hull and Assistant Superintendent Alliss were away when the order reached the factory. But General Manager McKnight didn't let that stop 3M from getting its first shipment out on time; with the help of the foreman, he supervised the production. After the first order from Briggs, other companies heard of the product and orders started coming in rapidly.

When America tooled to war production, THREE-M-ITE cloth, as well as other abrasives, were in high demand for the speedy manufacture of army vehicles, airplanes, munitions, and miscellaneous war materials. In line with 3M's sales policy, the salesmen worked beside the men on the production line of the factories, helping the workers select the proper coated abrasive for the job.

The success of 3M's new abrasive paper was in its flexibility. Soon after it was first sold, Bush reported that it would be much more successful if it were flexible enough for workmen to be able to bend the sheets to sand around moldings and other curved metal surfaces. McKnight tackled this problem as optimistically and thoroughly as he did administrative problems, even though he didn't have the slightest idea how to go about making sandpaper more flexible.

Factory workers were startled one morning to find McKnight and Plant Superintendent Hull sitting cross-legged in the middle of the factory floor, discussing a piece of THREE-M-ITE cloth. They were used to seeing McKnight and Ober, hats on, hands behind their backs, quietly strolling through the plant, checking production.* But the

*Affectionately, behind their backs, the workers referred to president Ober as "Uncle Sam" because they thought his long, thin face with steady, blue eyes and aquiline nose strongly resembled the Uncle Sam on World War I posters. General Manager McKnight was "Sandy Smooth" to the men, a nickname inspired by his red hair and ability to keep things running smoothly.

sight of the usually dignified McKnight sitting on the floor was unusual indeed. The men learned later that Hull and McKnight were working on the problem of flexibility. By sheer accident that day, Hull discovered the answer to the problem. He drew the sheet of the abrasive cloth over the sharp corner of an iron bar and succeeded in breaking the adhesive backing down in a way that made the sheet more flexible. The new flexible abrasive cloth immediately met with favor in industry. Now automotive and other production workers could wrap it around a hammer handle to get at otherwise inaccessible places on car parts they were sanding. Curved metal surfaces could be sanded with greater efficiency. Sales climbed higher.

3M's success in flexing brought trouble, too, and taught the company its first lesson in the value of patents. Carborundum Company was also producing an abrasive cloth made with an artificial abrasive, which they trademarked "Aloxite." Five years after 3M came out with the flexible variety, Vice-president George Rayner of Carborundum wrote President Ober warning him that 3M was infringing on the Carborundum patent covering the flexible feature of their "Aloxite" cloth. Ober was concerned. THREE-M-ITE cloth was 3M's first really profitable product; he wanted nothing to spoil its success. Worried, he wrote McKnight who was in Brookings, South Dakota, visiting his parents. All during McKnight's vacation, the two men corresponded. As they knew almost nothing about the patent situation, it seemed prudent to hire a patent lawyer. The word went out to staff members to see if anyone knew a good man. Within a short time Bush recommended Paul Carpenter, a Chicago patent attorney, who became one of Minnesota Mining's most colorful and valuable counselors.

The threat to 3M was serious if Carborundum's patent was valid. Ober's and McKnight's ignorance of patent laws made them exceedingly anxious about the situation.

Carpenter began investigations to determine whether 3M's method of flexing was infringing anyone's patent. All the time that he was checking patents, he wrote voluminous letters to Ober and McKnight from his Chicago office, briefing them on the intricacies and value of patents. His letters reveal a precise, legal mind with a literary turn. But the more prosaic Ober and McKnight didn't care how literary Carpenter got if he protected 3M's interest. He did, brilliantly.

After investigation of the situation, Carpenter wrote an opinion that the Carborundum patent was invalid. This opinion was based on the fact that the prior art showed the same things Carborundum claimed. He then notified Carborundum that 3M would continue production as before. Nothing more was heard from them.

The experience was an eye opener for 3M. They had been so busy worrying about production, quality, and sales that they had given little time to other than the routine legal problems which Dwan usually handled from Two Harbors. The incident gave 3M its first real patent consciousness. That they still had a great deal to learn, they were to find out later; but now they at least were aware of the value of a patent. Eventually, Carpenter was hired on a permanent basis and brought to St. Paul. The lawyer often wryly complained when dealing with patent infringers that 3M had "sent him to war with a feather duster." His reference was to 3M's dislike for law suits; the settled policy was to avoid litigation whenever possible. But while he complained, Carpenter kept 3M on sound ground patentwise; and, through his influence, 3M developed a profound respect for the power of a patent.

The problem of flexing and the problem of patents were settled without slowing the sales of THREE-M-ITE cloth. From the modest beginning of $15,110 gross sales for the six months in 1914, the product grossed an increasing volume

A.G. Bush, present chairman of 3M's executive committee, at his Chicago desk in 1919, when he was sales manager. Bush took the desk as payment for a delinquent account.

3M General Laboratory, 1924. Here the company's first formal product research began. The staff of nine set up scientific quality control standards for coated abrasives, and undertook the first chemical experiments to improve raw materials. Standing left to right: G.P. Netherly, E.C. Lund, S.L. Ruby, R.P. Carlton, R.G. Drew, L.A. Hatch. Seated at the desk: F.G. Meck and T.J. Miller. The ninth man, W.H. Siegworth, is not pictured. Only Mr. Ruby left the company. Mr. Hatch is now vice-president in charge of Research and Product Development. Mr. Carlton was 3M president from 1949 to 1953.

Cutting floor in 3M's St. Paul coated abrasives plant, 1925. Women ream sorters are shuffling sheets of sandpaper into quires (24 sheets). Women still perform this task today at 3M, and package orders as well.

3M's St. Paul office force, about 1930. Even during the depression, office space was at a premium, due to the company's steady growth. This office was on the top floor of Building 2, the company's second coated abrasives factory. Administrative employees got a building of their own in 1939.

each year. Soon its sales accounted for roughly 45 per cent of the total volume; the other lines of garnet, flint, and emery, the balance.

Before the THREE-M-ITE Brand and World War I, the annual sales volume was $263,000 and the company was in debt. When the smoke of the European conflict cleared away, Minnesota Mining and Manufacturing Company was a million-dollar concern. By 1919, the total volume of sales reached $1,386,383, with a net income of $439,407.

With the beginning of company prosperity, important changes were taking place within the organization. Once again 3M was developing a family flavor reminiscent of the early Two Harbors' days when the five founders gathered above John Dwan's law office to talk over their problems. Ober, McKnight, John Cable, Bush, and Hull worked on sales, office, and factory problems in close cooperation.* Their willingness to work long hours, and their optimism, persistence, and enthusiasm in solving all kinds of problems inspired a loyalty and unity of purpose among 3M's 65 employees. This spirit made possible high production during the war years in spite of inadequate equipment and production handicaps. The garnet still had to be heated for removal of oil, and sheets of THREE-M-ITE cloth had to be flexed by hand. Factory and office employees worked day and night to keep up with increased demand, but still the company was always behind on shipments. Back orders at one time amounted to $450,000. Finally, a large blackboard was set up in the factory and unfilled orders were posted daily as a reminder to employees that 3M was behind in production.

*There were few war-caused changes in personnel. As 3M was considered an essential war industry, both General Manager McKnight and Sales Manager Bush were deferred from the draft. Ober, of course, was beyond draft age. Only a handful of employees went to war, among them 3M's entire laboratory "force," William Vievering.

In 1915 and 1916, major changes took place on the board of directors for the first time since the 1905 reorganization when Ober and Ordway succeeded Henry Bryan and William McGonagle. In 1915, general manager McKnight was elected a vice-president. In 1916, 68-year-old Dr. J.D. Budd, vice-president, sold most of his stock and retired from active service to 3M in order to devote all his time to Budd Hospital and other Two Harbors interests. McKnight, who had been buying a few shares occasionally from small stockholders who wanted to sell, bought Dr. Budd's stock. Also, in 1916, D.D. Smith, the insurance agent who had come on the board with Lucius Ordway in 1905, was replaced by Samuel G. Ordway, the 29-year-old son of Lucius. Samuel was a graduate of Harvard and member of the St. Paul law firm of Sanborn, Graves, and Ordway. The new board of Edgar Ober, Lucius and Samuel Ordway, W.L. McKnight, and John Dwan met for the first time on June 3, 1916, in St. Paul following the annual stockholders' meeting. After the election of officers,* the first action was to make an official break with 3M's North Shore past. Although 3M hadn't mined any Crystal Bay "corundum" for years, nothing had been done about the tools, equipment, and buildings which were rusting and deteriorating on the shore of Lake Superior at Crystal Bay. The necessity of keeping a watchman on guard against theft and fire had become an unnecessary expense. At the June annual meeting, the board, not without a twinge of sentiment, resolved:

"It is no longer profitable or advantageous for Minnesota Mining to quarry, crush, grade and ship to its factory at St. Paul, the abrasive rock and mineral now located upon the so-called Crystal Bay property. [They agreed that] whereas the timber on said property is likely to become destroyed by fire and the build-

*Edgar Ober, president; W.L. McKnight, first vice-president; Samuel G. Ordway, second vice-president; L.P. Ordway, treasurer; and John Dwan, secretary.

ings on said property are likewise likely to be destroyed by fire, and are continually depreciating in value, and the machinery, equipment and tools on said property are no longer adaptable for the company's use, the timber, equipment, machinery, tools, dock and beach gravel, shall be sold to James Stubbs of Duluth, Minnesota, for $2,000 for conversion to a lathe and saw mill.*"

The directors voted to keep 3M's property in Lake and Cook Counties. A final severing of North Shore ties was made by changing the official headquarters from Two Harbors to St. Paul, a move long planned but delayed in deference to Dr. Budd and John Dwan.

The new board was called together again on August 11, 1916, for a special meeting. In the past, special meetings had always spelled trouble. This time the news was all good.

*Forty acres of 3M North Shore property were given to the State of Minnesota for Baptism River State Park in 1947, and forty acres sold to Rudolph Ilgen, a North Shore businessman who built a tourist resort near Crystal Bay naming it Ilgen City. Remnants of 3M operations in the early 1900's can still be seen on Crystal Bay beach, including concrete dock piers, an old iron cookstove, flooring timbers, and chains from the overhead tramway.

A LONG-AWAITED DAY

AT 10 A.M. on August 11, 1916, president Ober, W.L. McKnight, Samuel Ordway, and John Dwan gathered in the small office of the president and waited for Ober to open the special meeting of the directors. Ober's voice reflected his jubilant mood as he greeted his friends. "Gentlemen," he said, "this is the day we've been waiting for, the day some of us wondered would ever come. We're out of debt, and the future looks good. Business has more than doubled in the past two years; and, for the first time, we'll have enough left after expenses to pay a dividend. It will be a modest one, to be sure, but a dividend! I've called you together, as you know, to declare officially our first dividend to be paid for the last quarter of 1916." Ober leaned back in his swivel chair and paused a moment. "There are a lot of people who thought we'd never make it," he added, almost to himself.

At the meeting, the directors voted a dividend of six cents a share for the last quarter of 1916. 3M had proved to the skeptics that resourcefulness, optimism, hard work, and above all, unwillingness to give up, pay off.

The precise, formal, and brief report on the August 1916, meeting in the minute books does not reflect the full signif-icance of the event. The board meeting itself was comparatively undramatic, but the announcement of the dividend caused a minor sensation in many parts of the country.

For years, the smaller stockholders of 3M had been in general a very confused group. The directors had purposely kept them in the dark as to the true financial status of the company for fear competitors would learn how close to the brink of failure 3M constantly teetered. A planned price war might have pushed them over the edge. To confuse competitors, it was necessary to confuse the stockholders, too. Those who didn't attend stockholders' meetings had a hard time finding out just what was going on. Many wrote Secretary Dwan requesting information. They wanted to know how much the stock was worth and whether there was any market for it. Dwan would have preferred to write them all a letter telling just what was going on, but management had agreed on a keep-mum policy until business was better. So Dwan either ignored their letters or sent vague, ambiguous replies. In 1907, the standard reply to these inquiries ran like this:

"The annual meeting of the stockholders...will be held in Two Harbors, Minn. on May 5, 1908, at which time a full and complete statement of the Company's affairs will be presented. You will realize that statements cannot be kept on tap all the time; as the making of such a statement involves the taking of a complete inventory and the balancing up of the books and all of which takes a great deal of time and a tremendous amount of work and a considerable outlay of money.

For your information in general, I would say that the Company kept up its usual amount of business and usual sales until the financial depression came, since which time our business in common with that of all other business houses has suffered considerable shrinkage. Manufacturers have laid off many of their employees and consequently used less of our products than when running full force. In addition to this, most business concerns have adopted the policy of stocking up as little as possible with goods and, as a result of this policy, when business revives, most of our customers will be found with very little stock on hand in our line and buying is expected to be correspondingly heavy and for these reasons much of the shrinkage in our business has not been wholly *lost business*, but is to some extent merely *deferred* business.

Trusting this will be satisfactory for the present and that you will find it convenient to attend the annual stockholders' meeting, I remain...."

In 1914, when business had improved a little, but while the company was still in debt, Dwan replied a little more in detail. He was still not very specific, however. His replies were all similar to the one sent J.G. Seecamp, a tobacco distributor of Seattle, Washington:

"Yours of June 9, 1914, became mislaid, and hence the delay in answering same. There is no movement whatever in the Stock. None has been sold by the company for five or six years at least, and there have been scarcely any transfers by Stockholders. I can give you no information as to the market value of the Stock. The company is doing a very nice business, but is still heavily in debt.

All I can say is that its condition is improving from year to year. I beg to advise you that the Company's holdings on the North Shore are really valueless. It has developed that more suitable material can be purchased at less price than the cost of getting this out. You will now readily see that there was no value basis whatever for your original holding of Stock. Whatever value your Stock may have has been given to it by the present management.[2]"

As a result of the vagueness of Dwan's replies, stockholders who couldn't get to annual meetings didn't know whether to hang onto their stock, sell it, or try to buy more shares.

Such uncertainty and confusion were over with the announcement of the first dividend. 3M issued a full financial statement to all of its stockholders. In all, 193 stockholders were paid a total of $13,497 on 224,956 shares. There were many original investors in the group. Tilton

Lewis, one of the promoters of the original "corundum" proposition, held 1,500 shares. Rhoada Cable, widow of Hermon Cable, Hattie Swailes, 3M's first stenographer now working in St. Paul for President Ober, and John Cable all had shares. In California, Ralph Green, the chemist who had once tested Crystal Bay mineral and thought it to be a profitable abrasive, still owned 50 of the 100 shares 3M had paid him in 1903 for analyzing the rock.

On the North Shore, Dr. Budd lamented the fact that he had sold all but 3,382 of his 18,754 shares in 1915 and 1916–just a few months before the dividend. Within the company there were several pleased employees who had had the foresight to buy stock in 3M, including Orson Hull, C.C. Alliss, W.L. McKnight, and A.G. Bush.

To Ober and Dwan, the event was especially important. The dividend itself was small, but the fact that the company was out of debt and had a surplus for a dividend vindicated the two men who had so often persuaded people to risk their money. Ober especially felt justified in having talked L.P. Ordway into risking thousands of dollars more than he had planned on a seemingly unprofitable venture.

Since that first dividend in 1916, 3M has paid quarterly cash dividends of $80,683,201* on common stock without interruption. It has paid two stock dividends of 100% each,** and the stock has been split eight for one.*** One share which in 1916 may have cost $1 would now be thirty-two shares valued at the current market price. One share owned in 1916 and held through December 31, 1954, would have received $326.81 in dividends.

---

*Dividends paid through December 31, 1954; preferred stock dividends are not included in this figure.

**1920 stock dividend, 236,356 shares, making total outstanding shares 472,712.

1922 stock dividend, 472,712 shares, making total outstanding shares 945,424.

*** 1945, 2 for 1, November 13, 1945.

1951, 4 for 1, January 8, 1951.

For personal reasons, the dividend money was particularly welcome to E.B. Ober. During the summer of 1916, he learned that he had contracted tuberculosis and, under doctor's orders, he moved to Pasadena, California, with his family. The dividend money helped ease the expense of his illness which would have been difficult to manage with his modest salary from the railroad. He had received no compensation from 3M in the eleven years he had served as an officer and director.

Ober's absence left 29-year-old McKnight with the entire responsibility of the St. Paul operations. He had other new responsibilities, too. In 1915, McKnight had been introduced by Hattie Swailes to Miss Maud Gage, daughter of a St. Paul railroad engineer. On October 9, 1915, just six months from the date they had first met, they were married in a simple ceremony at the home of Maud's parents, Mr. and Mrs. Henry Gage. After a honeymoon in the East, they settled in their home on Laurel Avenue in St. Paul. Virginia McKnight, their only child, was born in 1916.

While President Ober was in California, the wires between Pasadena and St. Paul hummed with messages; for Ober had worked too closely with 3M problems to put them out of his life entirely, no matter what the doctor advised. There was much to consult about. The United States broke relations with Germany and there were problems of war production to consider. There was the question of whether 3M should build another plant and, if so, whether it should be in St. Paul or elsewhere. Ober's advice from California was that it should be in a city closer to both raw materials and the customers served. The company now had enough money to consider such a move. But for once, McKnight didn't agree with his friend and counselor. "The job of moving the entire plant to another city looked just too big to me," confesses McKnight today. "So we expanded in St. Paul and continued to be hampered by high freight costs."

Plans were made for a new, two-story building in St. Paul in 1917. However, the high price of labor and the shortage of materials due to the war made this impractical. Instead, a partial story, 85' by 30', was added to the original plant. The office and laboratory were moved to this new fourth floor, leaving the third story available for storage and manufacturing. Ober and McKnight shared a 16' by 28' office; the laboratory was next door in quite spacious quarters compared to its first home. There was room now for the chopping block inside the room as well as a new icebox and a cabinet to hold the 4" by 6" samples of sandpaper that had been tested. Later, a small machine for making experimental batches of sandpaper was installed.

3M's new prosperity provided the means to do many things the board of directors had had in mind for years. President Ober did not go back to the railroad on his return from California, since 3M offered him a salary of $5,000 a year as President. Dwan, who had also served without pay as secretary, was voted $300 a year. Ober, long a firm believer in employee profit-sharing, put through an unofficial stock purchase plan for key employees. His program blossomed into a full-grown profit-sharing plan in later years. McKnight, Bush, Hull, Alliss, Skillman, Cable, and others were allowed to purchase shares at one dollar par value from treasury stock. 3M stock now had an unofficial value of three dollars a share.

At Ober's instigation also, the board authorized a stock bonus of 5,000 shares for W.L. McKnight to make up for his low salary as sales manager and general manager from 1911 to 1916 and as a "reward for his valued services to the corporation and the improved condition of the company, due quite largely to such services."[3]

3M's high earnings after the Armistice reflected the general prosperity of the nation. During 1919 and 1920, spending was free and America was buying in increased quantities the products which needed sandpaper in their manufacture. As business prospered, the nation's consumption of abrasives increased sharply–49 per cent from 1914 to 1919–and in the latter year, the entire industry was employing the highest number of workers in its history.

Outwardly at least, the nation's mood was gay, although there was disillusionment over the war. It was all a preview of a gayer and even more prosperous decade to come, a decade in which 3M grew so fast it figuratively and literally pushed out the walls of the little plant on Forest Avenue in St. Paul.

FROM CURIOSITY, A NEW PRODUCT

THE TURBULANT TWENTIES were as hectic for 3M as for the rest of America. While hemlines went up and waistlines down and the nation went wild over stock speculation, 3M revolutionized the abrasive industry with a new type of sandpaper, developed the first of its famous family of "SCOTCH" Brand pressure-sensitive tapes, and quadrupled its sales volume.

The prosperous decade got off to a swift and successful start with the receipt of a letter by Vice-president McKnight one morning in January 1920, from a printing ink manufacturer in Philadelphia. The more McKnight thought about the letter, the more curious he became. What an unusual request, he mused, rereading the brief note typed on the sky-blue stationery of Francis G. Okie, "manufacturer of printing inks, bronze powders, and gold ink liquids." Wrote Okie, "Please send me samples of every mineral grit size you use in manufacturing sandpaper." This request wouldn't have been unusual had it been directed to H.H. Barton & Sons, Carborundum Company, or some other mineral supply house. But 3M was not in the business of selling bulk mineral. Why then, had Okie written the company?

McKnight's handling of Okie's request changed the course of 3M's history. He could have explained to Okie that 3M didn't sell bulk mineral, and there was consequently no point in sending samples. He could have ignored the letter. Instead, prompted by his curiosity, McKnight instructed 3M's Eastern Division sales manager, R.H. Skillman, to get in touch with Okie to find out *why* he wanted the grit samples.

As a result of this curiosity, the company acquired a new, revolutionary product. The new product zoomed sales, catapulted 3M into a position of world leadership in the abrasive industry, improved the health of laborers in many parts of the world, and helped the automotive industry solve a serious manufacturing problem.

When Skillman looked up Francis Gurney Okie in his little Philadelphia shop, he found an earnest young man working on an idea quite unrelated to the printing ink business. The idea, however, was definitely related to the sandpaper business and was one in which the alert Skillman knew Minnesota Mining would be most interested. Okie had invented a new kind of sandpaper, a type that could be used with water for abrading. In a word, it was waterproof.

Sitting amidst a clutter of samples of his sandpaper at an old, oak desk which he sandpapered almost out of existence, Okie told Skillman why he had written 3M for grit samples. "I had no idea of sharing my invention with anyone else," he said. "I had filed patent application and found financial backers when I learned I couldn't get a supply of mineral here in the East to go into the manufacturing of waterproof sandpaper. My backers started losing interest. Someone suggested I write the company in Minnesota that makes THREE-M-ITE cloth; that's how I happened to write you. I thought maybe you could sell me enough to get started."

Skillman saw great possibilities for Okie's sandpaper. With the inventor's permission, he wired McKnight to come to Philadelphia as soon as possible to talk to Okie about buying his patent rights. McKnight lost no time getting there. He, too, conferred with Okie across the battered oak desk, discussing terms and examining samples. McKnight was impressed with these samples. He saw a definite industrial potential in an abrasive that could be used wet or under water. With waterproof sandpaper, one of the major problems of sanding painted or varnished surfaces might be eliminated, that of sandpaper loading, which greatly reduced the abrading life of dry sandpaper. It was also apparent that smoother surfaces could be achieved by wet abrading. Too, the dust hazard which caused a high labor turnover in dry-sanding departments of factories might be cut down. These factors alone would make the new sandpaper a demand item in America's factories. Moreover, the Okie sandpaper was extremely flexible, which would make it easy for use in sanding moldings and crevices.

After many conferences, Okie was persuaded to sell his rights to waterproof sandpaper, and an agreement was drawn up between 3M and Okie on February 3, 1921. From that date, 3M became a leader in the abrasive industry, for the company had found a "first," a new product which industry needed and would buy in quantity, a product on which 3M could set its own price and make a reasonable profit.

How did Okie happen to invent waterproof sandpaper? In his own words* it occurred like this: "My uncle owned the shop where I worked in 1919. We made printing ink on the second floor of an old building. Our second floor neighbor was a man who beveled glass for a living. He used a grinding wheel, and there was considerable dust connected with the grinding. I often stopped to visit with him, and one day he mentioned something about wanting to get out of the glass-beveling business. I wondered why, as I knew it was a

*Told to the author by Francis Okie in 1951, at his home on White Bear Lake, Minnesota. Okie retired from 3M in 1941.

good trade. As I watched him working, though, I noticed the dust he had to breathe, and realized that this probably had something to do with his wanting to sell. After talking to him, I got to wondering why a person couldn't make a water-proof abrasive, a sandpaper that could be used under water. This would eliminate dust from abrading.

"The more I thought about it, the more I wanted to exper-iment. First I had to find out if there was such a thing as waterproof sandpaper on the market. I went to C. Schrack's in Philadelphia, one of the oldest varnish makers in America, and asked to buy some waterproof sandpaper. They were jobbers of sandpaper. The clerk said there was no such thing. That's just what I wanted to know."

"After leaving Schrack's, I went to work on my experi-ment. I bought small packages of mineral from Carborundum and H.H. Barton & Sons—that's all they'd sell me—and experimented with waterproof sandpaper in the ink shop. I mixed the adhesive or bonding agent, spread it by hand onto the paper backing, and sprinkled garnet on it. I had my neighbor, the glass beveler, try it out, and I tested it by sanding boards in my own shop."

"When convinced I really had something, I went to Baeder-Adamson and asked them to make me a trial run of sandpaper using my bonding agent. They agreed, and the sandpaper they turned out further convinced me I had a sal-able product. Funny thing, Baeder-Adamson never asked me anything about why I wanted the sandpaper or what I was doing with it."

"Then I got some people interested in backing me; and, when I couldn't get any mineral in the East, I wrote to Minnesota Mining," concluded Okie."

After arrangements were made with Okie, 3M immedi-ately plunged into production of waterproof sandpaper, which President Ober suggested should be trademarked,

"WETORDRY." At first Okie stayed in Philadelphia, mixing the waterproof binder there and shipping it to St. Paul in five-gallon buckets. 3M workers can still recall how laborious it was to empty the dozens of buckets of binder needed for a single run of sandpaper. By May 1921, samples were sent to customers, and the first sales were made in the same month. The Maxwell Motor Company, Buick, and Willys Overland were among the first customers. Customers were eager to try out the new sandpaper which 3M claimed could be used under water or while damp. Sales for 1921 reached $50,753, a promising start for a brand-new product.

Early in 1922, Okie moved his family to St. Paul. With his arrival, the prosaic life of the factory was considerably enlivened. 3M employees had never had an authentic inventor in their midst; and, although Okie was quiet and soft-spoken, he kept things humming in his own special way. He mixed experimental batches of waterproof adhesive in a huge washtub until someone thought to have him make smaller, more economical batches in a washbowl. He hated, in his own words, to be "confined to the specific," and many times applied this principle to his experiments, to the consternation of fellow researchers. For example, when he mixed a test batch of adhesive, he often failed to record the amount of each ingredient used. Consequently, when an experiment was a success, he didn't know exactly why, nor could he repeat it precisely. A laboratory assistant was finally assigned to him to measure and record all ingredients used.

Okie had many creative ideas, but they were not always acceptable to the sales department, for most of them were not practical. He was so confident of the cutting power of waterproof sandpaper that he once conceived the idea of shaving with it. He kept a piece of the material in his club locker and shaved with it before golfing. It was almost the parting of the ways between Okie and the sales department when he suggested that 3M salesmen board cross-country buses and demonstrate shaving with the abrasive paper as the bus traveled from town to town. Sales Manager Bush vetoed this idea, and 3M confined its efforts to selling its regular industrial customers.

The new waterproof sandpaper proved very disappointing during the early months of its life. In the first place, it was soon apparent that the Okie formula had serious defects. Laboratory tests and trials in the field showed that the mineral rubbed off too soon and the paper backing disintegrated too quickly. As competitors were now experimenting with waterproof sandpaper, the remedy of these defects in quality became an urgent matter.

The second disappointment was that the market which Ober and McKnight had envisioned for waterproof sandpaper failed to materialize. "We thought it would be duck soup to sell our WETORDRY sandpaper to furniture finishers," McKnight explains. "But we couldn't persuade them to use the new product."

The reason was simple. In 1921, all furniture was finished with varnish. Bulk pumice was used to rub down the gloss. Furniture finishers were tradition-bound artisans who had little inclination to change from the economical pumice to the more expensive abrasive paper, even though it gave a finer finish. It was 13 years before 3M could persuade them that the new product would work to their advantage, and then it was accomplished only through an intensive sales campaign.

So while the laboratory struggled to perfect Okie's formula, the salesmen worked to find a market for waterproof sandpaper. Within a few months the laboratory found that the paper backing also had to be waterproofed and that a sizing coat of waterproof binder had to be added on top of the mineral. These changes turned WETORDRY paper into a quality product. Meanwhile, a new market had been developed.

Once again, as with THREE-M-ITE cloth, it was the automotive industry that found the new type of sandpaper just what it needed. Two major markets developed in connection with automobiles: the auto repaint shops which had mushroomed all over the country in the Twenties, and the automobile manufacturers.

In 1921, as now, the finish on a car was very important. A car with a beautiful finish not only looked better but lasted longer and resold for a higher price. In 1921, however, finishing an automobile was a long, laborious process, whether done at the factory or in an auto repaint shop. The steel bodies had to be prepared carefully for a paint job. This task included the cleaning and sanding of the metal, the application of a metal primer, a glazing putty, an intermediate lead coat, a guide coat for use in sanding the surface smooth, and finally, color coats. After each application, a sanding job was required. Wooden moldings, doorjambs, and wheels had to be sanded, too, in the finishing process. All of this added up to a lot of sanding.

With dry sandpaper, which was the only kind available until WETORDRY waterproof paper was invented, the danger during the finishing process was that there would be too much friction. This would result in burning the surface or cutting too deeply, which would mar the finish. To overcome this, workmen tried dipping flint paper in varnish in an effort to make it waterproof, or treating dry sandpaper with oil to overcome the burning problem. Neither was satisfactory.

That was the situation when one of the 3M Eastern salesmen made the company's first call on an auto repaint shop. The salesman was making a call on a Philadelphia wagonmaker who suggested he demonstrate the new product to his upstairs tenant. With wagonmaking on the decline, the upstairs had been rented to an auto repainter to bring in an income. The salesman found the auto repainter using the traditional bulk pumice to rub down the car, and he wasn't too receptive to a demonstration of waterproof sand paper. He admitted the pumice got into the crevices of the car and had to be scraped out. He admitted, too, that the pumice sometimes cut deeper into the surface than he wanted it to. But he pointed out that pumice in barrels cost only six cents a pound, and a barrel went a long way. However, he finally allowed the salesman to demonstrate on a section of a car body. When the 3M man had finished sanding the surface, the auto repainter critically rubbed his thumb over the surface of the body. Immediately he called to his helper in the back of the shop. "Come here, I think this man's got something."

Spurred by his success with this shop, the 3M salesman called on every auto repaint shop in the Philadelphia telephone directory to prove to them, too, that he had something. He reported the enthusiastic response by auto refinishers to the St. Paul office, and soon 3M was calling on shops all over the country.* Sales began climbing at a gratifying rate.

At the same time, salesmen were calling on the automobile manufacturers and gradually persuading them that 3M had the answer to the burning problem. Waterproof sand-

---

*J.C. Duke, the salesman who helped introduce WETORDRY sandpaper to the repaint trade in 1921, became 3M's Eastern Division sales manager on July 1, 1936, and sales manager of the entire Abrasive Division on January 1, 1941. When sales manager, Duke also directed research activities of the New Methods group which was organized in 1941 to develop new markets for coated abrasives. Under his leadership, this group developed special machinery and contact rolls to utilize specialty items such as coated abrasive endless belts to do special abrading jobs. By the creation of many new methods of abrading and machinery to go with the new method, 3M greatly broadened the use of coated abrasives in industry as well as substantially increasing its sales. Duke was elected vice-president in charge of Coated Abrasives and Related Products on April 13, 1948. This is his position today.

paper could be used with either water or oil, which cut down the friction heat and allowed the workmen to produce a smoother finish on the new cars. Further, it cut faster under lubrication than was possible with dry sandpaper.

When 3M first started selling to the automobile manufacturers, cars were finished with varnish, a slow-drying process which often took as long as three weeks. Progress in methods of finishing cars had not kept pace with improvements in style and performance. From the first horseless carriage to the big, boxy cars of the early 1920's, many improvements had been made. But in the finishing of automobiles, developments had been slow. The tedious methods used for painting buggies, hearses, and carriages were adopted for painting the first automobiles. Practically the only improvements in a quarter of a century had been the elimination of a few coats of paint or varnish and improved drying methods to speed the process a little. The finishing process was a bottleneck in an otherwise speedy manufacturing operation. Finally, at almost the same time the new waterproof abrasive paper was perfected, lacquer was developed for finishing cars. For the first time, an auto body could be completed in three or four days, instead of the weeks required before. Not only was lacquer speedier in drying, but it was more durable and damage-resistant than varnish.

WETORDRY gained its real place in the industrial sun with the change-over to lacquer for finishing autos. Automobile manufacturers found it a necessity with lacquer. The primer undercoats and lacquer finish were too hard to cut with the traditional Bimstein rubbing bricks or pumice gangs. But WETORDRY sandpaper gave a smooth finish that polished to a high luster. There were die-hards, of course, who continued to use rubbing compounds. Gradually, however, the new paper replaced the old methods because it cut the sprayed lacquer to a perfectly smooth surface. Abrasives such as loose pumice and rubbing compounds followed the surface irregularities* instead of removing them.

By 1926, manufacturers and auto repaint shops were hailing WETORDRY Brand sandpaper as a product superior to ordinary sandpaper. Competition naturally was disturbed by 3M's waterproof sandpaper. In the first place, at least two abrasive manufacturers had had the opportunity of negotiating with Okie and had passed up the chance. It naturally piqued them that 3M had perceived what they had overlooked. Secondly, it was strongly felt by some that the marketing of waterproof sandpaper might hurt rather than help abrasive manufacturers. They pointed out that if it took less of the faster-cutting waterproof abrasive paper to do a job than with glue-bond sandpaper, the overall sales volume of sandpaper would be reduced.

3M calmed their fears, predicting that because waterproof sandpaper would cut faster and clog less quickly, it would be adopted by industry for many jobs where glue-bond sandpaper had not been efficient, and sales volume would probably increase. In 1924, Carborundum and Behr-Manning were licensed to manufacture waterproof sandpaper under 3M patents.

As predicted, the new product played a far greater role in the progress of industry than just that of a more efficient abrasive. It materially improved the working conditions of the sanders in the body departments of automotive plants where undercoat sanding was done. Before WETORDRY paper, attempts were made to control dust conditions with ventilators. Often a worker wrapped cheesecloth around his head, covering his nose and mouth. Both were unsatisfactory remedies for the unsanitary and often dangerous dust conditions caused by the dry sanding of automobile bodies. Even with ventilators, the worker inhaled a certain amount

---

*These surface irregularities are referred to in the industry as "orange-peel" surface, which is caused by imperfect application of the sprayed lacquer.

of dust. The cheesecloth idea obviously was uncomfortable and unsanitary. As the automotive industry grew, lead poisoning contracted in the body-sanding departments increased proportionately. By 1924, in Detroit, an average of 32 cases a year were being treated in hospitals. In Ohio, there were 104 cases in 1922.[1] While few cases were fatal, lead poisoning seriously impaired the workers' health, and few men would stay on a job where they had to sand lead fillers. When waterproof sandpaper was put on the market by 3M, it eliminated this dust hazard, bringing about an improvement in working conditions in industrial plants all over the country. And, as the labor turnover was reduced and the time lost through constant training of new workers eliminated, a saving was effected which could be passed on to the consumer.

After the technical problems were overcome and the product was generally accepted by the automotive people, 3M made another, and this time a successful, attempt to show the furniture manufacturers and refinishers that there were definite advantages to using waterproof coated abrasives. Realizing that the type of abrasive used for automotive finishing (with water as a lubricant) was not satisfactory for the furniture trade, 3M, in 1934, assigned one of its laboratory engineers to the problem of developing a special abrasive sheet that could be used as a lever to capture this business. After many months of field study and laboratory development work, the engineer succeeded in developing a WETORDRY abrasive sheet for furniture (where oil is the chief lubricant for rubbing). He also developed a complete finishing system that would cut costs, improve the finish, and speed production.

The next job was to sell the new abrasive and the finishing system to the trade. This was a difficult job because furniture finishing had always been done by artisans called "rubbers" who were proud of their work. They understandably thought their work could be done in no other way, and perhaps subconsciously sensed that it was a vanishing art which they should protect and keep alive. Consequently, they actively resisted any change from pumice abrading.

Again 3M resorted to its time-proved method of getting a 3M man in the plant to put the point over by demonstration. With permission of plant managers, the 3M laboratory engineer demonstrated that a man with no experience could be trained in a few hours to do the rubbing as satisfactorily and faster than men who had had years of experience. Even women could do the job now through the scientific application of controlled cutting speed with WETORDRY paper because it did not require the muscle pressure needed with pumice and oil.

Secondly, the demonstrations showed that the new abrasive was distinctly superior for cutting the new harder varnish and lacquer finishes adopted by the furniture trade. It would cut these finishes faster and with more effective results than old-style abrading methods.

Presented with such proof, plant managers one by one approved the 3M finishing system until it soon became the universal method in the furniture industry. Refinish shops, too, adopted the system, and homeowners found it an easy method to follow when doing over the dining room table or desk for the den.

XIII

KEY TO NEW HORIZONS

FROM THE MOMENT 3M bought the Okie patent, Vice-president McKnight began thinking about the European and British market for WETORDRY waterproof sandpaper. The idea of developing a substantial foreign trade had always appealed to McKnight, but 3M had never before had a product outstanding enough to compete with foreign products. Glue-bond sales abroad had been negligible so far. They accounted for less than four per cent of the total sales volume in 1919 and 1920, with England purchasing roughly half of all the sandpaper shipped overseas. France and Germany were purchasing no sandpaper directly from 3M.

England looked especially good to McKnight. For years, the British had been trying to eliminate lead poisoning among workers who had to dry-sand paint finishes which contained white lead. There was a difference of opinion in England as to the best solution of the problem. One faction wanted white lead eliminated from paint; another faction argued that this would put lead industry workers out of employment. Still others believed too much fuss was being made over a relatively minor occupational hazard, and that energies should be directed toward eliminating more serious occupational dangers such as those in the coal mines.

The lead industry had been working on the problem of eliminating poisonous dust conditions but with only minor success. Experiments had been made with paint containing no white lead, but most of the industry thought this paint would be commercially unsatisfactory. Neither were efforts to perfect a waterproof sand paper producing satisfactory results.

To McKnight, WETORDRY paper looked like the solution for the British. As 3M's new abrasive could be used while damp, it would keep the poisonous dust from flying about when painters sanded, and there would be no need to eliminate the white-lead base from paint. Auto workers in America had already found that the paper improved working conditions by eliminating lead dust during the sanding of undercoats.

The new product was far from perfect early in 1922, but McKnight began to sound out British industry as to the possible foreign market. He obtained a list of manufacturers in England and wrote to them, asking their opinion as to possible foreign sales. At the time, he had no idea anyone in England was working on a waterproof sandpaper.

One inquiry was directed to Brimsdown Lead Company, Ltd., a prominent lead manufacturer in Brimsdown, Middlesex. In his letter, McKnight outlined the three types of waterproof 3M had developed: "AUTO WET" flint paper, an inexpensive abrasive paper for use by painters; WETORDRY garnet paper for use by auto repainters and furniture finishers; and "WETORDRY TRI-M-ITE," a higher priced but more durable abrasive paper made with the artificial mineral silicon carbide, for use by automobile manufacturers.

The response from Brimsdown was immediate. Their research manager, C.A. Klein, replied that they were definitely interested. Public concern in England had reached a new high over the lead poisoning problem, and Brimsdown agreed that a waterproof sandpaper would be the solution.

In November 1921, the International Labor Organization had met in Geneva and had passed a formal resolution recommending that all member countries adopt legislation prohibiting the use of lead paint in internal painting, and regulating the use of lead paint in external painting. The English Parliament was considering the passage of a lead paint bill which embodied this recommendation. According to Brimsdown's research manager, such legislation would deal a severe blow to the British lead industry. Brimsdown was working on a waterproof sandpaper that would make dry sanding of lead paint safe, but it hadn't been able to iron out the technical difficulties. Klein asked for samples of 3M's product, which McKnight sent in July 1922. They tested and examined these samples in their laboratory and also had them tested by the Amalgamated Society of Operative and Ship Painters. Their first reports were that the paper wouldn't stand up well enough to satisfy the British trade, but they encouraged further experimentation. Klein expressed the hope that 3M's product might be the means of forestalling Parliamentary action on a lead paint bill.

While McKnight and Klein were exchanging letters, the former sent 3M's Eastern Division sales manager, R.H. Skillman, to Europe to establish distributorships for 3M products, particularly WETORDRY sandpaper. The directors, at McKnight's request, set aside a $75,000 reserve for construction of English and foreign plants.

Skillman established connections with several distributors in Britain and Europe in the shoe, metalworking, and woodworking industries. The chief one of these was R.W. Greeff and Company, Ltd., of London, primarily a distributor of chemical supplies, including lead. Greeff began selling 3M's waterproof paper in quantity after Skillman's visit; British sales jumped from $189 in 1922 to $68,391 in 1923.

While Skillman was in Europe, American abrasive manufacturers formed a Webb-Pomerene Export Corporation for the purpose of promoting the sale of their own brands of abrasives to the woodworking, metalworking, shoe, and electrical industries, and the paint and hardware trades overseas. The corporation, formed early in 1923, was called the American Surface Abrasive Export Corporation. 3M became a member along with its nine major competitors. Headquarters were established in New York City. The formation of the corporation, according to publicity released to trade journals at the time, was for the purpose of capturing the "European, African, and South American abrasive business, principally controlled by European agencies."

Joining the corporation did not change McKnight's intentions for 3M in Europe, for A.S.A.E.C. was organized solely to assist in the export of abrasives from the United States and not to acquire stock in foreign concerns, foreign patents, or plants. McKnight considered all of these necessary if the foreign markets were to be successfully entered by the American manufacturers.

While Skillman was establishing distributorships abroad, patent attorney Paul Carpenter was working on a strong foreign patent structure for WETORDRY waterproof sandpaper. It had been learned that the National Lead Company had a patent, which 3M succeeded in purchasing.

The foreign patent situation was complicated; and, in March 1924, McKnight went to Europe to talk to abrasive and other industrialists of England, France, Germany, Belgium, Switzerland, and Italy. Skillman accompanied him. It was McKnight's first trip abroad, and he found the prospect of negotiating for foreign patents and abrasive business challenging. The young American executive had given himself quite an assignment. He spoke nothing but English and knew comparatively little of the inner workings of European industry.

In England, McKnight called on Klein of Brimsdown
Lead Company to discuss acquiring the patent that had
been issued in the name of C.A. Klein and Robert Brown,
and which they controlled. Klein, who had been so interested in WETORDRY paper, changed when he learned that 3M
wanted to acquire control of their patent. He alleged that
3M was infringing on their patent, and negotiations to
acquire it made little progress on McKnight's first European
visit in 1924.

McKnight called on R.W. Greeff & Company, Ltd., too,
and the other distributors of 3M sandpaper, and discussed
the sales potential of the product. Greeff, the English distributors for the National Lead Company of New York,
brought McKnight up to date on the fight in England
against lead poisoning which had reached a boiling point
that spring of 1924. The bill introduced in Parliament in
1922, called the Lead Paint (Protection Against Poisoning)
Bill, embodying the recommendations of the International
Labor Conference in Geneva, was to come up for debate in
June 1924, to determine whether it should get a second
reading. Those involved in the fight were gathering forces.

In order to learn firsthand about the lead poisoning situation, McKnight hired a car to drive through the poorer sections of London. Whenever he saw house painters working,
he stopped to talk to them. His question was, "What do you
think about waterproof sandpaper?" To his disappointment,
they were not much interested. McKnight recalls, "They
didn't seem to care much about improving the old method of
dry sanding and didn't want to be bothered by using water
with their sandpaper. It meant more work."

As it turned out, the parliamentary legislation did not
have too great a bearing on the ultimate sale of 3M's sandpaper. The British lead paint bill came up for second reading June 20, 1924, and waterproof sandpaper did figure
prominently in the stormy debate on the bill. Mr. Rhys

Davies, undersecretary of state for Britain's Office of Home Affairs, speaking for his government which was anxious to carry out the international agreement at Geneva, pointed out that from 1910 to 1923 there were 1,500 cases of lead poisoning with 300 deaths. He regretted that passage of the bill would put any persons in the white lead industry out of work but explained that under the provisions of the bill, they would have three years to find other, more healthful, employment. Then he went on to say,

A new idea has cropped up since this Bill was suggested. It is that some inventor...has found out that if you can manufacture a waterproof sandpaper which will do wet rubbing-down, all will be well. The Home Office experts have examined this proposal and are satisfied that it does not meet the case. In fact the house painters, the Operative Painters Society, sent out a questionnaire to their 590 branches in May last asking for information as to the number of firms using the wet rubbing-down process. The information received was to the effect that only 43 firms had adopted the system in 27 towns. If the opponents of the Bill are so keenly interested in the welfare of the painters who are liable to this disease, they ought to have it very much more widely adopted than appears in the result of this inquiry.[1]

Opponents of the bill in the House of Commons said in rebuttal that waterproof sandpaper was a new discovery since the Geneva conference; that had the conference known about it and had such a product been available at the time of the conference, no recommendation concerning lead poisoning would have been made. Opposition members further argued that experts had found that waterproof sandpaper was an absolutely safe method of sanding down paint containing white lead.

After heated debate, the bill was approved; and in 1926, the Lead Paint Act became law. The Home Secretary was given the power to make regulations for the protection from lead poisoning of persons employed in the painting of buildings. But the act did not, as the International Labor

Organization recommended, completely prohibit the use of lead paint in the interior of buildings as the lead industry had feared, and dry sanding was not entirely banned.

Consequently, the hardware stores and paint supply houses did not become major customers for waterproof in England. Instead, the bulk of the orders came from the automobile manufacturers and the railroads. The largest consumers were Morris Motors, Ltd., Cowley, Oxford; Sunbeam Cars, Darracq Motors, and Citroen Cars, London; Humbler, Ltd., Coventry; Vauxhall Motors, Ltd., Bedfordshire; and Royal Body Corporation, Surrey. Also, Short Bros. Seaplane Works, Kent; the Gramophone Company, Hayes, Middlesex; and Columbia Graphophone Company, London.

From England, McKnight went to France. He had ambitions to buy the major French abrasive plant, *Centrale des Emeries*. Through an interpreter, he arranged for conferences with the two plant owners who had indicated a willingness to talk about selling. They said they couldn't speak English. At the daily conferences the interpreter would explain McKnight's offer to the two French men who would then verbally fence at length with the interpreter. McKnight, understanding no French, was forced to sit by and wonder what was going on. "What are they saying? What are they saying?" he would impatiently ask the interpreter when he could break into the conversation. "Are they willing to sell?"

No matter how long the Frenchmen had been talking–fifteen minutes or a half hour–the interpreter would report the same thing, "They said 'No!'"

This went on for about a week with the same results. ("They said 'No!'") McKnight found out afterwards the two Frenchmen could speak some English and could understand what *he* said! In spite of all his efforts he did not succeed in making a satisfactory deal with these French abrasive manufacturers.*

Nor did he get anywhere in Germany. The German industrialists in the abrasive field treated him well. They entertained him at their plants and in their homes and seemed willing to do business. After looking the situation over, however, McKnight decided it would be prudent to stay out of any deals with them.

After his first trip to Europe, McKnight decided that he had better learn at least one language before he returned. He asked his secretary, who spoke French fluently, if she would give him a lesson each morning. McKnight's spirit was willing but his tongue inept. No matter how hard he tried, "bon oncle" always came out a harsh "barnacle," and he finally gave up and decided to continue to depend on interpreters.

In 1925, McKnight returned to Europe, this time with attorney Paul Carpenter, to work out the patent problems which needed solving before Minnesota Mining and Manufacturing Company could manufacture in England.

In all, McKnight made five trips to Europe between 1924 and 1929 to negotiate on matters relating to foreign expansion. The trip in 1924 was strictly a business trip, which caused Skillman some disappointment. He had hoped that McKnight would spend some time sightseeing with him, but found that his employer preferred to see new factories going up rather than old churches in decay. When he finally persuaded McKnight to visit the Louvre, Skillman complained that he went through faster than any man he'd ever known—in about twenty minutes. It wasn't that McKnight

---

*There is an interesting sequel to this event. In July 1951, the owner of *Centrale des Emeries*, who was one of the Frenchmen McKnight conferred with in 1924, wrote 3M asking if the company were still interested in purchasing his company. After a year of lengthy negotiation, 3M bought the French plant.

actually disliked sightseeing, but he felt that this first visit to Europe was strictly a business trip, and time couldn't be wasted on personal pleasure. He took his family with him on his 1925 trip to Europe and at that time combined business with pleasure.

After the third trip overseas in 1927, and many stormy conferences, a satisfactory patent arrangement was finally worked out with the British manufacturers. They agreed to the organization of a corporation in which Minnesota Mining and Manufacturing Company, the Associated Lead Manufacturers, Ltd.* of Newcastle and London, and R.W. Greeff and Company, distributors, would each have one-third interest. The company was named "British WETORDRY, Ltd.," incorporated for £30,000, and through McKnight's efforts a cross license agreement was negotiated in which waterproof sandpaper could be manufactured by the new corporation employing the Brown and Klein and 3M patents.

McKnight hoped to get British WETORDRY, Ltd. into production before competition in the United States learned of its organization. He almost succeeded. A young engineer from 3M's St. Paul plant was sent to England to get a factory equipped for the new British corporation. He sailed for England in May 1928, carrying a typical McKnight memo of instructions:

> We want you to feel it is up to you to keep posted on all developments in the waterproof sandpaper field. I do not want you to feel that you are to wait until you are told. You have the responsibility of asking for information.[2]

Upon his arrival in Newcastle the engineer with the help of Associated Lead Manufacturers leased an old warehouse for British WETORDRY, Ltd. It contained 30,000 square feet

---

*A company which had acquired Brimsdown Lead Company since McKnight's 1924 European trip.

of floor space and was located in Hepburn-on-Thyne, a suburb of Newcastle. It had once been part of a plant for manufacturing lead pipes and white lead. It was located in a shipbuilding area where unemployment at the time was high and unskilled labor consequently plentiful at twenty to twenty-five cents an hour.

The engineer immediately began getting the plant in order. Sandpaper manufacturing equipment was ordered, and alterations were started on the old plant, which needed a new roof. The old roof was taken off preparatory to putting on the new one. That's as far as British WETORDRY, Ltd. got.

While the Newcastle building was standing without a roof, President F.S. Tone of Carborundum Company learned of the plans for the British company. Greatly disturbed, he immediately got in touch with McKnight, who was now in St. Paul, and warned him that if 3M built a plant in England, Carborundum had no alternative but to build one too, adding that undoubtedly other competitors would do the same thing. This was in December 1928.

McKnight knew that the English market wouldn't support more than one American factory and realized that Tone's threat warranted consideration, particularly because the Carborundum Company already had a large grinding wheel manufacturing plant capable of diversification. He cabled a terse message to the 3M engineer in Newcastle:

HOLD EVERYTHING AND STAND BY.

McKnight was in a dilemma. The Newcastle plant stood with the roof off, leaving it exposed to rain and wind. The machinery had been designed and was ready for delivery from St. Paul. English capital was at stake as well as that of Minnesota Mining and Manufacturing Company. Seeing that he couldn't proceed with British WETORDRY, Ltd. without serious financial risks, McKnight saw no alternative but to confer with Tone and the other competitors. All through

December 1928, and early in 1929, the conferences continued while the engineer and the laborers stood by in
Newcastle. Eventually, all nine abrasive manufacturers
were in on the conferences, and a plan began to take shape.

One of the original impelling reasons for the formation of
British WETORDRY, Ltd. was to protect the patent structure
by manufacturing waterproof sandpaper in England. Under
English law, if a patent owner does not make the product in
England within a certain time, the government can grant
licenses to others. During the discussions with the other
American sandpaper manufacturers, it was discovered that
there also were American-owned patents covering other
abrasives which would be lost if the patented products were
not manufactured in England. After many conferences
among the lawyers of the companies involved, it was
decided that the United States abrasive manufacturers
could legally form a holding corporation to acquire and own
the capital stock of foreign corporations and to manufacture
patented and other abrasive products in those foreign countries where patent laws required that this be done. A corporation was organized under the name "Durex." The capital
stock was apportioned among the nine companies on the
basis of their exports during a certain period. Ownership of
Durex Corporation was as follows, in the order of the number of shares held: Carborundum Company, Behr-Manning
Corporation, Minnesota Mining and Manufacturing
Company, American Glue Company, Armour and Company,
H.H. Barton & Sons, United States Sandpaper Company,
Baeder-Adamson Company, and Wausau Abrasives
Company.

At the same time that the Durex Corporation was
formed, the same group of nine abrasive manufacturers
decided they could cut exporting costs and improve their
service to other countries by combining under the Webb-
Pomerene Act. They then could sell a single brand of coated

abrasives through a single worldwide sales force instead of maintaining nine separate sales forces and nine brands, as was the case under the American Surface Abrasive Export Corporation. Accordingly, a Webb-Pomerene corporation was organized, the Durex Abrasives Corporation, for this purpose. The old A.S.A.E.C. was abandoned. The officers elected for the new corporation were: A.J. Sidford (vice-president of Behr-Manning Corporation), president; F.J. Tone (president of Carborundum) vice president; W.L. McKnight (vice-president of 3M) vice-president; R.W. Young (vice-president of American Glue Company) treasurer; and L.K. Southard (formerly secretary of A.S.A.E.C.), secretary.

Plans were then made by Durex Corporation to build a plant in England, provided McKnight could make satisfactory arrangements with his partners in British WETORDRY, Ltd. This presented quite a problem, for he wasn't sure whether the other two members would agree to sell their interest in the company. Unless he could make satisfactory arrangements with them, Durex Corporation couldn't function in England as planned. McKnight returned to Europe and solved this problem by persuading Associated Lead Manufacturers and Greeff to exchange their one-third interest in British WETORDRY, Ltd. for an eight per cent interest in a British company to be organized under the name of Durex Abrasives Limited. This cleared the way to get out from under the lease covering the partly finished plant in Newcastle, as this plant was not large enough to serve the needs of the new company.

McKnight and an officer from the Carborundum Company then bought a modern building containing 125,000 square feet for the Durex plant in Birmingham, and the 3M engineer who had stood by through all the Durex conferences from February to July 1929 helped get Durex started. 3M also helped organize a quality-control laboratory. The other members of Durex furnished technical help.

Labor was recruited, of course, in England. The sandpaper machinery originally ordered for British WETORDRY, Ltd. was purchased by Durex Abrasives Ltd. Production in England started early in 1930. This was an inopportune time in view of the economic depression, but Durex Corporation, which later acquired plants in other foreign countries to manufacture coated abrasives, tape, adhesives, and coating compounds made under license contracts with 3M, soon was doing a satisfactory business.

After the European situation had been brought under control in 1930 by the formation of Durex, W.L. McKnight found he could, for the first time in five years, give more of his attention to 3M's domestic affairs. It was definitely needed, for the United States was in the Great Depression.

PATTERN FOR GROWTH

THE TWENTIES were critical as well as prosperous years. Until World War I, 3M's task had been to survive. Now the problem was to allocate a growing surplus wisely. The future of the company depended on how well this was done. The board of directors could have traveled any of several roads. Most of the stockholders, remembering the lean years, undoubtedly would have welcomed a distribution of the surplus in dividends. Those who had served in responsible positions for so many years with small compensation would have appreciated substantial pay increases. Or the directors could plow the surplus back into the business.

The directors were in complete agreement during the decisive years between 1920 and 1930. The original dream was not to be altered–3M was to grow. Surplus was to be turned into cash reserves for emergencies, product research, physical expansion, defense of patents, and similar uses. The dividend policy was to remain conservative.

Fortunately, the company's profits were so substantial after World War I that the board could set aside the desired reserves every year, pay regular quarterly dividends, and also give two 100-per-cent stock dividends to the shareholders. This brought the total number of outstanding shares to

472,712 in 1920 and to 945,424 shares, held by 138 individual stockholders, in 1922.*

These policies on surplus, set in the Twenties, have never been changed. A substantial percentage of earnings has always been put back into the company for research, expansion, and other reserves. Dividends have remained modest. All of which has, in the terms of economists, made it a textbook example of a "growth" company.

Other important policies were formed during the '20s, also. President Ober had always felt that the employees should share in profits as an incentive to help the company prosper. Early key employees like C.C. James and H.W. Boynton had been stockholders, and, through the '20s, Ober saw to it that all loyal employees in positions of responsibility were able to share profits through various informal sharing plans. From time to time, for example, key employees were allowed to purchase shares from treasury stock whenever it became available. These employees could no longer buy it for the pittance of earlier years, however, for in 1920 the value of 3M stock had risen from the much-derided "two shares for a shot" to $2.40 a share.

Under another profit-sharing arrangement sponsored by Ober, certain employees responsible for increasing company profits were issued what were called "dividend participation certificates." Those holding such certificates were paid dividends on them at the end of each quarter at the same rate paid to stockholders owning actual shares. This plan had been put into effect soon after 3M declared its first dividend in 1916.

Vice-president McKnight, as well as Ober, had always been a strong advocate of the principle of profit-sharing and, when he became president in 1929, continued the policy.

*On November 27, 1922, capitalization was increased to 1,000,000 shares at $1 par.

Major changes were made, however, in the dividend participation certificate plan, as further experience showed it was not providing the most effective profit-sharing plan for 3M employees. The drawback was that the employee felt he was not actually participating in earnings as earned, a feeling which defeated the basic purpose of the plan–incentive to increase company earnings. Employee feeling on this score was justified. The company was paying relatively small dividends in relation to earnings. Under the policy of plowing a large part of earnings back into the business, the amount paid on the dividend participation certificates did not bear a direct relation to actual earnings in any year.

To correct this situation, all dividend participation certificates were recalled in 1935, and a new plan was put into effect. Under the new plan, the number participating in profit-sharing was increased to include division heads and more executives broadly responsible for overall operations. Only a handful of employees had been eligible for the original plan. The new one provided for the allotment by letter of management profit-sharing shares to executives responsible for overall profits. These shares entitled them to participate in the overall profits of the company. These executives were paid quarterly an amount per share on their profit-sharing shares equal to the amount the company earned per share on its outstanding capital stock. To a division head, an allotment of commodity profit-sharing shares was made, entitling him to participate in the profits made on the commodity produced in the division for which he was responsible for profits. Division heads were paid quarterly an amount on their commodity profit-sharing shares determined by dividing the earnings of each division by the number of shares of outstanding capital stock.

The purpose of this experimental plan was to extend profit-sharing to employees who had a direct influence on profits. In announcing the plan to the key men allowed to participate, McKnight said, "You are placed in the same relation to profits in your department of the business as a stockholder or partner in the business. It is recognized that this is an experiment and is subject to change as we gain experience, or replacement by some other plan if it proves impractical."[1]

The plan was successful; and, on January 1, 1937, profit-sharing was extended even more broadly to cover, with certain restrictions, almost all employees not already participating in a profit-sharing plan. The addition of the 1937 plan gave 3M three kinds of profit-sharing: management profit-sharing which had been in effect in some form since the company was organized; commodity profit-sharing, and general profit-sharing.

The basic principle of the 1937 general profit-sharing plan was that ten per cent of the net profits of the company in excess of a reserve representing a percentage of the net worth of the company would be set aside as a fund for profit-sharing purposes. The amount of this fund was divided by the total eligible payroll to determine the profit-sharing percentage. This percentage was then applied to the salary or wages of eligible employees to determine his or her profit-sharing payment. Employees with long periods of service were to participate to a greater extent than those with short. A little booklet was given to all employees participating in the profit-sharing plan, in which president McKnight outlined the goal and made suggestions on how to make greater profits:

The amount of profit-sharing disbursement will be largely dependent on the combined efforts of the entire organization toward increasing the net profits of the company by

Improving the quality of our products.

Reducing mistakes to a minimum.

Constant efforts toward reducing costs.

Eliminating lost time and delays.

Better planning of each job.

Avoiding waste and spoiled work.

Saving materials and supplies.

Developing more efficient methods.

Better care of equipment and tools.

Increased individual effort.

Completing each job promptly.

Continuous study and training.

The 1937 general profit-sharing plan had every chance to succeed, for at that time Minnesota Mining and Manufacturing Company possessed the requisites considered conducive for the success of such a program:

(1) Its employee relations were good. Most key employees had started in the company early, shared its hardships, and helped bring about its success. There had never been any labor trouble of any consequence. Any labor problems had been settled round-table fashion, with employees always having representation. Under these circumstances, 3M employees could be counted on to make the most of a profit-sharing plan. (2) Wages paid by 3M were comparable to those of other industries in its area, so income from the profit-sharing plan would be over and above already adequate wages. (3) The company was making money and had every reason to believe it would continue to do so, which meant there would be substantial profits to share.

General profit-sharing was successful until the late Forties. By that time, several factors were decreasing its effectiveness; namely, there was a large increase in the capital investment in the company, heavy taxes, and a large increase in the payroll due to a rise in the number of employees and an increase in salary or wages paid to each participant in profit-sharing. The larger reserve necessary to cover returns to stockholders and the heavy increases in taxes had some adverse effect on the amount available for profit-sharing. But the most important factor was that the large increase in payroll resulted in a progressive decrease in the percentage applicable to the participant's income for profit-sharing even though there was a substantial increase in the overall fund available for profit-sharing distribution. This contributed to dissatisfaction with the plan, and in 1952, general profit-sharing was discontinued as it had ceased to fulfill the purpose for which it was intended–that of providing an incentive. Management and commodity profit-sharing were retained.

There were losses in the prosperous '20s, as well as gains. In 1920, 3M founder John Dwan died unexpectedly. He was taken ill in October while on one of his frequent business trips for the Minnesota State Fair Board. He died October 10 in Detroit before he could be moved to Two Harbors. His loss was deeply felt by both Two Harbors and the company he had helped found. For the first time in Two Harbors' history, business was suspended and flags flown at half mast in honor of a local citizen. Dwan was the last of the original founders on the board of directors. His thorough knowledge of company affairs, his intense faith in 3M's future, and his devotion to carrying out responsibilities of his 3M work were greatly missed.

His son, John C. Dwan, who as a boy had earned ten cents a morning doing janitor work in the original 3M office above his father's law office on Poplar Street, was elected a vice-president and to the board of directors in November 1920. He is still a director.

In 1927, the company had a serious misfortune. In an effort to save money, McKnight, in 1920, had approved the building for the new maker of waterproof sandpaper without fireproof construction. On December 3, 1927, fire broke out in this building in the midst of a raging snowstorm.

Firemen battled the blaze in the wind and snow, but it was almost impossible to control. A huge stock of highly inflammable varnish-coated sandpaper fed the flames. The building and the stock of sandpaper were destroyed. Firemen were hampered by hundreds of spectators attracted by the billowing, oily smoke and flames. At one point, the lives of bystanders were threatened when a high tension wire carrying 4,000 volts was loosened, but the danger was averted by cutting the wire. When the flames broke through the roof of the waterproof maker, the nearby glue-bond plant as well as three 1,000-gallon tanks of linseed oil were threatened. These were saved in a seven-hour battle by the firemen. Fortunately, the company's 150 workers normally in the factory had ended their day's work just before the blaze broke out.

The loss was covered by insurance, but the fire stopped production of WETORDRY sandpaper at a most crucial time. The new product was beginning to catch on, and 3M was anxious to make immediate delivery on all orders. The fire wiped out the stock as well as production facilities.

Vice-president McKnight was in Europe at the time of the fire, getting British WETORDRY, Ltd. started. He recalls that this was the one time President Ober relaxed the company rule about cabling. Ordinarily, cables had to be sent in code to cut down their length. This time, Ober wired McKnight in detail and without code, telling him what had happened in St. Paul.

"I guess Ober thought I'd have heart failure before I could translate a code message about the fire," explains McKnight, who hurried back from abroad, took a look at the ruins, and with a flash of wit, said, "I don't like the looks of things around here. When can we get into production?"

As an incentive to the workers, he promised a big banquet "on the house" if they could rebuild the plant by February 1928, which was less than two months away.

Through the exceptional teamwork so prevalent in 3M, the goal was reached two days early, and McKnight gladly paid up. The new building was announced in the plant newspaper, *Three-M-News*, with the editorial comment

The Three-M Company is at the threshold of what appears to be a new era of accomplishments. Out of the ruins of a fire that destroyed the WETORDRY unit December 3rd has arisen, with unbelievable speed, a new and better building, equipped not only for greater production, but also for a better waterproof sandpaper. Somewhat as the famous Chicago fire is said to have wiped out a large city to make way for a larger one, so our apparently crushing disaster now looks like a blessing in disguise.[2]

In August, 1929, 3M had another loss, this time in the unexpected resignation of its president, Edgar Ober. Illness had plagued Ober for more than 15 years; his doctors had repeatedly warned him to retire from business and take care of his health. For years he had planned to resign and take life easy, but he liked hard work and kept putting retirement off. In 1929, he felt that 3M was on a solid foundation. It appeared that only success was now ahead; he could retire with a clear conscience. Over the protests of all who worked with him, he resigned in August.

Leaving wasn't easy for him. 3M had been a major interest in his life since 1905 when he had rescued it from insolvency through the help of his friend L.P. Ordway. Before he left, he was moved to make a statement to the press, one of the few he ever released:

In all my years of business contact I have never known a more competent, loyal and forceful lot of men than those now in charge of the affairs of our company, and, I might add, they never know when to quit working, and they all pull together. Many new lines of specialties have developed, all of which strengthen the company's position and materially increase its profits. Much as I regret being forced to give up active business, I am glad to know it is left in such able hands as those of Mr. McKnight and his able lieutenants. Its success is due to the combined efforts of many men, and all of them are now with the company and about of an even age, with the best years ahead of them.[3]

Ober's resignation meant the loss of the man most responsible for putting 3M on its feet in 1905; the man who had helped employees not only with company problems, but with personal ones as well; the man who had helped build an incomparable spirit of loyalty within 3M; the man who had served as friend, advisor, and inspiration to W.L. McKnight, who succeeded him as president. The board of directors paid the following tribute to their president on his retirement, August 12, 1929:

It is fully recognized that the survival of the company during the early years of its existence was due entirely to Mr. Ober's personal determination and persistence. The growth of the company in later years has been due largely to his organizing ability and his friendly and personal interest in the employees, which has built up a spirit of loyalty to the company that cannot be measured. In retiring, Mr. Ober leaves a place as a friend and businessman that can never be filled.[4]

Before Ober resigned, he decided to sell his 3M stock. At the time he had purchased his shares, he had paid $1 (par) or less for most of it. They were sold for $12.50 a share. At the time he be came a stockholder in 3M, the company was nearly insolvent and owned only the Crystal Bay deposit of "corundum," and was heavily in debt. When he resigned in 1929, 3M had nearly a $2½ million surplus, investments of more than $1 million, and plants and equipment valued at $831,236. Earnings since 1923 had averaged 80 cents a share on the stock. Another major change was that 3M had become a Delaware corporation, having incorporated under the laws of that state in 1929 to provide the company with the form of corporate organization best suited to its business needs. It has been operating under the Delaware law ever since. Too, export business by 1926 was in excess of the total

1915 sales volume. 3M salesmen could be found calling on industry all over the world.

Such rapid growth had brought one problem which even today is not completely solved: that of expanding manufacturing facilities and office space fast enough to keep pace with growth. By one means and another, the increased volume of business brought by World War I and THREE-M-ITE cloth was handled in the small St. Paul plant on Forest Avenue. Additional facilities were badly needed, but the high cost of building and company concentration on war effort forced the postponement of expansion. A partial fourth story added in 1917 to Building 1 had to do until the spring of 1920. Then Building 2–a $96,000, two-story brick plant for glue bond sandpaper production–was built on the corner of Forest Avenue and Fauquier, adjacent to Building 1. The building committee of McKnight and Orson Hull, always economy-minded, proudly saved the company the 7½ per cent architect fee by drawing the plans for Building 2 themselves with the aid of a contractor. By 1921, the addition of WETORDRY sandpaper overtaxed facilities again; and Building 3–a plant for manufacturing waterproof sandpaper only–was built in 1922 at a cost of $111,000. This is the building that burned in 1927 because 3M had tried to save money by not making it fireproof. In 1924, another story was added to Building 2 to house the general office help. In 1925, a plant for manufacturing the adhesive binder for WETORDRY abrasive paper was built.

In 1928, a plant for mineral grading and storage was constructed at a cost of $144,000. In addition, between 1920 and 1930, a series of miscellaneous buildings were acquired or built in an effort to alleviate overcrowding. A small building was constructed for coal storage, a frame shed acquired for general storage, an open shed for company automobiles, and a wagon shed and horse barn were purchased from a dairy company. In addition, two more sandpaper-making units were built.

St. Paul had paid scant attention to 3M when it moved into the East Side from Duluth in 1910. More glamorous enterprises absorbed the city's attention. By 1926, however, 3M could be ignored no longer. The St. Paul *Daily News* commented at length on 3M's growth in its 24-year history, on August 29, 1926. Like the Duluth *News Tribune* in 1906, the *Daily News* referred to 3M as the "world's largest manufacturer of sandpaper":

From obscurity to its present place as the leader in the coated abrasive manufacture field is the record made by Minnesota Mining and Manufacturing Company. At the beginning of the 20th century this company was unknown. Today it is the world's largest manufacturer of sandpaper.

The plant today consists of 10 production departments and 20 service departments. Making Departments No. 3 and No. 4 where the WETORDRY waterproof sandpaper is made have within them the largest bake ovens in the sandpaper industry. Each oven has a capacity of 24 miles of sand paper. The abrasive material manufactured by this company in 1925, made in 24-inch and wider strips, could be stretched out across the United States 6,818 miles. This means that approximately 100,000,000 units upon which the words "St. Paul, Minnesota" appear in large type are sent out each year to all parts of the United States and to many foreign countries.

But this recognition was an exception. The company usually wound up as an unidentified industry in the miscellaneous column whenever a history of St. Paul was written. The "Industrial and Civic Survey of St. Paul of 1928" by Charles J. Moos, Postmaster, is an example. For years, relatively few people knew much about the company in spite of its growth, for 3M deliberately shunned publicity whenever possible, and, until the '20s, the company did not advertise except by direct mail because of limited funds.

The no-advertising policy was finally reversed in 1921 when for the first time the company had a small surplus. In the early days, when the company began manufacturing in Duluth and C.C. James was its sales manager, advertising was confined to direct-sales letters and circulars. James was in charge of this direct-sales advertising and personally wrote innumerable letters to prospective customers expounding the virtues of Crystal Bay "corundum" paper. They were bold, confident letters, signed with a rubber stamp, advising customers if they ordered Crystal Bay corundum paper and it wasn't equal to garnet paper, to send it back. As often as not, that's just what they did. With his letters, James enclosed little buff-colored pamphlets containing a sales talk which he had composed on Minnesota Mining and Manufacturing Company. The inside of the pamphlet was always the same, starting out with a bright, "Good Morning. I represent the Minnesota Mining and Manufacturing Company and wish to interest you in their Crystal Bay products." The titles on the outside of the pamphlet varied, however. Two choice examples were "A Smooth Talk on a Rough Subject" and "Hard Facts at the Hardware Store."

When Ober, Ordway, McKnight, and Bush took over management of 3M, they, too, felt that the direct-sales effort was more practical than "good will" advertising in magazines and other media for a company operating on a limited budget. In 1921, however, they decided to push the sale of retail packages of sandpaper. To back the campaign, advertisements were placed in The *Saturday Evening Post* in order to reach a wide audience of homeowners. Bush and McKnight collaborated on the copy for these ads and look back with much amusement on their amateurish results. Through these one-column advertisements, 3M advised homeowners to give their homes a "new look" by painting their woodwork and furniture, and sandpapering first, of course, with 3M flint paper. Farmers were told to "pretty up" their cows with 3M flint paper to get them ready for the State Fair. Car owners were advised to use 3M flint paper to smooth out spots which needed repainting on their automobiles.

The *Post* ads were to run every two weeks for a year but at the end of nine months, the nation went through a brief but acute postwar depression which spoiled the success of 3M's sales campaign. The ads were discontinued.

Advertising was not resumed until 1932 when the decision was made to launch an ambitious program in various media. A particularly intensive and unique advertising campaign now referred to as "monkey business" was directed at the auto refinishing trade. Arrangements were made with English cartoonist Lawson Wood to draw a special series for 3M of his famous monkey cartoons, for use on advertising folders. Space was provided inside the direct mail folders for a sales letter to the auto refinishing trade by various branches of the company. These "monkey" letterheads carried not only sales letters, but announcements of new products or price changes. Monkey cartoon posters were enclosed with shipments of 3M materials, and soon the walls of auto repaint shops all over the country were plastered with these pictures.

The monkey pictures had no direct connection with the product advertised, but soon the auto refinish trade identified the cartoons with 3M and thought of the company whenever they saw one. This "monkey business" was so appealing to customers that when 3M slackened its sales campaign, complaints were so numerous that the company had to resume the cartoon mailings. They are still used today.

The monkey series was not without its troubles. Wood once included a bear in a cartoon. Unfortunately a bear was the trade symbol of one of 3M's competitors and strong objections quickly reached Minnesota Mining.*

During World War II, the monkey cartoons were employed in still another manner to advertise 3M. Stationery was made up featuring the monkey cartoons on the back and distributed to 3M employees to use in writing servicemen.

Since the '30s, the Advertising Department has constantly expanded and today has a staff of over 80 people.

*A similar amusing incident occurred in 1951. An advertising agency cartoonist unthinkingly showed a picture tacked to the wall. 3M quickly reminded him that the picture should be shown taped to the wall with SCOTCH Brand cellophane tape!

TRIAL JOURNEY

WETORDRY sandpaper gave industry a new, valuable tool, and at the same time it led 3M down a trail which had long been beckoning and which McKnight believed would lead to greater profits and growth. This was the road marked "diversification."

The first excursion into diversification, however, was not a planned trip, in spite of the fact that for years McKnight had wished 3M could manufacture something besides sandpaper. The directors didn't decide that "3M will now diversify its products." To the contrary, the company was not thinking in terms of diversification at all when they developed their first nonabrasive. They were merely trying to remedy a situation which had put the sale of WETORDRY sandpaper in jeopardy.

3M's waterproof paper had been in use only a short time in 1921 when it was found that, while it satisfactorily smoothed the lacquer finish on the auto bodies, unfortunately it dulled the natural shine of the lacquer and destroyed the eye appeal of the finish. If it was to be a commercial success, some way had to be found to restore the luster. This problem did not exist with baked enamel and varnish finishes which dried to a natural shine.

To both the sales division and the laboratory, the obvious way to restore the luster was with an auto polish, and as there were no suitable polishes on the market for use with waterproof sandpaper, 3M decided to develop one. Okie was assigned the job of concocting a polish, and he tackled the job in his own inimitable manner of trying this and that until he had a formula that worked.

He mixed up a paste wax and a sanding liquid, too; and each concoction was taken into a field and tested on a car, either in a St. Paul repaint shop where sandpaper was also tested, or in a large automotive plant in Detroit. Finally, Okie had three products ready for sales, Lacqua Polish, Lustra Wax, and "3M Sanding Liquid", and 3M salesmen bravely sold them along with Wetordry sandpaper.

The volume on these products was negligible that first year, 1924.* But 3M didn't mind. The important thing was that the company was keeping Wetordry abrasives on the market and also helping the automotive industry with a production problem.

For several years the abrasive salesmen sold polishes and wax under several different trade names and as many different formulas. A change from the name Lustra Wax to Lusterize brought a complaint from the manufacturers of "Simoniz" that the name too closely resembled theirs. 3M was not anxious to tangle with so well-established a firm and changed the name of its entire car maintenance line to Retsul (luster spelled backwards).

The Retsul line, however, was never to be a breadwinner like Three-M-Ite or Wetordry abrasives. Volume remained small and profits low. Competition, while minor at first, soon grew to substantial proportions. Polish and wax were easy to manufacture, and small businessmen all over the

*$920. This does not give an idea of how much polish, wax, and sanding liquid was manufactured. A great many free samples were furnished for trial purposes that year.

country began whipping up their versions and supplying their own immediate areas. Then national competition entered the picture. McAleer, Simoniz, Du Pont, and others developed successful polishes and sold special retail kits not only to automotive manufacturers and auto repaint shops, but directly to car owners as well.

3M made only one major attempt to put RETSUL into this competition in the retail field. Early in 1929, the retail market looked especially attractive, for car sales that year were nearing the $5 million mark, the highest thus far in the history of the automobile business. Every car owner was a potential customer for car maintenance items like polish and wax. Big plans were made by 3M for a nationwide campaign to sell RETSUL products to garages, service stations, hardware stores, and other retail outlets. General sales manager Bush appointed a special campaign sales manager. St. Louis was chosen as the test city for the campaign. This was considered a difficult area, and if the program were successful there, it was 3M's intention to campaign in Chicago, Cincinnati, Detroit, Cleveland, Akron, St. Paul, and Pittsburgh. Spring was considered the best time to sell a maintenance item like polish, and spring came early in St. Louis. This would give the salesmen some experience selling the new product before spring came to other cities. Newspaper advertising was scheduled to coincide with the salesmen's efforts in St. Louis.

Optimistically, Okie and his staff manufactured a whole carload of RETSUL items and shipped it to the small 3M warehouse in St. Louis. Old-time St. Louis employees will never forget the day it arrived. The small warehouse was already nearly full of regular sandpaper stock, and they spent hours trying to make room for the carload of cartons.

Plans for the campaign were made in the most prosperous months of the jazz age. With car sales at their peak, a campaign to sell auto maintenance items seemed astute sales programming. No one dreamed the economic picture of the nation would change overnight.

In February 1930, when it was time to put campaign plans into action, 3M was in a dilemma. The stock market crash had plunged the nation into a depression. No one knew how long it would last, or how far surplus dollars would have to stretch. They did know the campaign would be costly. A special sales force had to be hired for each city. Newspaper advertising was an added expense. Profits, even with substantially increased volume, would be problematical because of the high cost of introducing the products.

Unused to turning back after plans had been made, however, McKnight and Bush gave the campaign sales manager a green light. In February, 1930, he went to St. Louis to hire a crew of eight special salesmen to call on every potential retail outlet.

The campaign selling point was to be the fact that 3M's polish left no oily film on the car as did other polishes. Okie had worked day and night to perfect this no-film feature of the polish. By Friday, February 28, the St. Louis crew had been carefully briefed on this feature and equipped with demonstration samples. They were ready to canvass the city. Friday afternoon the sales manager made a horrifying discovery. While demonstrating a can of polish, he found that it *did* leave an oily film on the car and was no better, therefore, than competitive polishes. At least the can of polish from which he made the demonstration left a film. He tried more samples with the same result. Close examination disclosed that the pigment which Okie had incorporated in the polish formula to give it the special no-film component had solidified in the bottom of the can. The campaign was to begin Monday. Frantically the sales manager summoned the entire 3M St. Louis staff of five—the office manager, the sales manager, the shipping clerk and his assistant, and the regular local salesman. With their help, he spent the entire weekend at the warehouse, ripping open carton after carton, can after can, to see if there were any good stock. Every single can was alike; the pigment had gathered into a lump in the bottom.

Everything was tried to restore the pigment to suspension in the polishing fluid. The polish was stirred with sticks and electric stirrers. The cans were thoroughly shaken. Nothing worked. The whole carload had to be thrown away. The campaign either had to be called off, which would mean losing the entire initial investment, or it had to be put on without a special selling feature. The newspaper ads had already been set for the Monday morning papers to support the salesmen's calls on the retailers.

It seemed more sensible to go ahead. Meanwhile the sales manager telephoned Okie to find out what he thought was wrong. The laboratory worked day and night that weekend, and it was finally figured out that the vibration of the freight car in which the RETSUL was shipped had caused the pigment to gather in the bottom of the cans. No one in the laboratory had found this defect in the routine testing. By working around the clock that weekend, Okie and his staff made up new samples for the St. Louis sales crew, and the campaign went ahead as scheduled. The only delay was in filling orders.

This intensified sales effort in 1930 increased polish and wax sales a little, but production and merchandising costs were too high; profits too small. Before the campaign, sales of all car maintenance items had run between $50,000 and $150,000 a year. The special effort pushed the volume to $170,371 in 1930, but it dropped sharply in the ensuing years to $66,569 in 1932.

By 1931 prices were breaking; competitors' retail prices ran as low as 75 cents for polish. 3M had to charge a dollar a can or lose money. In the words of A.G. Bush, "The volume of business brought by these products was not sufficient to satisfy the appetite of a young, ambitious company intent on further growth." The RETSUL products were gradually discontinued in the early '30s.

The low-profit wax and polish business had never caught the imagination of growth-minded McKnight and Bush, but in 1925, a laboratory worker had an idea for a new product which did. Richard G. Drew, a 26-year-old laboratory assistant, got the idea for a new kind of industrial masking tape urgently needed by the automotive industry. There was no other tape like it on the market; it would be profitable. It had all the potential for the kind of diversification program wanted for 3M.

Drew was encouraged to develop his idea and money was furnished for research. In 1925, the tape was marketed, and in a short time 3M had another product as salable as THREE-M-ITE aluminum oxide cloth and waterproof sandpaper. The tape, the first major nonabrasive item in 3M's growing list of products, was christened "SCOTCH" Brand masking tape and became the nucleus from which more than a hundred pressure-sensitive industrial tapes evolved, including the famous "SCOTCH" Brand cellophane tape.

BIRTH OF THE "SCOTCH" CLAN

MINNESOTA BORN Dick Drew, though an individualistic youngster, hadn't been particularly ingenious in his childhood in St. Paul. Like most boys, he had been interested in mechanical toys. He dismantled well-running clocks, played with erector sets, and once built a miniature railroad in his back yard. In his teens he was interested in cars, as were all his friends, but no more intensely than they. In high school, he liked mathematics and chemistry fairly well, but took no special interest in them. What he did like was playing the banjo, an instrument then indispensable to a dance band. When Richard Drew was graduated from St. Paul, Minnesota Central High School, he was a prank-loving, banjo-playing teen-ager, with nothing on his record to point to a future of international fame.

Earning his way by playing the banjo with Twin Cities' orchestras, Drew completed two quarters of engineering at the University of Minnesota, but he soon found staying up nights and attending classes by day too much. He dropped out of college in 1920 and made his living playing in the dance band. He was still interested in engineering, however, and enrolled in a mechanical engineering course with International Correspondence Schools. In 1921, young Drew decided to try to get a job with a future and began watching the want ads. At this same time, in 1921, 3M decided to double the personnel of the research laboratory. William Vievering was to get an assistant to help with quality control of waterproof sandpaper. In business fashion typical of the times, 3M ran a blind ad in the St. Paul *Dispatch*, merely stating in it that a St. Paul concern had a good opening for the right young man. Interested applicants were asked to write stating their qualifications.

Richard Drew was one of a dozen or so who answered the ad. In his reply he described himself as just the type of young man 3M was always looking for–eager, enterprising, and willing to work. He outlined his engineering training at the University of Minnesota and the correspondence work. And for an impressive touch, he wrote the letter on International Correspondence School stationery:

DEAR SIR:

I am taking this opportunity to answer your ad which appears in the St. Paul *Dispatch*. I am a graduate of Central High School, St. Paul, and have completed a year in Engineering College at the State university. At the present time I am studying the Mechanical course offered by the I.C.S. schools. I have not as yet been employed in commercial work and am eager to get started in this kind of work. I realize that my services would not be worth much until a certain amount of practical experience is gained and would be glad to start with any salary you see fit to give. You may be sure that I would put forth every effort to do that which was required of me and I would continue my I.C.S. work evenings.

At present I am a member of the Athletic Orchestra, taking this means to earn enough money to finance another year of school, but having found the International Correspondence School's work and instructions to be of high caliber, am looking for just such an opportunity as you are offering and have not the intention of returning to the University. Upon closing I wish to say that I am accustomed to physical labor, if this be required, as I drove a tractor and did general farm work for two years.

William Vievering was impressed with a young man so determined to get ahead and he telephoned Drew early one morning to arrange for an interview. Drew, groggy from a late job with the band, buried his head in the pillow and almost let the telephone keep ringing. Luckily for him, and for 3M, however, he finally answered the call.

Richard Drew found his work at Minnesota Mining and Manufacturing Company far different from playing the banjo. He spent the first two years checking raw materials and running tests on sandpaper. One of Drew's jobs was to take samples of Okie's waterproof paper to St. Paul auto body refinishing shops for testing. At that time, everyone who bought a car wanted a two-tone finish, which the automobile manufacturers had just introduced. They were beginning to be sorry they had, for two-tone painting was causing headaches on big production lines and even worse ones in small body-repaint shops all over the country.

Because a straight, sharp demarcation between the two colors was essential when a car was being painted two colors, one area of the car had to be masked off while the other was being painted. In addition, glass windows, upholstery, rubber mats, running boards, bright metal parts, and other sections had to be protected from the lacquer, which was sprayed on with automatic spray guns. The new, quick-drying lacquers and automatic spray guns had made possible beautiful finishes with mass production speed, but the assembly line was creaking to a standstill on two-tone jobs because an adequate and efficient method of masking off one area from another had not been found.

The problem was to keep a clean, sharp edge where one color met another without sacrificing the speed made possible with the spray guns. The most satisfactory method of masking in the early '20s was to separate the two areas to be painted by old newspapers. These were glued to the body and windows with ordinary library paste, a cloth-backed surgical tape, or a paper-backed tape with a water-soluble glue coating. The idea of masking off the straight line was good, except that the homemade glue concoctions and cloth-backed surgical tapes used to hold the newspapers in place created new trouble. The glue often stuck too tightly and had to be scraped off, which ruined the paint finish. The cloth-backed tapes permitted the lacquer to seep through, and they, too, stuck to the surface the tape was supposed to protect, leaving a messy paint job.

Wherever Drew delivered sandpaper samples, he heard a story of grief from the men painting the two-tone jobs. One day at a small repaint shop in St. Paul, in 1925, Drew heard a particularly violent outburst of profanity from a worker who was disgusted with the mess the crude masking method had made of his paint job. It was a rush job, and the carefully sprayed paint had been ruined when the car painter removed the gummed tape used to mask off the upper part of the car body. The paint had come off with the gummed tape, leaving a blotchy stripe around the car. Without knowing quite what possessed him, Drew sympathetically told the painter he could make tape that would do a better job than anything they were using. He could back this promise with neither experience nor know-how. He didn't even know exactly what was needed, but he had the optimism of youth, and back in his mind he wondered whether some of the Okie concoctions for waterproof sandpaper couldn't be used to make a masking tape. Drew returned to 3M and explained his idea to management. They encouraged him to work on it, authorized an investigation of the patent situation on masking tape, and provided money for experiments. Drew set to work.

What the auto industry needed was a masking tape that would stick tightly, yet pull off easily without leaving a gummy residue or taking the paint with it; a tape that wouldn't let the solvents in lacquer seep through and ruin the paint job underneath; a tape strong enough to provide a sharp, clean edge for the two-tone job. Preferably, it would be a tape that didn't need water or any other activator to make it stick to the car as tape of the water-soluble type stuck too tightly. As yet there was no such tape.

Drew experimented first with the vegetable oils Okie had mixed for WETORDRY sandpaper. He tried smearing this tacky mixture on ordinary Kraft wrapping paper. The resulting "flypaper" tape, as it was quickly nicknamed, stuck readily enough and came off easily, but it bleached the paint.

It was a start, however, and during the next few months, Drew and his assistants, in a laboratory of their own now, cooked dozens of batches of various sticky substances using linseed oil, various resins, gum chicle, and naphtha. The laboratory finally ended up with a formula containing a good grade of cabinetmaker's glue kept sticky with the addition of glycerine. With this mixture, they came close to the answer to the painters' problem. The tape adhered easily to the car and also pulled off easily without leaving a gummy residue. It gave the painter a sharp, clean edge on the two-tone jobs. This first successful tape was called simply, "3M Non-Drying Tape."

But many problems were still unsolved. The Kraft paper backing used for this tape had no extensibility, or stretchiness. This meant it couldn't be pressed flat around curved surfaces, an essential feature for a successful masking tape. Too, the tape stuck to itself when in roll form, which was the only practical way to manufacture it. When unwound from the roll a gummy residue remained on the back of the tape. To counteract this, Drew decided to add a cheesecloth liner to the roll to catch the gummy residue. This added materially to the production cost.

3M struggled along with the combination of cabinetmaker's glue, ordinary wrapping paper, and a cheesecloth

liner for about three years. The tape wasn't entirely satisfactory, but automotive manufacturers were desperate, and
whatever Drew dreamed up, they tried. However, the automotive industry rejected increasing quantities of this
cheesecloth-lined, nondrying tape and before long competition had developed a cheap, cloth-backed, surgical tape for
masking purposes. Drew's staff doubled their efforts to
improve the product. While they worked, 3M managed to
stay in the tape picture mostly for one reason. Solvents in
the auto paint didn't penetrate the Drew tape as it did that
of competition.

3M finally named this new product "SCOTCH" Brand
masking tape and has been trying to explain why ever since.
The trouble is that no one remembers exactly how the name
"SCOTCH" did come about. One story has become a plausible
legend. When the masking tape was first sold, the company,
as an economy measure, applied adhesive only to the outer
edges of the two-inch strips, leaving the center plain. One
edge was to be taped to the paper, the other to the car to
hold the masking paper in place. 3M's stinginess with the
glue turned out to be a new headache to car painters, for the
partially coated tape didn't stick too well, and the story is
that these painters growled at 3M salesmen, "Why be so
Scotch with the adhesive?" Soon, the tape was officially
trademarked "SCOTCH" Brand.

As Drew's staff stumbled along with tape experiments,
vice president McKnight began to worry about the effect of
this poor quality tape on 3M's reputation for high-quality
products. He approved of Drew's research, but was skeptical
of the wisdom of ever selling a poor product. Much as he
hated to dampen young Drew's enthusiasm, McKnight
finally wrote a memo to the young laboratory assistant. "I
think it would be better if you returned to your job of helping Mr. Okie with this waterproof sandpaper," was the gist
of the note.

Drew reluctantly reported back to Okie in the sandpaper laboratory, but his mind was still on tape. His first assignment from Okie was to go to the top floor of the plant to see if there was a roll of crimped, towel-type paper used once before in an experiment. Okie wanted to try this paper once more for WETORDRY sandpaper.

Drew remembers vividly that hot, summer day when he dutifully climbed to the third floor of the plant. His mind was still on tape as he began to hunt for the jumbo roll of paper. He found it in a corner, covered with dust, and took it to the laboratory to make up a sample of sandpaper. "As I cut off a piece of the paper, it suddenly occurred to me that *this* might be the right paper for the tape. I became very excited," remembers Drew. "The paper was an absorbent Kraft paper almost identical with the hand towels used in washrooms. It had that feature we wanted most–stretchability, or extensibility–because of the crimping. I couldn't wait to try it."

Forgetting all about sandpaper, Drew made up a sample of masking tape out of the crimped paper. When he finished testing it, he knew that finally he had found the key to a more satisfactory product. Hurriedly, more experiments were made to determine the best adhesive formula for the new type of backing. It was found that when this creped paper was treated with a glue-glycerine solution, the fibers of the paper became so unified that the tape could be unwound from a roll without laminating the paper backing. This new nondrying masking tape could be pressed on the car with finger pressure, it stayed tight while the worker painted the car, it ripped off easily without leaving a sticky residue, and it didn't allow solvents to seep through it. It had extensibility. With this tape, two-tone jobs were no longer such a headache, and one of the automotive industry's most annoying and expensive production problems was eased.

A new difficulty soon became apparent in this tape, however. It wouldn't perform properly if more than about 30 days old. When kept in stock too long, the glue-glycerine adhesive dried out, the tape lost its tackiness, and then would not stick to anything. So Drew and his laboratory staff began a new set of experiments to overcome this problem. Meanwhile, 3M dreamed up a stopgap measure to keep the masking tape on the market. Someone suggested that 3M sell small electric heaters to the automotive people along with tape to reactivate it and make it usable. A small shop in St. Paul agreed to manufacture a heater which consisted of a small heating coil curved under a brass plate two inches wide. When a painter was ready to use the tape, he slid it over the heated brass plate. The heaters sold for $10, the cost to 3M.

The aging problem was finally solved fairly satisfactorily with a third type of nondrying masking tape in which the adhesive formula was changed from a glue-glycerine to a rubber base. Glycerine had caused the adhesive to take on moisture in high-humidity areas and give off moisture in low humidity, making the tackiness of the tape variable and unpredictable. The new formula made it possible to abandon the heaters and to assure the customer that he could keep tape in stock a reasonable length of time with proper storage care. The new rubber-based SCOTCH Brand masking tape was sold until 1935 when still another major improvement was made, this time in the treatment of the paper backing. The glycerine 3M had been using in the solution to treat the paper backing absorbed and gave off moisture (as had the old-style adhesive); this in turn affected the uniformity of the finished tape. Now a carefully balanced formula of rubber and special resins was developed as a substitute for the glue-glycerine saturating solution, which overcame the variable caused by the use of the glycerine. This type has been sold successfully ever since. From this basic masking tape, 3M branched out into the manufacture of dozens of industrial pressure-sensitive tapes. Some of the more successful variations are decorator's tape, tape for shoe manufacturing, electrical tape, and filament tape for heavy duty packaging.

SCOTCH Brand masking tape made an amazing sales record right from the start, in spite of all the problems. Yearly volume grew steadily from $164,279 its first full year on the market to $1,151,023 in 1935, and on up to a multi-million-dollar gross, where it has remained. Definitely, masking tape was the kind of diversified product 3M wanted!

THE FAMOUS ONE

3M's MASKING TAPE was only five years old when Drew came up with another ingenious, multimillion-dollar idea. This time, he conceived the product which brought 3M not only new recognition in the industry but fame throughout the world.

His second invention was "SCOTCH" Brand cellophane tape, the filmy, but sturdy, colorless tape for which the world has discovered a thousand and one uses neither the inventor nor anyone else in 3M had in mind. In no time at all after it was invented, farmers found it handy for patching cracked turkey eggs, secretaries discovered it would patch torn fingernails, and housewives found it useful for removing lint from clothing, holding cheese on mousetraps, and for taping cracked plaster to the ceiling.

It was early in 1929 when Drew began work on a sealing tape with Du Pont's new moistureproof, transparent cellophane. His 1929 tape was not marketable, but it was the embryo of a product which was to prove more spectacular than anyone could imagine. Without realizing it, Drew was developing a tape which not only replaced string and other sealing devices in the small packaging field to a great extent, but became an indispensable supply item in homes and offices around the globe. Most important to 3M, overnight it equaled prior company products in earning ability.

Romantic legend has it that Drew stumbled on the idea for SCOTCH Brand cellophane tape "somewhere between a thought and a daydream." There is truth in the legend of course, for no one will dispute that much thought and not a few daydreams go into most inventions. Drew, now technical director of the Product Fabrication Laboratory and as individualistic, philosophical, and unpredictable as ever, half-humorously remarks that when he stumbled on SCOTCH Brand cellophane tape, perhaps he was blessed with serendipity–the gift of finding valuable or agreeable things not sought for. More seriously, he feels that the "pinpoint of origin" of any invention is difficult to determine and that an invention is really the work of many, regardless of who thinks of the specific idea which makes the product a reality. "If it hadn't been for earlier research in 3M on adhesive binder for WETORDRY abrasive paper, there might not be any masking or cellophane tape today," points out Drew.

Actually, SCOTCH Brand cellophane tape, like its predecessor, masking tape, came about because 3M was looking for the answer to a production problem of one of its customers. Masking tape had been developed to aid the automotive industry in the two-tone painting of cars. Cellophane tape was invented while Drew was trying to solve a packaging problem for a St. Paul manufacturer. Ordinarily, this manufacturer, the Flaxlinum Company, sold insulation for houses, but in 1929 it had an order for insulating material for several hundred railroad refrigerator cars. In trying to fill the order, Flaxlinum found that their regular material would have to be wrapped and sealed to protect it against moisture in the refrigerator cars. Unwrapped, it developed a most objectionable odor. Flaxlinum turned to Minnesota Mining and Manufacturing Company for help in finding something that would seal the wrapped slabs of insulating material and make them waterproof, thinking that perhaps 3M's masking tape was the answer.

Drew and his tape laboratory made innumerable attempts to find a solution for the Flaxlinum Company, all unsuccessful. He tried wrapping a slab of insulating material 2 feet by 3 feet by 1 inch in Kraft wrapping paper like any package, then sealing the seams and folds with SCOTCH Brand masking tape to make the package moistureproof. It didn't work. The backing on the masking tape was not sufficiently moistureproof to insulate the package from moisture. Then Drew tried to make an entirely waterproof, pressure-sensitive masking tape out of a Kraft-type waterproof paper which consisted of two pieces of paper sealed to each other with asphalt. This didn't work either, since the waterproof paper couldn't be successfully unwound after the adhesive was applied and the paper made in roll form.

3M then tried to seal the insulating material without any tape at all. Drew coated the entire surface of a waterproof wrapping material with pressure sensitive adhesive, then folded this coated material around the insulating slab like a pillowcase. He sealed the folds in such a manner that the package would be waterproof. This was an improvement, but it still was not sufficiently waterproof.

During the experiments for Flaxlinum, another tape-laboratory worker was considering packaging 3M's masking tape in Du Pont's new moistureproof cellophane to protect the rolls of tape from heat, cold, moisture, and dryness. (Du Pont cellophane by 1929 had already made its mark on the packaging field. The brittle, sparkling cellophane had been first adopted by candy and cosmetic manufacturers and bakers. Then, when Du Pont chemists made cellophane moistureproof, it was adopted by meat packers, chewing gum manufacturers, and other food distributors.) One day he showed Drew the sheets of cellophane and discussed how he proposed to do the packaging.

At that moment, it could be said, SCOTCH Brand cellophane tape was born, for Drew looked at the cellophane and thought to himself, "Why couldn't that stuff be coated with adhesive and used as a sealing tape for the Flaxlinum slabs? It's moistureproof."

Drew lost no time. He ordered 100 yards of moistureproof Du Pont cellophane for experiments on June 28, 1929. When it arrived, he cut the cellophane into six-inch widths so that it could be pulled through the laboratory knife-coating equipment. Using the standard masking tape, rubber-base adhesive, which was a dirty amber color, he coated several six-inch strips. Then he made the usual routine checks used for masking tape to see if the adhesive-coated cellophane tape had any possibilities. A one-inch strip was removed from one edge of the hand-spread sample, placed on the back of an uncoated side of cellophane, pressed down with an old chair coaster to insure contact, and then ripped off again. This was to see whether the cellophane had sufficient strength to resist splitting or rupturing on the surface, and whether it had sufficient anchorage to the surface on which it was coated so that the adhesive would not transfer to the uncoated sheet.

The test showed that there was a possibility of using cellophane as a backing for pressure-sensitive tape, and Drew elatedly went to work on more samples in the hope of solving the difficulties of the Flaxlinum Company. As it turned out, SCOTCH Brand cellophane tape was not what they needed, but it showed great possibilities as an aid in packaging other products, and research was continued. It took more than a year before 3M had a salable tape, a comparatively short time for research and development of such a successful product, but some of the longest and most discouraging months in 3M's history.

Drew and his assistants found that cellophane didn't act like any backing with which 3M had had experience. It posed one dilemma after another, all seeming to defy solution. It curled near heat and split in the process of coating by machine; the adhesive wouldn't adhere evenly, and bare spots were left while other areas were too heavily coated. The dirty amber color of the adhesive ruined the filmy sparkle of the colorless, transparent cellophane. It broke and tore before enough could be coated for a full roll. At the end of each day, stacks of spoiled cellophane were piled several feet high on each side of the experimental coating machine. It took a truck to remove the waste for burning.

Meanwhile, many companies were approaching 3M for help with packaging their products. Waldorf Paper Products Company of St. Paul, Vander Bie's, Inc., the St. Paul meat packing plants, and others needed a waterproof-type sealing tape. Most anxious of all were the companies using Du Pont plain, transparent, and moistureproof cellophane for packaging both nonperishable and perishable products. No satisfactory means had been found for sealing these packages. String wouldn't work. It spoiled the looks of the package. Rubber bands could be wound around the package, but they ruined the eye appeal. Stapling was unattractive and awkward. No known way of sealing a package made it moistureproof.

One inquiry in particular interested 3M. A Chicago firm which specialized in the printing of cellophane–Shellmar Products Corporation–wrote 3M to see whether masking tape could be suitably manufactured for sealing fancily printed cellophane used for wrapping bakery goods. Shellmar didn't know that 3M had already begun work on a transparent sealing tape which might be just right.

In June, 1930, 3M discussed the possibilities of manufacturing both transparent and colored, pressure-sensitive cellophane tape with Shellmar.

The anxiety of all these companies, and Shellmar in particular, served as a driving force for Drew and his assistants. One by one, production difficulties were overcome. It was found that if a primer coat was first applied to the cellophane, the adhesive would coat evenly. Special machinery was designed to overcome splitting and breaking. New adhesives which were almost colorless were developed so that the coating wouldn't ruin the transparency of the cellophane.

It took all the ingenuity of both nontechnical and technical personnel, plus infinite patience and perseverance, to develop the tape to a marketable stage. Almost everyone was tempted to give up after nearly a year of discouraging attempts to perfect the tape, but the laboratory wearily kept on experimenting. The tape had to have a proper balance of adhesiveness, cohesiveness, elasticity, and stretchiness. It had to perform in temperatures from below freezing to 110 degrees and in the relative humidities from two and three per cent to 95 per cent in such cities as Seattle, New Orleans, Galveston, and Houston.

Finally, on September 8, 1930, a roll of SCOTCH Brand cellophane tape which 3M felt met these requirements was sent to Shellmar Products Corporation. On September 24, 1930, after examining and testing the sample, Shellmar advised 3M: "It seems that the practical nature of your gum [adhesive] is such that it will adhere to glass or practically any surface. It needs no moistening or smearing and is so easily applied, that it would appear this would be a very ideal means of sealing moistureproof packages for cakes, cookies, etc. You should have no hesitancy in equipping yourself to put this product on the market economically as it will be quite evident that there will be a sufficient volume of sales to justify the expenditure."[1]

Even with encouragement from the trade, 3M was cautious and conservative as always in announcing its new product to stockholders. Only a brief statement appeared in the 1930 annual report:

During the year a new product known as SCOTCH Brand Cellulose Tape was introduced. It consists of cellophane coated with a transparent pressure sensitive adhesive. Although it has many uses its largest utility is in sealing packages wrapped in moistureproof cellophane. In view of the present popularity of cellophane as a wrapping medium, this market appears to have large possibilities.

The world was to show 3M just how large. The new tape had been on the market only a short time when everyone realized that there was no need to worry about the demand for it. Sales manager Bush first pushed cellophane tape in the packaging field, but ingenious Americans, and eventually the world, began devising all sorts of other uses for it.

SCOTCH Brand cellophane tape was put on the market the first year of the depression, a most inopportune time for what seemed to be a luxury item. But luckily, Americans had been forced into thrift and soon found that the filmy, colorless tape could be used to make old things do. They found it was fine for mending torn pages of books, window curtains, sheet music, and even small rips in clothing. Soon this new tape replaced the only other mending tape on the market that was anywhere near transparent–a French paper tape called AP which had been introduced in America shortly after 1900.

As the depression deepened, new uses were found: for mending broken toys, sealing opened cans of evaporated or condensed milk, and attaching labels on home-canned food. Insurance companies used it to mend torn policies, banks their torn currency, and all business found it useful for mending torn documents.

Almost daily, new ideas for using the tape popped up from the public and 3M salesmen. Laundries began using it instead of glue to seal the paper bands wrapped around freshly laundered shirts–the glue had often dropped on the shirt, requiring it to be laundered again. Ribbon manufacturers used the tape in place of pins to prevent rolls of ribbon from unwinding; a pin had always been objectionable because it punched a hole through several layers of ribbon.

Stores of all kinds used the tape for attaching price labels to articles where ordinary gummed labels wouldn't stick and on metalware which might be damaged by the use of a china pencil. Housewives and businessmen discovered that coins to be mailed could be held in place on cardboard with the tape.

One of the most unusual uses was by Goodyear Zeppelin Corporation. This company used large amounts of SCOTCH Brand cellophane tape in the manufacture of its lighter-than-air craft, to cover the inner ribs and beams of its dirigibles. The tape served as an anticorrosive shield.

The volume for this tape, however, was in the field for which it had been developed–packaging. Bakeries were the largest consumers those first years. Then retail grocers learned that vegetables, cookies, and other foods kept better when wrapped in cellophane, and the "cracker barrel" era began to disappear.

At first 3M abrasive salesmen sold the new cellophane tape but it was soon obvious that an entirely separate sales force would have to be hired. In the beginning, these new tape salesmen had huge territories–eight to ten states a piece. One salesman had the entire Pacific coast area. When the salesmen began calling on retail grocers, they found in many cases that in order to sell cellophane tape, they first had to sell the grocer on the idea of packaging foods in cellophane bags. For months, tape salesmen took orders for both cellophane bags and SCOTCH Brand cellophane tape. Finally, practically all grocers had adopted cellophane bag packaging, and 3M dropped out of the bag business.

After connections with bakeries and grocers were established, 3M made surveys of the drug, dry goods, hardware, ready-to-wear, shoe, and stationery stores to determine possible outlets for the new tape. By now, 3M had developed a small roll for home use as well as its large one for commercial purposes. The sales staff discovered that selling tape was just a matter of sending out enough salesmen to cover the territory. Everyone wanted the tape after they heard about it.

There were still many production and merchandising difficulties, however. For one thing, the tape wouldn't keep in stock very long. Humidity, heat, or cold could spoil it. Heat caused the adhesive to soften and ooze out from the roll, making it hard to handle. When the tape was used to mend books the stickiness caused the pages to stick together. A package wrapped with tape became sticky in warm weather. On the other hand, cold caused the tape to stiffen and lose its "tackiness," or pressure-sensitive qualities, and then it wouldn't stick properly and broke off easily in unwinding. While the laboratory tried to overcome this "aging" trouble, the sales department was forced to warn customers to keep the tape away from radiators and windows. However, this warning often was unheeded, and many a roll was returned by jobbers as unsatisfactory until 3M overcame the difficulty.

Another serious obstacle arose. When the tape was first put on the market there was no easy way to unwind it from the roll. As there was no way to keep the tape free after a piece was cut or torn off, the loose end rolled back in place on the roll, became almost invisible and hard to locate, and had to be picked loose with a fingernail or sharp instrument by the user. Too often, small pieces of tape broke off instead of the desired longer strip. When the user finally succeeded in unwinding the necessary length, it had to be cut off with scissors, which was time consuming and awkward, or it had

Auto repaint shops are major users of 3M coated abrasives. An abrasive disc is being used here to rough finish a car fender that has been bumped out. The metal will be sanded again with discs of finer grits before the surface is painted.

Do-it-yourself fans use 3M coated abrasives extensively in home workshops. For more than 30 years the company has offered sandpaper especially designed for finishing furniture.

3M's black plastic electrical tape is one member of the company's large family of electrical tapes. Others made with backings of treated paper, cotton cloth, acetate cloth, film, and glass cloth are used in the construction and repair of electric motors, appliances and electronic equipment.

In middle Twenties, 3M masking tape helped automotive plants do a speedier, neater job on two-tone cars. Manufacturers and repaint shops soon used it for all automobile paint jobs. More than 300 variations of pressure-sensitive tapes followed this invention.

Permanent mending tape, another 3M specialty, becomes practically invisible on paper as shown above.

Tape slitter slicing a six-foot wide sheet of treated cellophane into rolls of "SCOTCH" Brand pressure-sensitive tape.

Many miles of cellophane speed through 3M's tape makers each week to meet demand for this versatile product.

3M Roofing Granules plant, Corona, California, built in 1951 to serve the Pacific Coast market.

3M Roofing Granules plant, Wausau, Wisconsin.

to be haphazardly torn crosswise, an equally unsatisfactory method. Then, as there was no way to keep the loose end free, the next user had to go through the same troubles. A way to facilitate easy and speedy unwinding and cutting of the tape was urgently needed. Storekeepers were losing their tempers and valuable time trying to pry the end of the tape free from the roll, unwind it, and cut off the desired strip to wrap a package while the customer waited impatiently.

3M first designed an inexpensive–and clumsy–dispenser made of tin, for use by bakeries and retail stores. This dispenser held the roll of tape in place while the user unwound the strip and cut it with scissors or tore it off. It had to be inexpensive, for the depression was in full swing, and no one could afford an expensive dispensing gadget. These 25 cents to a dollar, light-weight dispensers were nailed or taped to the counter, and were annoyingly inefficient. Storekeepers constantly complained about them. The dispenser didn't allow the user to get hold of the end of the tape to pull it free, or to cut a strip neatly and quickly. The need for something better was essential, but it took about a year and a half of experimenting before the sales manager of the cellulose tape department designed an efficient dispenser with an incorporated cut-off-knife.* With this new type of dispenser, the tape could be unwound, cut off, and applied in a few seconds. A special feature of the dispenser was that it

---

*This dispenser which contributed so substantially to the success of pressure sensitive tape, was the invention of John A. Borden, sales manager of the cellulose tape division. Borden started his career at 3M on October 14, 1925 in the statistical department, served as assistant to W.L. McKnight for a short time, and in August, 1929, was named sales manager of masking tape. In 1930 he was given complete responsibility for sales development of SCOTCH Brand cellophane tape. He became general manager of cellulose tape products in January 1937, general manager of SCOTCH Brand Tapes in 1941, and vice-president in charge of Tape in April, 1948. In April, 1954, he retired from 3M but still serves as Consultant on Pressure-Sensitive Adhesive Tapes.

kept the end of the tape free for the next user after each strip was cut off. The new dispenser had a very favorable effect on sales; many in 3M feel that without it, SCOTCH Brand cellophane tape might have quickly waned in popularity. This style of dispenser with the built-in cut-off knife is still in use. There is a heavy model for commercial dispensing, and a lightweight model in plastic or metal for home and office use.

In these early years, only one setback in sales of the new tape occurred, and that was minor. Du Pont had experimented with many ways of sealing cellophane so as not to mar its sparkling transparency. Solvents had been tried, but this method was obviously unsatisfactory for sealing packaged bakery goods. SCOTCH Brand cellophane tape was one satisfactory answer. Another sealing method, found by Du Pont around 1928, was by heat. This temporarily spoiled some 3M sales in the packaging field, and at first, 3M feared its new tape was in serious jeopardy. But they had nothing to worry about. America had found so many uses for the versatile, transparent tape that the drop in sales volume caused by the adoption of heat sealing was more than offset by other sales. In fact, the sales volume grew so rapidly that by the middle '30s, it was evident that the tape department, which had been housed with the Coated Abrasives Division, would have to have quarters of its own. A new building was not possible immediately, since the unfavorable tax situation in Minnesota in 1936 to 1938 caused a delay in all 3M expansion plans. Not until 1941 was construction started on a special tape plant. In the summer of that year, facilities for manufacturing both masking and cellophane tape were constructed on Fauquier Avenue and Mendota in St. Paul diagonally from the coated abrasives buildings. The new space was badly needed by the time it was ready. In the years since masking tape was first marketed in 1927, the department had grown from a laboratory staff of six, and a hand-

ful of salesmen, to more than 700 factory, research, and
sales people, 300 of whom had been hired in 1940 and 1941.
The tape department was filling orders for nearly
$14,000,000 worth of tape a year, and the volume was grow-
ing each month, so substantially that it was evident, even
before the new tape building was completed in 1941, that
still another unit would be needed, especially in view of
defense demands. To meet this need, a second tape plant
was built in early 1942 just west of the first building. This
was also a three-level structure with the same amount of
floor space as the first. In a short time even these two were
not adequate, and in 1949, 3M built a tape (and adhesive)
manufacturing plant in Bristol, Pennsylvania, to serve
Eastern markets, and in 1951, constructed a block-long,
three-level building on Reaney Avenue between Arcade and
Mendota Streets in St. Paul, adjacent to the other tape
buildings. The new steel and masonry structure in St. Paul
cost over a million dollars, and on its completion, the company rearranged and consolidated its tape production facilities and laboratories to provide the finest arrangement
possible for development and research in the tape field.

NEW ROOFS FOR OLD

AVIATORS winging over America in the middle '30s saw a great change taking place on the earth below them. The vast patchwork of brown and green fields and grey cities was bursting into a riot of color during those years of the Great Depression. The change was in America's housetops; in fact an evolution was in progress, and the aviators had a ringside seat. American homeowners were swinging from drab wood, slate, and tile shingles to brightly colored roofs made with a new kind of roofing–asphalt shingles coated with artificially colored granules. Eye-catching red, blue, green, and buff roofs were replacing the grey, brown, and black housetops which had predominated for generations.

3M contributed substantially to the progress of this evolution from drabness to color in American homes. Many of the artificially colored roofing granules in the new type of asphalt roofing were a Minnesota Mining product, created in 1930 by the research laboratory. In that year, 3M unexpectedly got into the roofing business, all because president McKnight bought a mountain.

3M's research division had no sooner focused its microscope on the baffling problems of its newest invention, SCOTCH Brand cellophane tape, when McKnight tossed it a new question to explore. "What," he asked his laboratory staff, "can you do to make a mountain of quartz profitable?"

President McKnight was talking about a real mountain. Early in the fall of 1929, he learned that 3M's only Midwest competitor, Wausau Abrasives Company of Wausau, Wisconsin, was for sale. He moved quickly, and in December, 1929, when the echoes from the stock market crash were still reverberating across the nation, purchased the company for $260,000. Wausau was 3M's first acquisition. Included among its assets were one 1923 Nash Roadster, three Reo Speedwagon trucks, a sandpaper manufacturing plant, a mineral crushing plant, and one mountain called Rib Hill. The mountain contained an unlimited supply of silica quartz from which Wausau Abrasives made flint sandpaper and other abrasive products.

Wausau had produced only low-profit items, and when McKnight acquired the company, he felt greater profits could be realized from the unlimited supply of Rib Hill mineral. He immediately called a conference of top management and key laboratory personnel and posed the question. In answer, the laboratory created a new product which added another successful chapter to the company's history. The product was "COLORQUARTZ," an artificially colored roofing granule which helped make possible the evolution in housing referred to earlier.

The idea for COLORQUARTZ wasn't the first one suggested for Rib Hill quartz, however. A few unsuccessful ideas came first. Soon after McKnight held the conference, one of the varnish specialists from the sandpaper laboratory came up with a thought: Why not crush Rib Hill quartz and make smalt? The smalt he referred to was a deep blue pigment made by fusing silica, potash, and oxide of cobalt, and grinding the fused mass into powdered form. Sign makers sprinkled this powdered pigment on painted outdoor signs to add color and produce highlights.

This suggestion plunged 3M briefly into the sign material business. A sign maker was called in as a consultant, and the varnish specialist was put to work on his idea. Not only was smalt made for a short time, but attempts were made to produce a granular material like smalt in a wider range of colors by crushing and coloring Rib Hill quartz. The quartz was colored by tumbling a mixture of crushed granules and short oil varnish, containing red, green, or yellow pigments.

The smalt idea was carried one step further. Utilizing its knowledge of adhesives and backings, the laboratory made up sheets of prefabricated sign material by sprinkling the colored Rib Hill quartz onto an adhesive-coated backing with the idea that from these prefabricated sheets, sign makers could cut out letters which could be quickly and easily tacked onto a blank signboard.

An attempt was made also to manufacture still another type of prefabricated sign which could be used for marking airport hangars and landing fields. The colored granules were pressed onto a roll of asphalt-impregnated felt, with the idea that from this roll, sign letters 30 feet high could be cut and nailed onto airport hangar roofs and landing fields.

These various projects didn't progress much further than the experimental stage, however. It was soon realized that the market for sign materials such as smalt was much too limited, and the whole idea was dropped. Meanwhile, other uses for Rib Hill quartz were studied, such as for flint on matchboxes, a base for scouring powder, an inert in asphalt road compound, and for the lithographic industry. These markets were all found to be too limited and competitive.

Then one day, a 3M employee learned that roofing manufacturers were looking for a colored granule to coat asphalt roofing shingles which would not fade from the sun or deteriorate under other weather conditions. The informant was Sifo Products Company, St. Paul, who told 3M that all roofing granules developed up to that time faded, leaving a blotchy, unsightly roof. Sifo said further that if 3M could produce a colored roofing granule that was weather resistant, they would gladly purchase the material, and undoubtedly other roofing manufacturers would also.

Stimulated by Sifo's encouragement, 3M delved a bit into the roofing business and turned up some interesting information. They learned that Sifo was right. A colored roofing granule that would keep its color under all weather conditions was definitely in demand by roofing manufacturers. American homeowners were turning more and more to brightly colored exteriors, as well as interiors, in decorating their homes, and all evidence indicated that they were anxious to buy colored roofing, provided it would keep its color and prove an economical investment.

They learned, too, that in 1932 there were many different kinds of roofing materials on the market but that few were attractive as far as color was concerned. Among these were asbestos cement shingles, natural slate shingles, tin and sheet metal, asphalt shingles coated with crushed slate, wood, roll roofing, tile, corrugated iron, zinc, and corrugated asbestos. In fact, the history of color in America's housetops had begun less than thirty years before, when roofing manufacturers found that shingles made with asphalt-impregnated felt* would last up to 500 percent longer if they were coated with some kind of fine granular material. This discovery led to the first colored rooftops. Until 1900, American homeowners had purchased mostly natural wood, slate, or tile for their roofs–sturdy but drab roofing which fitted into the early American taste for conservative colors.

---

*This was a type of composition roofing in roll form which had to be powdered with mica to keep it from sticking together. It was not popular for homes because of its lack of resistance to sun's rays and other weather conditions and because of its inflammability. Further, though economical, it was unattractive.

Between 1900 and 1918, roofing manufacturers tried coating asphalt shingles with various kinds of crushed particles. Crushed slate, slag, sand, feldspar chips, crushed pottery, brick, and fired clay were all used with varying degrees of success. Each experiment made one fact clear: The particles made the shingles last longer under all weather conditions.

Crushed slate asphalt shingles were the most satisfactory, and as natural slate is either green, red, or blue-black–depending on the quarry from which it comes–Americans got their first taste of color in their housetops and liked it. These colors were not strong. The green looked more like gray than the "cool sage green" described in magazine ads on roofing; the red more like faded rust than "Indian Red." Advertisements in popular magazines pictured the new crushed slate asphalt roofs as fire-engine red and grass green, but this was the result of limitations of 1921 two-color presses, not the fault of the advertiser. But red and green crushed slate started a trend and the appetite for color was whetted. Homeowners demanded more. To meet this demand, roofing manufacturers tried to "paint" these slate granules brighter colors, but painted granules lost their color quickly and peeled from weather exposure, particularly from the sun's rays.

In 1930, Flintkote Company, Inc., was the only manufacturer producing a colored asphalt shingle in any quantity. They worked under a license agreement with an Ohio roofing company which controlled a patent to color crushed slate granules by coating the granule and fixing the color coating by firing the granule at high temperatures. Flintkote's first experiments were conducted in the early 1920s. They tried a broad range of colors, but found that the slate wouldn't stand the high temperatures needed to fuse the color on the granules, and impurities in the slate adversely affected the color. They were producing these colored granules only for their own roofing shingles at the time 3M began manufacturing colored roofing granules in 1930.

The quick survey of the roofing business persuaded president McKnight and sales manager Bush that there was an unfilled demand and a good market for a colored roofing granule if it could be made weather resistant. A chemist from the sandpaper laboratory was put in charge of a full-scale research project on roofing granules. The research department knew little about color-coating a roofing granule but by now they knew enough to call in the experts. An artist, several 3M chemists, and a roofing specialist collaborated on the experiments, which had to be conducted on makeshift equipment until 3M learned what was needed. The laboratory had no instruments to test weathering quality of the granules—the most important feature—so the laboratory simulated weather conditions the best they could without the necessary Weatherometer. Green and fire-engine red were the only two colors tried at first. The red was soon abandoned; it was not a pleasing color.

3M produced its first "painted" Rib Hill quartz granules in quantity in 1930, and as promised, Sifo Products was their first customer. They bought all that 3M made in both 1930 and 1931–about 1,026 tons. Because the quartz had to be shipped from Wausau to St. Paul where the coloring was added, the granules were much higher in cost than natural crushed slate. The latter could be sold to roofing manufacturers for $6.75 a ton, while 3M's painted granules ran from $25 to $30 a ton.

To 3M researchers it was obvious that painted granules could not be successful, for the life of the paint in outdoor weather is too short to be economical for roofing. The color on a painted granule would last perhaps five years, whereas it should last approximately 15 to warrant the necessary investment by the homeowner. The only thing to do was to find a type of coating that would answer the requirements.

The chemists, artists, and roofing specialist went to work again.

Meanwhile, patent attorney Paul Carpenter investigated the patent situation and found that there were several existing patents which might be infringed by 3M coated granules. Most were controlled by roofing manufacturers who had not been able to produce a marketable product with their patent. No one was making a granule with the same quartz base as 3M, which was one advantage, and within a short time, Carpenter worked out license agreements for all existing patents.

In seeking a weather-resistant coating for Rib Hill quartz, the laboratory worked at a terrific pace. They knew that there was a tremendous market waiting to be served and that competition was experimenting along the same lines. Experiment after experiment was conducted to find a method of making a nonfading, weather-resistant, artificially colored granule at a cost that could compete with the slate shingles already on the market. Finally, the laboratory decided to coat the quartz granules ceramically with powdered pigment. The idea seemed practical and a study of ceramics was made. Green chromium-oxide pigment was the most stable and economical in a ceramic process, 3M found. This was fortunate because green was one of the most popular colors with homeowners.

September 10, 1931 might be called the official birth date of 3M's successful roofing granule. On that date, less than two years after McKnight bought Rib Hill, one of the chemists working on the project set up an experiment for a new type of ceramic coating which he thought might be the solution. Experiments were conducted in a formal, orderly fashion now. Gone were the sketchy, penciled jottings of the early days. Carefully, the record was prepared for mimeographing:

COLORQUARTZ Experiment

Object: To investigate the possibility of making

COLORQUARTZ by application of a ceramic

glaze to surface of grains.

Equipment, time, and place were all carefully entered on the record. Only a tiny amount of crushed Rib Hill quartz was used for the experiment–about a pound. The granules were mixed with green pigment, put in a container, and heated over a gas burner. The mixture was stirred while it was heating, then the granules were poured in a little heap on a table to cool.

The chemist anxiously studied the green-coated granules spread on the table. Anxiety soon turned to satisfaction, for the results indicated that Rib Hill quartz could be coated by a ceramic process and would be both weather-resistant and eye-appealing. At least, laboratory tests showed these results. How well the granules would stand up under actual weather conditions could not be determined with existing laboratory equipment. Neither did 3M know as yet how much it would cost to produce the granules, but management was intensely interested in the new product. If 3M could make a satisfactory colored roofing granule, the company could serve an entirely new market, one which would need practically no sales force. One or two men could service the twenty roofing manufacturers who made asphalt shingles. This would mean a low sales cost for the product to offset high production costs. Further, the ultimate market to be served was very large. In prosperity or depression, man had to have a roof over his head.

Following the pleasing results of the first experiment, more ceramically coated granules were made, and in December, 1931, 3M took samples to the Chicago branch of Bird & Son, Inc., veteran roofing manufacturers, to get their opinion on the possible market. Bird was most interested.

They had been working on similar experiments and agreed to test the new roofing material in their laboratory, which was especially equipped for testing roofing. In February 1932, Bush and the chemist in charge of COLORQUARTZ research returned to Bird & Son for an opinion. They had scarcely sat down when the Bird executive fired the question, "What guarantee do you make on your granules?" This was a touchy question, as 3M didn't know what guarantee they could make, but Bush replied with equal force, "You tested the sample and approved it. We can only guarantee to duplicate it." To this, the Bird executive answered, "Well, when can you deliver two carloads?"

Although 3M had no equipment for manufacturing COLORQUARTZ, delivery was unabashedly promised by April 1, less than two months away. The St. Paul factory was astounded by this promise, but in a spurt of cooperation reminiscent of the time 3M employees got the sandpaper plant into production after the 1927 fire, they accomplished the seemingly impossible again. By April 9,1932, the factory had produced the two carloads of COLORQUARTZ, in spite of the fact that they had never made it before, and the laboratory had produced it only in experimental quantities of a pound or less. There were only seven employees in the new division, but men from other departments offered their help. While the men in Wausau crushed and shipped the quartz to St. Paul, the abrasive laboratory started a quest for equipment for manufacturing the granules. No one knew what kind was needed. The chemists thought a rotating kiln would be best for glazing, and on March 2, 1932, conducted experiments with makeshift equipment to test this theory. A large flower pot was set at an angle on a rotating device to provide an action similar to a concrete mixer, placed over a gas burner, and a batch of granules was glazed in this device. As the rotating action of the flower pot spread the glaze coating evenly on the granules, the theory was tested further by glazing more granules in an experimental rotary kiln at the University of Minnesota School of Engineering. This worked, too, and final experiments were made in a full-size rotating furnace at the U.S. Smelting Furnace Company, Inc., Belleville, Illinois. These tests were satisfactory, and a rush order was placed with the furnace company. By the time the rotating furnace arrived, there were only a few days left before the deadline for Bird & Son. Production started immediately and by working around the clock, two carloads were finished and shipped on April 9, only nine days later than promised.

After this, business developed so rapidly that 3M could scarcely keep up with orders. In spite of the fact that 3M had to charge nearly four times more for its roofing granules than the price for natural slate granules, and that the country was in the depths of depression, the product was in tremendous demand. From 1931 to 1935, A.G. Bush personally called on the roofing manufacturers along with personnel from the new division. There were between 20 and 25 of these manufacturers, and soon most of them became customers. They had to be shown that COLORQUARTZ would be worth the cost, which volume production finally brought down to about twice that of natural slate. Weather resistance and color appeal were the two selling features, though rather shaky ones considering the fact that 3M didn't know exactly how long the new roofing would stand up under various weather conditions. The main appeal of the product to homeowners was its color, and the laboratory worked hard to broaden the range of colors. In a short time, they produced red, green, blue, and buff granules. Green continued to be the most popular color. Even without a regular sales force, volume grew from $26,413 for the first year, 1932, to $255,379 in 1933 and $657,402 in 1934.

In 1932, 3M production facilities in St. Paul became entirely inadequate to meet the demand. The board of directors faced the difficult decision of whether or not to expand without knowing (1) the long-range future for roofing granules; and (2) whether 3M roofing granules would last the desired length of time on a roof. The prospects for new home building looked bleak; it was the worst time of the depression. But the demand was so great it was decided to invest $45,000 in a new plant in Wausau.* It was opened the day the banks closed across the nation in March, 1933. The 3M employees who made the trip from St. Paul to Wausau had barely enough cash among them to finance the trip.

McKnight felt that business conditions everywhere would be improved if industry expanded where possible during the depression. In announcing the new plant, he told the press:

If every business concern which can afford to do so would undertake now to do work required in the reasonably near future, it would stimulate employment and hasten the return of prosperity. Such companies would find that surprisingly low building costs prevail.[1]

In April, 1934, it was apparent that even the new plant wouldn't take care of demand for roofing granules, and 3M stood at an unmarked crossroad. Should more new plants be built? Or should the division remain static? It was a hard decision to make and different from any connected with sandpaper or tape. It had to be most carefully considered

---

*Management of Wausau was given to Lloyd A. Hatch, a chemist in the WETORDRY sandpaper laboratory, on January 1, 1937. He served as general manager of the Roofing Granules (COLORQUARTZ) Division until April 9, 1946, when he was elected vice-president in charge of Roofing Granules. Under his direction the division developed color-fast granules in many shades, built two additional plants, and pushed sales volume into the multimillion-dollar bracket. Hatch was the first chemist hired by 3M for its WETORDRY sandpaper laboratory. He joined 3M on July 2, 1923, and soon developed a grading system for very fine minerals which assured uniformity of grit size for 3M's coated abrasives. His "flour grading" system was greatly responsible for the success of waterproof sandpaper. On October 1, 1949, Hatch was elected vice-president in charge of Research and New Product Development.

from every angle. On April 24, 1934, the problem was brought up for action at a board of directors meeting. Briefly, McKnight reviewed for the others the history of the development of the product and the outlook for the future.

"The question," he explained, "is whether or not we should expand our roofing granules plant in Wausau at this time."

On the negative side, McKnight pointed out that no one could be positive that 3M roofing granules wouldn't eventually fade, and investing more money until this was definitely known was a decided risk. No one could be positive that a ceramic granule would stick to the asphalt base for the life of the shingle, and until this was known, investing more money was hazardous. There was a possibility that Wausau would declare 3M operations in the city a public nuisance. And finally, someone might produce a better or cheaper granule and reduce the 3M sales volume.

The reasons favoring expansion were pointed out also: Expansion would be a safe risk because there was a large demand for permanently colored roofing granules; 3M was first in the field and had a good reputation with the trade even if competition should develop a cheaper roofing granule. 3M's supply of base material (quartz) could not be duplicated in the Midwest, so the company had a favorable commercial position. 3M's superior research department should be able to keep the company in a favorable position with the trade.

McKnight then pointed out that if 3M did not invest additional capital now, after such a substantial initial investment, and if the trade were not adequately served, competition might enter the field and take away 3M's existing business. "And," McKnight finished, "the roofing granule business fits in with our policy of diversifying."

The reasons in favor of expanding outweighed those against it, and on McKnight's recommendation, $300,000 was approved for building another crushing and coloring unit in Wausau. Nine months later, it became necessary to build a $200,000 warehouse in which to store a supply of roofing granules to fill orders in peak months when production could not meet demand.

The $500,000 had no more than been spent when a situation arose which made it look as if the board of directors had made a serious mistake in expanding operations at Wausau, and that the entire COLORQUARTZ investment was in jeopardy. It was discovered that 3M's gravest fear for its roofing granules had come true. In some areas they were popping off the asphalt shingles in quantity, leaving the black asphalt exposed and creating blotchy, deteriorated roofs.

"It was the most mysterious thing we'd ever seen," recalls one chemist. "We just didn't know what was causing the granules to pop off the shingles." Those who had worked for 3M in 1915 remembered with a shudder the olive oil incident when garnet mineral was dropping off sandpaper for no apparent reason, and the sandpaper business had been almost ruined. It looked very much as though 3M would be out of the roofing business, for the value of their roofing granules depended primarily on their long-term weather resistance.

Unlike the olive oil incident, however, the roofing granule trouble was tracked down scientifically and systematically. Working with the roofing manufacturers, 3M researchers found that in certain parts of the country, sunlight was penetrating the Rib Hill granules, causing the asphalt to oxidize. This destroyed its adhesive qualities, and the granules became loose and popped off the shingles like water from a hot griddle.

3M was doubly fortunate in connection with the incident. The trouble was caught early, and the company had a supply of another more opaque rock which could be used as a base for a roofing granule. Some time before, when it was discovered that Wausau quartz wouldn't take a blue coating, the company geologist had located another type of rock which would, just four and one-half miles from the Wausau plant. The laboratory tested this graystone and found that sunlight didn't penetrate it as it did Rib Hill quartz. Without interruption in production, 3M switched to Wausau graystone base for its roofing granules. The laboratory began to hunt for another use for Wausau quartz.*

At about the same time the first complaints were heard on the roofing granules, trouble cropped up from another direction. A Copley, Ohio, firm named R.J. Funkhouser Company began infringing on patents covering 3M granules. Repeated warnings to cease manufacturing the granules were of no avail. Primarily a manufacturer of slate roofs, Funkhouser was also making a ceramic granule using a silica sand base supplied under contract by a firm named the Columbia Silica Company. 3M preferred not to litigate, but as Funkhouser continued to infringe, it appeared there was no alternative. Relations became extremely strained between all parties concerned. The dispute involved other roofing manufacturers who had interests in pertinent patents and license agreements. However, when faced with a lawsuit, Funkhouser agreed to sell its Copley granules coloring plant. 3M also bought Columbia Silica Company. These two acquisitions gave 3M an additional 50,000-ton capacity nearer Eastern markets until 1947, when the Copley quartz deposit ran out.

Between the Wausau and Copley plants, 3M could adequately serve all Midwestern and some Eastern roofing

*In December, 1941, 40 acres of Rib Hill were deeded to the city of Wausau for park purposes and for skiing.

manufacturers but not those of the West and South as it desired. In order to serve these areas, 3M located and purchased a quarry of syenite near Little Rock, Arkansas, and built a $3,000,000 plant at this site. Construction was begun in 1945; the plant was opened April 24, 1947. The capacity of the Little Rock plant is 200,000 tons of colored granules a year. A similar move was made to serve the Pacific Coast area, a quarry being purchased at Corona, California, and a plant built there in 1951.

From the very beginning, the roofing granules division realized that the success of its product was eye-appealing color and that research should be concentrated on developing as many shades of granules as possible. The task was not simple. Some pigments–yellow, for example–will not resist the sun's rays effectively. But through intensive research, the laboratory added new colors which would stand the sun and at the same time increase the attractiveness of roofing. Between 1930 and 1941, green, red, blue, buff, brown, black, and gray were perfected. Each time a new color was added, the demand for asphalt shingles coated with colored granules increased. Each new color made it possible for roofing manufacturers to create not only new one-color shingles, but multicolored combinations with mottled or variegated patterns to meet specific decorating schemes of homeowners.

Another impetus was given the color trend when 3M introduced a silver-gray ceramic granule in 1941. The overnight popularity of this color in California and the Gulf States indicated that lighter shades might be popular in the warmer states, and the laboratory immediately started work on a line of pastels. By 1952, pastel shades of green, blue, and coral were introduced. Other new shades are still in the experimental stages.

In recent years, 3M has cooperated even more closely with roofing manufacturers by helping them work out new color combinations. Today, even brick siding and natural wood shingles can be simulated with asphalt shingling by properly mixing various shades of granules.

Thus through the years,3M has helped turn the trend of the '30s into an established vogue for bright and gay roofs. Through its promotion of color for roofing, the swing from drab gray and black shingles to color is almost complete. Today, nearly all of America has colorful housetops.

ANSWERS TO A NEED

FROM THE EARLIEST DAYS of the horseless carriage, automobile shows have been an important event in the lives of travel-loving Americans. Since 1900, when the first National Automobile Show was held in Madison Square Garden, millions have flocked to unveilings of new models to see what change in design or performance has been made to increase their driving pleasure. At these shows, the vast driving public has witnessed dozens of innovations which have changed the one-cylinder carriagelike cars to today's powerful, streamlined beauties. They had learned of the advantages of each new change—the steering wheel, wind shields, canopy tops, shock absorbers, demountable wheel rims, headlights, new finishes, the all-steel body, free wheeling, over drive, power steering, and an endless list of other improvements. But there's one thing American motorists never have and never will learn at an auto show, and that is about the headaches, often migraine size, caused on the production line by most changes in car design or performance.

Almost every change has outmoded some method of manufacturing and forced automobile manufacturers to develop new ones which would make the design change workable. And for each of these production headaches, someone had to furnish an aspirin in the form of a new assembling tech-

198

nique. Suppliers were often called upon for aid, and several times, 3M was able to furnish the remedy. This was particularly true in the '20s when WETORDRY abrasive paper made possible the switch from varnish to lacquer finishes, and SCOTCH Brand masking tape made it possible for Americans to drive two-tone cars.

In the early '30s, a whole family of headaches broke out on the automotive industry's production lines, and again it was 3M who came to the rescue. The advent of the all-steel body created the need for a new method of attaching upholstery, of installing sound deadener to the inside of the car, and of attaching trim inside the car. To meet this need, 3M developed a new line of special adhesives designed to speed production and cut costs on the assembly line. And once again, the company added a multimillion-dollar division.

Actually, 3M had dabbled in commercial production of adhesives before the all-steel body created a volume need for them. Perhaps the real beginning of this division was when 3M learned that Fisher Body Company was looking for a more effective way to attach fabric cartops to the wood frame of bodies, and when Franklin Motor Car Company needed a special rubber cement for bonding rubber sheeting to running boards. In each case, a special adhesive was compounded to solve the problem.

Anyone who owned a car with a fabric top in the very early Thirties will remember that the top was tacked to the crown molding and the constant jolting over rough roads and prolonged outdoor exposure often loosened the tacks. Then the fabric pulled away from the molding, moisture seeped in and eventually the wood frame rotted. Fisher wanted a sealer to replace the tacks, and 3M, drawing on its experience with adhesives for abrasives and pressure-sensitive tapes, tackled the problem and came up with an adhesive with the sealing qualities needed. It would bond fabric to wood, withstand drastic climatic changes, and remain flexible enough to withstand constant stress and strain, all of which meant the sealer would keep out moisture.

For the Franklin Motor Car Company, the laboratory resurrected a gooey concoction originally mixed as a tape adhesive but long since set aside as unsatisfactory. This particular cement had caused endless difficulty by sticking to the metal rollers of equipment, and on a hunch, the laboratory tested it for running boards. It turned out to be just what Franklin needed.

There was little sales volume from these products, however, because just about the time they were introduced, both fabric tops and running boards were discontinued.

The all-steel body construction of automobiles created the first substantial demands for 3M adhesives. With the new construction, upholstery could no longer be tacked onto the car frame. Neither could inside trim. And worst of all, the all-steel body set up such reverberations on the road that unless sound-deadening material was installed inside the car, the motorist would be virtually deafened. Abrasive salesmen, through close association with the automotive industry, learned of these problems in the blueprint stage and immediately alerted the St. Paul laboratory to get to work on special adhesives to solve them.

The first adhesive developed and sold in volume was for attaching trim (upholstery on arm rests, seats and head linings). Adhesive for trim had to be strong enough to bond the upholstery fabric to metal and had to do the job without penetrating or staining the fabric. For these trim jobs, 3M mixed an adhesive with a rubber base and a gasoline type of solvent.

Shortly after this, in 1935, things began to happen fast in the infant adhesive department. The automotive industry adopted the 3M trim cement for attaching sound-deadening material, such as Kimpak or felt, inside its cars. Adhesive sales climbed higher and higher. Within a few months, the sale of rubber cement to the automotive industry increased to a point where a special plant was needed for the Adhesives Division. During the division's first two years, rubber cement had been manufactured in the tape adhesive compounding department. The quarters were improvised in a wagon shed and blacksmith shop near 3M's other plants. The only storage space for raw materials was in the stalls of the old wagon shed, and there was no room at all for storing the inflammable solvent used in the rubber cement formula. Manufacturing equipment was overtaxed.

There was no question about the advisability of expanding the division. Profits were satisfactory, and the product fitted into the company's policy of diversification, which had already proved so profitable. The all-steel body had greatly increased the market for cement, and the general consensus was that the market would continue to be good. As equipment to make a good adhesive was quite expensive, and considerable technical knowledge was necessary for its manufacture, competition was relatively limited. 3M was in good standing with the large automobile manufacturers, and the addition of rubber cement to its line of abrasives and pressure-sensitive tapes meant an even closer relationship. "And," president McKnight pointed out at the time, "the manufacture of rubber cement might conceivably lead to the development of still other new products, 3M's primary method of growth."

However, management was divided on where the new plant should be built. Some advocated a St. Paul site near other 3M operations; others, Detroit, on the argument that this division should be near the automotive industry. They pointed out, "There may be other markets, but it is doubtful that they will ever approach the automobile market in volume." The faction against decentralization felt that the

adhesive business was too much of a gamble to warrant setting up a separate division outside of St. Paul. Approximately $300,000 would be needed to build in Detroit, and it
was felt that it would be unwise to risk this surplus, which
had been carefully conserved in depression years, on something as uncertain as adhesives.

At the height of the debate over decentralization, a tax
situation arose in the state of Minnesota which not only
caused 3M to locate the Adhesives Division in Detroit, but
again to consider moving all of its manufacturing operations
out of Minnesota.

In 1935, the Farmer-Labor administration under
Governor Floyd Olson, in a burst of zealousness to raise revenue for the state, proposed enforcement of a corporate-
excess tax law which had been put on the statute books in
1878. The law had been originally and primarily designed to
tax public utility companies only. The plan of Governor
Olson's administration to apply it to general business corporations threatened the life of many major Minnesota industries.

Under the Olson administration's interpretation of the
1878 law, the state of Minnesota planned to tax corporations
on the difference between the book value and the market
value of their stock. This could spell economic disaster for
3M and many other Minnesota corporations whose stock
had a market value (representing intangibles such as good
will, patents, and trademarks) far higher than its book
value (representing tangible assets such as plant facilities
and inventory). The danger lay in the fact that the state
administration, in order to carry out such a plan, would
have to put a cash figure on intangible values for the purpose of taxation, and in doing so might "go all over the lot"
in arriving at a figure.

The tax situation started a bitter fight between the state
administration and the threatened Minnesota corporations.

President McKnight, who was almost ready to have 3M "pick up its toys and leave the state of Minnesota," publicly campaigned against a proposed political measure for the first time in his life.

In one of the first press releases he had ever issued, he announced that 3M would expand no further in St. Paul in view of the unfavorable tax situation. He declared, "It is our intention to continue to maintain headquarters and present operations in St. Paul, but the officers and directors of the company feel they would not be justified in enlarging the capital investment of their stockholders in Minnesota at the present time."[1]

Although he thoroughly dislikes to speak in public, McKnight joined other Minnesota businessmen in a tour around Minnesota to muster help against the proposed tax. The group paid its own expenses, traveling by auto with two or three men in each car.

Some newspapers joined the fray against the Farmer-Labor administration on this issue. Among these was the St. Paul *Pioneer Press* which carried on an editorial crusade against the administration's tax policies, using Minnesota Mining and Manufacturing Company as a prime example of the disastrous effect enforcement of the 1878 corporate tax would have on Minnesota business. (3M, with 1,091 employees on its $1,300,000 payroll, was now one of Minnesota's larger manufacturers.) The first of the editorials appeared February 5, 1936, after 3M had decided to establish its Adhesives Division in Detroit:

The policy of hamstringing, penalizing, and hazing business in Minnesota now begins to bear fruit. Confronted with the need of expansion to handle a new product, the Minnesota Mining and Manufacturing Company has decided to expand in Michigan, not in St. Paul as it has always done in the past. The company has bought a plant in Detroit equal in size to all of its St. Paul properties. Quite evidently the officers of the company look forward to quite sizable operations in their new branch of production.

In the 26 years the company has been...in St. Paul, the number of persons employed has risen from 20 to more than 1,000. These figures convey an idea of what industry means in new wealth to the city and state, also what a city and state lose when through rash and reckless policies industries are driven elsewhere....

For months, the outcome of the tax situation was in doubt. Meanwhile, the Adhesives Division moved to Detroit near the automotive industry and located on three acres of property purchased from the Studebaker Real Estate Corporation on January 31, 1936. Included in the transaction was the original production plant of the Ford Motor Company which had been built by Henry Ford about the time 3M was starting to quarry "corundum" in Crystal Bay, Minnesota, on Lake Superior. This plant, situated on the Michigan Central Railroad, is now used by 3M for both storage and manufacturing. Ford moved from this plant to major operations in Highland Park, where he established the $5-a-day minimum wage which caused such excitement in the industrial world. After 3M purchased the building, Ford made a personal visit to the plant and selected two pieces of machinery for the Ford museum at Greenfield Village. Other original Ford machinery still stands in this building.

The new Adhesives Division had a total of 84 employees when it opened in Detroit. This included factory workers, office and sales personnel, and researchers for the new adhesive laboratory set up when the move was made.

The Minnesota tax situation was finally settled as far as the 1878 law was concerned, by a Minnesota State Supreme Court decision which ruled in the case of Bemis Bros. Bag Company vs. Wallace (1936) that the tax had been repealed by implication. With this tax situation eased, president McKnight announced a half-million-dollar expansion program in St. Paul. His statement was carried by the St. Paul *Dispatch* September 2, 1937:

The legislature and the tax commission have recognized the importance of payroll and industrial development in the state. They have also recognized, in a small measure, the fact that Minnesota industries cannot continue to be taxed as heavily as industries more favorably situated in other states and nearer industrial centers. For these reasons, the directors of the company have decided to carry out their complete plans for meeting the full needs of the business which will mean additional expenditures beyond the cost of the building now started.

The next morning, the St. Paul *Pioneer Press*, which had fought earnestly for easing taxes on Minnesota industry, greeted 3M's decision with the following editorial:

The announcement of Minnesota Mining & Mfg. Company that it will expand its already large St. Paul plant is particularly welcome because of what it signifies for the industrial future of this city and state. This was one of the important industrial companies which felt obliged to hold in suspension plans for needed expansion because of fears which grew during the last regular session of the legislature that tax policies would be instituted which would make practically impossible the continued existence in Minnesota of business competing with the national market.

St. Paul and indeed the entire state owes a debt of gratitude to the State senate for the fact that although very severe increases were enacted on business, and income taxation, a more moderate counsel prevailed at the end.

That this insistence on a moderate policy has averted what would have been a first class calamity the action of this St. Paul company indicates.[2]

The Detroit plant opened September 14, 1936, and in less than two months was in serious trouble with the automotive industry. The 3M adhesive being used for bonding silencer pads to the metal floors of cars and in trunk compartments was causing a serious fire hazard on the assembly lines. Fumes from the solvent in the adhesive were highly inflammable, and being heavier than air, collected close to the floor where ventilation was insufficient to clear them away. Day after day, flash fires occurred on the assembly line where the silencer pads were being installed. The fire hazard was unexpected; the same adhesive had been used without trouble in the trim shops, where apparently, fumes had been dissipated by normal room ventilation before they could build up dangerously.

One incident on the assembly line brought the whole matter to a crisis. One day a flash fire occurred which completely destroyed a car. The automotive people were ready to scratch 3M from its list of adhesive suppliers unless something was done immediately to replace the inflammable adhesive with a safer one. As so often in the past, 3M was in a very tight spot. The company had no other adhesive to sell for the job. Years before, developmental work had been done on a water-dispersed adhesive which would be safer, but the product had never been perfected because no commercial possibility could be seen at the time for it. These early experiments showed that water-dispersed adhesives were slow to develop strength in the bond, which was one of the major obstacles to their use.

Production was virtually stopped in Detroit. Workers at 3M were put on a short work week while management frantically tried to figure out what to do. Then, at that crucial moment, General Motors employees went on their famous sit-down strike which eventually spread to not only 50 General Motors plants, but to all auto plants with the exception of Ford Motor Company. It lasted from December 30, 1936 to February 11, 1937, just long enough to allow 3M to get out of its predicament. During the strike, adhesive production in Detroit was suspended, and in St. Paul, a typical 3M laboratory marathon was organized in an effort to find a substitute adhesive. The men worked day and night for those six weeks trying to perfect a formula for a water-dispersed adhesive. They succeeded at practically the same time the strike ended and hurried back to Detroit to start commercial production, realizing that with the strike over, the automotive people would want action immediately.

The Adhesives Division's troubles were not yet over, however. When the factory in Detroit tried to manufacture the new formula on a commercial scale, the compound just wouldn't come out right. It took another two weeks to find and correct the difficulty, which was caused by lack of control of important variables. The water was boiling out of the compound, and it was necessary to retain just the right amount. This apparently simple problem caused many a sleepless night.

The water-dispersed adhesive completely eliminated the fire hazard and, in addition, could be sprayed on instead of brushed on. This speeded the job substantially, and reduced the cost of attaching silencer pads and other materials to the all-steel bodies. To the relief of all, 3M was solidly in the adhesives business again.

Not as solidly as it wanted to be, however. Competition was still selling the greatest share of the adhesives business created by the general adoption of the all-steel body. For example, a substantial volume of adhesives was needed to bond sound-deadening insulation to the floors and inside trunks and the new turret tops which had been introduced in 1935. The adhesive that competition sold for installing sound-deadener pads to turret tops was a cheap asphalt emulsion. On the production line, this emulsion was poured into the inverted turret top and swabbed around in a circle by a mechanical arm; then the silencer pads were slapped on. It was a crude operation and not too satisfactory, as the pads often failed to stick to the roof after the car had been in use for a while. But the car manufacturers thought it was the most economical method.

In order to capture this turret top adhesive business, 3M had to persuade the car manufacturers that even though its adhesive cost nearly eight times more than the asphalt emulsion, it would be more economical in the long run because of its superior quality. To do this, the company resorted to its traditional policy of getting a 3M man on the assembly line to demonstrate the superiority of 3M's product and help work out the most effective and economical way to do the whole job. Adhesive salesmen spent long hours with the automotive workers. Together they developed an installation system, using 3M's adhesive, which took less labor and was more satisfactory and more economical than the former method. Under the new system, pressure was applied mechanically to bond the felt pads to the turret top, and this insured a more permanent adhesion. By early 1938, most of the industry was converted to 3M's adhesive for turret tops.

By this time, the company realized that the policy of "tailor-making" adhesives to meet specific industrial needs was fairly profitable and a good one to follow in the future. Gross annual sales had steadily risen from $14,685 for the first year, 1933, to $1,458,330 for 1937, with the automotive industry purchasing more than 70 percent of production. This volume was made up not only of sales to the trim shops, and to plants for silencer pads and sound deadeners, but also of special adhesives for attaching weather stripping, another requirement of all-steel bodies.

The fact that such a high proportion of 3M's adhesive business was with the automotive industry brought about the second major financial crisis in the new division. When World War II halted production on passenger cars and non-defense vehicles in February, 1942, practically all of the adhesive business evaporated. As the amount of nonauto-motive* (industrial) business at this time amounted to only

*Nonautomotive or industrial customers were the auto repaint and repair shops, the furniture manufacturers, railroads, building trades, and other outside automotive production plants.

15 percent of the total volume and was insufficient for profitable operation of the Detroit plant, something had to be done immediately.

Forced by this crisis to drastic and decisive action, the Detroit sales division began an intensive hunt for new business which would tide them over until car production was resumed. The salesmen began pushing every doorbell where they thought adhesives could be sold. The result was that in a surprisingly short time such an extensive industrial market was developed that Detroit not only was kept operating during the war, but sales were tripled by 1946. If the crisis hadn't occurred, it probably would have taken years longer to develop an industrial market of such proportions and give the Adhesives Division the greater security achieved through wide diversification of customers.

3M had known for some time that a wide industrial market existed for adhesives outside the automotive production plants, but not until the industrial business was actively sought from 1942 on, did everyone realize just how extensively America was "glued" together and how many products could use a 3M cement. To list even a small portion of the markets 3M eventually sold is impossible within the limits of this book, but the reader need only look around him to see how many manufactured items are held together in part or total by an adhesive. The little, felt "feet" on telephones, for example, are attached with an adhesive. Furniture, children's toys, TV cabinets, sponge mops, refrigerators, plumbing installations, apparel accessories such as pocketbooks, shoes, and jewelry all take adhesives. So do candy wrappers, farm machinery, scientific instruments, bathroom tile, acoustical ceilings, and other parts of house construction.

The pocketbook industry was one of the first new industrial accounts to help tide Detroit over the lean war months. Until the war, pocketbook manufacturers had used an inexpensive rubber-base adhesive to glue parts of purses together. When rubber became a critical item, their adhesive supply became critical, too, and they had to look for a new supply source. 3M heard of their plight and mixed a formula made with reclaimed rubber which provided a substitute. The shoe industry experienced the same problem, and 3M aided it, too. To find still more business, 3M asked the Federal Government what adhesives might be needed in defense materials. They found that a waterproof adhesive was required to seal packages consigned overseas. In military operations, supply packages had to be waterproof because they often had to be floated ashore. Many civilian export packaging operations as well required a waterproof sealer. 3M compounded a special adhesive for packaging purposes, which was used extensively throughout the war and is still in demand.

Then 3M learned that the aircraft industry was in need of numerous adhesives for bonding parts of planes together. These bonds had to be resistant to weather and to oil and other fuels, in addition to maintaining a high bond of strength at temperatures from substratosphere cold to high desert heat. 3M furnished these.

Spurred by their wartime success in expanding industrial accounts, adhesive salesmen continued their aggressive campaign in postwar years. Still operating on the original policy of making a special adhesive for each specific industrial job, the company developed more than a thousand formulas. Around three hundred and fifty of these compounds are in regular production; the others are made to order. By 1952, 3M was selling adhesives to more than eighty different industries in addition to the automotive. These industrial accounts include manufacturers of machinery, chemical and allied products, stone, clay, and glass products, fabricated metal products; transportation equipment (nonautomotive); the government; wholesale merchants; the mining industry; ordnance manufacturers; radio and television broadcasting industries; apparel accessory manufacturers; and others. These accounts now account for two thirds of the division's total sales compared to the less than 20 percent of prewar days, a healthier condition by far than dependence on one or two major customers.

World War II had another unexpectedly favorable effect on the fortunes of the Detroit Division. As an indirect result of the war, one of 3M's products which had failed to click before became one of Minnesota Mining and Manufacturing Company's best selling items. Millions of motorists now know the product as "UNDERSEAL" rubberized protective coating for car underbodies.

In 1934, the tape laboratory of the St. Paul factory not only began making rubber cement for commercial sale for the first time, but it also developed a rubberized coating which could be sprayed on the metal and nonworking underparts of cars to stop rust and corrosion, prevent abrasion, and deaden engine noise for the motorist. The product was called simply, "3M Underbody Protective Coating." Plans were to sell this coating to the automotive industry, and in 1935, some was used in Chevrolet production. In those depression days, however, automobile manufacturers were reluctant to add any more to the cost of production, and there was no general acceptance of the product. The first sustained commercial usage was by the railroad industry, not the automotive.

At this time, the railroads had just put on the nation's tracks the streamlined, high-speed trains, and had found that their high speed caused severe abrasion to the underside of cars from flying roadbed materials. This roadbed abrasion was particularly severe in mountain areas. The axle generator on the undercarriage, which supplied electricity to the car, was one example of a vital part which couldn't stand this severe abrasion and needed better protection than the quarter-inch steel plate covering it. These steel plates were being destroyed in one round trip to the Pacific Coast by Union Pacific streamliners, and something had to be done immediately to give better protection.

3M, which had sold heavy-duty abrasive paper to the railroads for years, learned of this problem and suggested its protective coating. Experiments were made by the Chicago & North Western Railway Company, which found that the coating would protect the axle generator from the roadbed abrasion for several months. The railroads became the first volume customer.

It was not until late 1942 that 3M was able to sell this protective coating to the market for which it was originally invented, the automotive. When passenger car production was halted in 1942, everyone began to realize that the family car might have to last a long time. To help car owners, the automotive manufacturers started promoting car conservation through their dealers. 3M strongly felt that its underbody protective coating should be a part of any conservation program and again approached Chevrolet on the idea of promoting this product through its dealers. This time they took to the idea and agreed to include 3M's underbody protective coating as part of Chevrolet's national car conservation program. Chevrolet was convinced of the wiseness of this decision when they later saw pictures of cars parked on the streets of the Gulf city of Freeport, Texas. The pictures, taken by Detroit's sales manager, clearly showed that unprotected metal parts of the cars were being badly corroded from the sun and salty, humid air, and Freeport was typical of many coastal areas where the climate was destructive to unprotected metal.

3M actively aided Chevrolet and its dealers in the campaign to show the public the value of conserving its cars. A 3M representative personally called on every dealer, and a great deal of work was done by direct mail. Other large car manufacturers soon instituted similar conservation programs through their dealers. The public was not easily persuaded to use protective coating, as it was an added expense. Through intensive effort on the part of the dealers and 3M, however, car owners came to see its value and orders steadily increased. Soon, 3M could not produce enough of this coating in Detroit, and to meet consumer demands, a plant was built at Lemont, Illinois in 1946. Some manufacturing was also given to a subcontractor. UNDERSEAL protective coating was a welcome addition to the lines of both the car dealers and 3M.

From 1936 to 1944, Detroit operated very much as the other divisions, with sales, production, and laboratory facilities of its own. Their department heads were responsible to corresponding department heads in the St. Paul home office. Then, in June, 1944, a major departure was made in 3M's organizational structure by giving Detroit a near-autonomous status, the first given any division. A general manager was appointed to assume direct responsibility for the profitable operation of this division. He was given authority over sales, production, and laboratory activities, and instructed to consult the home office only on matters of policy and in connection with important actions within his division. He was to be, in effect, "president" of his own group, responsible directly to top management in St. Paul.

This was the company's first experiment with a vertical type of organization. If successful, it meant other divisions could be given the same status.*

*Louis F. Weyand, sales manager of adhesives, was named general manager of the Detroit Adhesives and Coatings Division on November 1, 1944. The success of this division under this direction convinced 3M that they could successfully shift to a vertical type of organization under which all divisions would be given near-autonomous status. Weyand began his career in 3M as an abrasive salesman on September 1, 1915. He served as sales manager of automotive products from 1935 to 1941, and of automotive products and cements from 1941 to 1944 when he became general manager of the Detroit Division. On April 9, 1946, he was elected vice-president of the Adhesives and Coatings Division in Detroit. In April of 1950 he was named a director of 3M, and on January 29, 1952, was elected executive vice-president in charge of Tape and Allied Products. On March 15, 1955, Weyand was promoted to Executive Vice-president–Director of Sales.

Adhesives and UNDERSEAL rubberized coating were not the only products successfully sold by the division. Still a third line, closely allied to adhesives and coatings, was developed in 1935, and also became an important part of the Detroit operation. This line was industrial sealers. Sealers, like adhesives, were developed on the principle of tailoring each to fit a particular job, and a substantial business was built up through this policy. The first sealer was the one for Fisher Body for attaching fabric cartops to the crown molding, as described earlier. Gradually, 3M produced all kinds of industrial sealers. They are used to caulk wooden boat decks; to seal parts of auto bodies and refrigerators; for auto wind shields and windows; for various types of fuel tanks; for aircraft cabins; for trailer bodies; and for a multitude of other jobs.

By 1952, the business of the Adhesives Division was keeping five plants busy. As the markets for adhesives, coatings, and sealers outgrew the Detroit area, new plants were located in other sections of the country to serve customers better and reduce freight costs. In addition to the Lemont, Illinois plant, manufacturing facilities were built in Los Angeles in 1947; in Bristol, Pennsylvania in 1949; and in Wayne, Michigan in 1950. The Wayne plant absorbed the Lemont operations in 1952, and the latter plant was sold. With these strategically located plants, the division now serves an ever-expanding market all over the nation, as well as the all-important Detroit area where the division got its start.

W.L. McKnight, then 3M president, leveling the cornerstone of the company's first administration building in St. Paul in 1939. This ultramodern, four-level structure was outgrown during World War II.

Aerial view of 3M's St. Paul plant area in early Thirties. 3M started business in St. Paul with one small three-story building on this site.

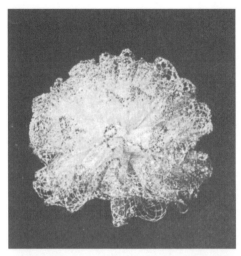

"LACELON"
Sparkle Bow

Decorative wrapping ribbon, one of 3M's many specialty items. These are the three attractive synthetic fiber ribbons— "LACELON," "SASHEEN," and "DECORETTE" Brands, developed through the company's knowledge of coating techniques.

"SASHEEN"
Magic Bow

"DECORETTE"
Informal Bow

3M laboratories conduct endless experiments in their search for better quality and new products. Above, a test is made to determine the bonding strength of a special adhesive in adhering plexiglass to plexiglass.

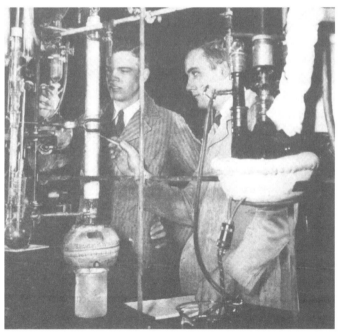

Through its pioneer research in fluorocarbon chemistry, 3M has produced a series of new compounds with unique physical and chemical properties. Semicommercial production of these "fluorochemicals" is under way at the company's Chemolite plant at Hastings, Minn.

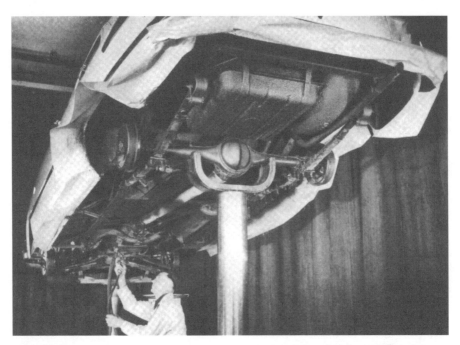

"UNDERSEAL" Brand rubberized coating, a product of 3M's Adhesives and Coatings Division, protects vital parts of a car from road salts and chemicals, moisture, and roadbed abrasion.

The company's only major disaster which destroyed this St. Paul mineral building on February 8, 1951, killed 13 men and injured 60 others.

THE GREAT DEPRESSION: A GOLDEN ERA

3M was a depression phenomenon in the industrial world. While many other firms were slashing payrolls, discontinuing dividends, or going into the red, Minnesota Mining and Manufacturing Company made front page news with new product development, physical expansion, continuous dividends, and growing sales volume.

The natural question is "How did 3M do it?" One obvious, but incomplete answer is, "Through research and aggressiveness." Actually, 3M's stability through the great depression is attributable to many factors. For one thing, 3M's prosperity during the '20s was not an unsound one as was the nation's. Rather, it was the product of conservatism and sound fiscal policies. Surplus was not recklessly invested, but put back into product research; dividends were paid out prudently. The same strong leadership that had brought the company from obscurity to prosperity saw to it that these conservative policies were not changed in the '20s. These are only partial reasons why the depression years were to be a golden age of research and growth which eclipsed even those of the '20s.

The single major factor which kept the company moving forward while others were going under or barely breaking even, was the acquisition of a competitive abrasive firm,

Baeder-Adamson Company of Philadelphia, Pennsylvania, the oldest sandpaper manufacturer in the United States.

In 1930, McKnight had the foresight to purchase Baeder-Adamson when he learned the American Glue Company was planning to sell it. Through his earlier planning, 3M had sufficient cash reserve to enable the company to make such an acquisition following the country's worst financial collapse.

Baeder-Adamson was purchased just nine months after the fateful October, 1929, stock market crash, for approximately $2,000,000. The purchase price was met by $658,175 in cash, 22,825 shares of 3M capital stock at $10 a share and a new issue of $1,100,000 in ten-year, 6 per cent debenture bonds. The latter, which did not involve any property mortgage, were taken by the American Glue Company. They constituted 3M's first long-term debt since the financing by L.P. Ordway. This time 3M retired the entire amount by 1933, seven years ahead of schedule.

By shutting down the Baeder-Adamson plant in Philadelphia and bringing everything to St. Paul, 3M increased its dollar volume more than 25 per cent, with little added cost in production. Looking back on this move, McKnight explains, "Without this increase, we too would have suffered losses. But the added profits from the acquisition gave us courage to go ahead with our research program. If we had had to fight harder to keep our heads above water, we probably would have curtailed product development appropriations. As it was, we kept our research going, and the 1930–1940 period became known as our golden era of research."

This was 3M's first major acquisition. The prior purchase of Wausau Abrasives had made little change in St. Paul operations. The Baeder-Adamson purchase increased 3M's payroll by a hundred and twenty-five persons,* and its sales volume by 25 per cent. This was approximately the percentage that 3M's normal business had dropped off in the months following the crash.

While 3M was acquiring Baeder-Adamson Company, its largest competitors were also making acquisitions. The Carborundum Company acquired the assets of the Walpole, Massachusetts, sandpaper plant of the American Glue Company. The Norton Company acquired the Behr-Manning sandpaper business and operated it as a wholly owned subsidiary under the firm name of Behr-Manning Corporation. The latter acquired the United States Sandpaper and the H.H. Barton companies. After these changes, there were four major sandpaper manufacturers in the United States: 3M, Carborundum Company, Behr-Manning Corporation, and Armour & Company. As these companies were all strong financially and good merchandisers, sandpaper prices remained fairly stable throughout the entire depression period, another factor which helped 3M maintain profits through the depression.

3M made the front page again by pioneering in the field of employee relations. On January 1, 1932, the company established, on an experimental basis, a program of unemployment insurance for its employees to be financed from company earnings. It was one of the first of its kind in the nation, and caused considerable comment in business and labor circles. At the time, the whole country was preoccu-

---

*Baeder-Adamson's vice-president and sales manager, George H. Halpin, transferred to 3M's staff at the time of the acquisition as sales manager. During his many years of service to 3M, Halpin's skillful direction of salesmen, his prestige with the trade, and his sound sales policies have been major factors in keeping the sales curve moving steadily upward. He became a director of 3M on March 14, 1939, and on December 10, 1940, was elected vice-president in charge of sales. In 1949, he was elected executive vice-president in charge of sales, and served in this capacity until March, 1955. Today he serves as executive vice-president.

pied with unemployment and its problems. There had been much talk but little action. The Federal Government had toyed with various plans but rejected them all. State governments hesitated to take the initiative for fear of putting home industry at a disadvantage in interstate commerce through extra costs. The subject was discussed in June, 1930, at a governors' conference. As for private industry, only a handful of companies had provided any kind of program for their employees although the topic was under constant discussion. Those who had programs included the Dennison Manufacturing Company of Framingham, Massachusetts, who had pioneered with the first company unemployment reserve system in 1916; 14 companies in Rochester, New York, who inaugurated the same plan, the Unemployment Benefit program, and a few others.

President McKnight felt deeply that the problem of unemployment was partly the responsibility of the employer, and on June 10, 1931, he recommended to 3M's board of directors that it inaugurate a plan to supplement the company's old-age pension system and sickness and disability insurance program. In a letter to the directors, he wrote:

From my point of view there are two good reasons for unemployment benefits:

First, I think every employer has a real moral responsibility to regular employees who are paid only a living wage and that responsibility, to see that they are able to secure life's necessities during the time of distress, increases in direct ratio to the length of time they have been employed. Industry already has gone quite a way in recognizing its responsibility in sickness and old age of its employees, but until now little has been done regarding unemployment.

Second, as this country becomes more industrial and less agricultural, the larger proportion of its population becomes dependent upon so-called "capital," and unless capital finds a way to give labor some feeling of security, in my opinion it leaves itself open to socialistic and communistic attack. One way for capital to contribute to that sense of security is to assure, as far as possible, some income to its old and valued employees (and such employees are a substantial percentage in most organizations) in times of unemployment, distress, sickness, and old age. The sense of security can only be developed by definitely assuring permanent employees these benefits. A mental reservation that you are going to do it is of little value in respect to the employees' sense of security or as a political safeguard.[1]

McKnight's recommended plan was patterned after the Rochester, New York, Unemployment Benefit Plan, and was put in effect on January 1, 1932. The heart of the plan was the accumulation of a reserve fund out of company earnings sufficient to pay unemployment benefits for a five-year period. The reserve set aside equaled 2 percent of the 1932 payroll.

In announcing the plan, McKnight said, "I have purposely relieved the employee of any participation in the cost of the plan, as I do not think the employee whom we are trying to reach can afford any more income deductions beyond the pension and sickness and accident benefit to which he is already contributing."[2] In an extreme emergency, however, and if the company fund became depleted, the company planned to make deductions from salaries of the employed to aid the unemployed.

To be eligible, an employee had to have been with the company at least three years and earn less than $45 weekly, and be a participant in the company's old-age pension and group insurance plans. More than 450 of the company's 735 employees were covered by February, 1932. Eligibility terminated if the employee got a job elsewhere, or was involved in a layoff due to a labor dispute.

Unemployment benefits were to range from $7 to $17.55 a week, payable for from 10 to 17 weeks in a year, depending on the length of service with the company and wages normally received. The plan was to be administered by a special committee appointed by and subject to the general control of the board of directors. For example, an employee normally earning $25 weekly and with three years of service to his credit would receive $9 a week for 10 weeks of continuous unemployment. If the same man had 10 years of service, he would get $12.15 weekly for 17 weeks. A person earning $45 weekly would be eligible for $13 a week for 10 weeks if he had three years' service, or $17.55 for 17 weeks if he had 10 years' service.

In launching the program, McKnight said further:

There are three major problems common to most wage earners. These are old age, sickness or disability, and unemployment. The Minnesota Mining and Manufacturing Company has attempted to solve the first two by old-age pensions and by sickness and disability insurance for its employees. Now the company, after long and serious consideration, has embarked on an effort to remove the worry of unemployment from its organization. The difficult period of business depression through which we are passing impresses us with the fact that no management can in sure continuity of employment to all its employees. Therefore, it becomes desirable from every standpoint that industry should take voluntary steps to provide for unemployment relief. Our plan is, of course, an experiment. We have purposely been conservative in its provisions, hoping that later experience will justify liberalization of the program. I consider it wholly practical for most American industries eventually to work out unemployment plans of a similar nature. Programs of this character should be recognized as a legitimate part of the cost of doing business, to be considered in accounting just as any other cost item.

American industry will profit itself, its employees and the entire nation by carrying out a progressive, forward-looking program which will enable it to care as much as possible for its own unemployed in periods of business stress. Should municipal, state, or federal governments undertake to care for the unemployed, as under the English dole system, the cost in taxation will be tremendously greater than if industry cares for its own. There would be inevitable waste and inefficiency in any government dole or benefit system, and, in addition, it would pauperize the recipients of the aid. This would not be true where an industry keeps its own workers protected.[3]

Another provision in the 3M program was, "This [plan] will be discontinued in case the United States or any state to which the company pays taxes shall enact any statute appropriating money raised by taxation to the payment of any dole, benefit, or other unemployment relief." Interestingly, the one state in which 3M operated a plant outside of Minnesota, the state of Wisconsin, was the first state to pass an unemployment compensation measure. It was called the Groves Bill and was passed in February, 1932, under Governor Philip F. La Follette. The bill became effective July 1, 1933, and provided for employer contributions to a state fund for unemployment compensation with a segregation for each employer's account, but a pooling of the funds. The state scheme was not to take effect if Wisconsin employers established their own system before the effective date; in such cases, the employers would manage their own systems. Because of the provision that the 3M plan would not apply where a public plan was in effect, 3M employees working in Wausau became ineligible for 3M's unemployment insurance plan.

McKnight and other industrial leaders who had inaugurated unemployment compensation programs in their firms had hoped other industries all over the country would follow their lead and forestall government action. But by 1935, only about 37 companies had any kind of a program. These varied from special agreements with unions to full-fledged unemployment insurance programs like that of Minnesota Mining. Most of the firms were in the East.

As it turned out, however, no payments were ever made under 3M's program. In the first place, the company's all-around foresightedness kept it a growing company, and consequently, while there were pay cuts, there were few layoffs. The few that were dropped were not eligible for compensation. To avoid layoffs, the work week for hourly-wage employees was shortened from fifty hours a week to as low as a four-day, 32-hour week during the worst months. By December 19, 1932, it was obvious that 2 percent of the payroll was more than was necessary as a reserve for unemployment payments, and the amount was changed to a flat $10,000 fund.

Secondly, as the depression wore on, a new and keen interest in not only unemployment insurance but other social security measures arose across the country, especially in the Federal Government. Agitation grew for state or federal action. In 1935, the federal unemployment compensation program was established and the states there upon proceeded under the provisions of the act. In accordance with 3M's original reservation, its plan was discontinued after passage of the federal law.

But even though McKnight's unemployment compensation program was never used, the fact that it was instituted had a reassuring effect on the morale of the employees, and helped them through the worst years of the depression.

As America climbed painfully out of the depression, Minnesota Mining and Manufacturing Company occupied an enviable position in industry. By diversifying as fast as possible and through sound fiscal policies, a strong patent structure, and aggressive selling, five flourishing businesses had been developed: abrasives (glue-bond and waterproof), masking tape, cellophane tape, roofing granules, and adhesives. Except for brief setbacks in 1930, 1931, and 1932, each business had grown. During the era of economic disaster 3M had brought its gross annual volume from its 1929 figure of over $5,500,000 a year to more than $15,000,000. While black blizzards rolled over the dust bowl and Hoover desperately tried to bring back prosperity, 3M continued to pay regular dividends without interruption, and only once (1932) was forced to dip into surplus to do so. By 1937, only 37 percent of the total volume of business was from abrasive products, compared to 100 percent from abrasives in 1920. This was a ratio much more to management's liking.

Under its program of diversification, 3M by 1940 had established not only these five businesses, but also had invented a myriad of variations of each major product. The Abrasives Division had developed 10,000 shapes, widths, lengths and grits of abrasives made with three kinds of bonding adhesive materials and three kinds of backing to serve almost every type of industry including the automotive, metal working, stainless steel, electrical, lumber, woodworking, furniture, railroad, airplane, glass, plastics, hat, and shoe industries.

The Tape Division had created special tapes for use in the electrical, shoe, decorating, and photographic industries; and general industrial tapes for bakeries, banks, chain stores, confectioneries, department stores, drugstores, florists, grocers, hardware stores, homes, jewelers, meat dealers and packers, offices, schools, stationers, and the textile trade, as well as the automotive production plants, repaint and repair shops, airplane manufacturers, and memorial craftsmen (SCOTCH Brand sandblast stencil).

Adhesives had branched out to serve furniture manufacturers and repair shops, as well as the automotive industry. Its rubber cements were being used by the refrigerating, air-conditioning, furniture, railroad, building, and many other industries.

3M roofing granules were being produced in six colors and were gaining regularly in popularity for homes, farms, and industrial buildings. Silica quartz from the Wausau plant was also being sold to lithographers, foundries, paper mills, and the glass and cast stone industries.

In addition, miscellaneous products were developed through research such as 3M lapping and grinding compounds, TAN FIBRE oil sheet packing and gaskets, and TAN

FIBRE shoe covering. Such items were bringing in $452,970 a year.

Such impressive development could never have occurred without the most expert technical direction, a fact McKnight had luckily recognized in 1921. In that year, he advertised for a technically trained man for 3M's laboratory. The young engineer hired for the job breathed life and form into a rather shapeless research program, skillfully coordinating research, manufacturing, and engineering activities for 28 years. Ultimately, he succeeded William L. McKnight as president.

A MAN WHO LOOKED AHEAD

RICHARD P. CARLTON was just the type of ambitious, talented young man 3M was always looking for, but W.L. McKnight hesitated about hiring him when he applied for a job in answer to the company's blind ad for a laboratory assistant in the fall of 1921.

It wasn't that the 27-year-old engineer, recently out of the army, didn't have the qualifications to work in the sandpaper laboratory, for he did. Carlton held a B.S. degree in engineering from the University of Minnesota (1921); had worked as a draftsman for the state of Minnesota, and had been a partner in an electrical contracting firm doing business in South Dakota before World War I. His personality was pleasing; he was affable, poised, and alert. As a matter of fact, McKnight felt sure he would be a decided asset to 3M, yet debated about putting him on the payroll.

Carlton, he felt, would be too high priced for 3M's budget. He had been earning more than twice the salary 3M could offer, and McKnight believed a man of his caliber might not be satisfied in the job 3M had in mind, which was that of making routine tests. He pointed this out to Carlton, but to McKnight's surprise, the young engineer told him that 3M couldn't get along without technically trained men like himself and, to McKnight's further surprise, offered to take the

$65 a month which 3M offered. For although Carlton had been earning $200 a month, he had decided 3M was a company that was going places, and he wanted to go along.

Carlton's offer was quickly accepted, and he joined the laboratory staff October 26, 1921, with the distinction of being the first technical man in the company with a degree from an accredited college.

Carlton's title to begin with was factory engineer, but this hardly described the many responsibilities he quickly assumed. His first accomplishment was to switch the laboratory program onto a more technical track by supplanting trial-and-error methods of quality control with more specific scientific standards.

Under McKnight's earlier direction, the laboratory had developed an elementary set of quality control standards for testing sandpaper, and following these standards was the laboratory's only function until Carlton took over. Under his direction, elementary tests were refined and highly technical tests were devised to measure the abrading performance of sandpaper. He designed a special wood-sanding machine for making these tests, and with the information obtained from actual abrading of various woods in the laboratory under scientifically controlled conditions it was possible to determine the factors which most greatly influenced the quality of sandpaper during the manufacturing process. Under this program quality improved rapidly.

In 1925, Carlton and his staff published a manual of technical information for the laboratory, factory, and sales personnel.[1] Carlton was trying to accomplish more effectively the very thing that McKnight had written Ober about years before: greater cooperation between manufacturing and sales. In this manual he expressed in writing for the first time the important 3M technical policies which undeniably account for much of 3M's success:

The time to get closest control of your product is during your manufacturing process. What you do after this is just history except in isolated cases.

Close factory control, in its strictest sense, is the factor that has permeated 3M policy. Every instrument which can aid in controlling our product is installed.

There is no room for a thin-skinned man in this organization. Carelessness cannot exist. The day of "rule of thumb" method has passed in the 3M organization long ago, and the future is building even more exacting requirements as refinements on machinery can be designed to meet the demand. The technical phase has passed from the laboratory to the production department; and the coordination of departments had evolved a laboratory and technical phase run with the sole idea of production in mind. A free interchange of data and ideas, we hope, will always be our policy and creed.

The laboratory of the modern industrial plant must have something more than the men and equipment to do control work. It must possess a two-fisted generating and testing department for ideas. This work, dressed in its best Sunday clothes, is termed "Research."

No plant can rest on its laurels–it either develops and improves or loses ground. Every idea evolved should have a chance to prove its worth, and this is true for two reasons: 1) if it is good, we want it; 2) if it is not good, we will have purchased our insurance and peace of mind when we have proved it impractical. Our company has adopted the policy, "Research in Business Pays."[2]

Included also in the manual were data which the laboratory had compiled on special standards for belt-sanding, disc-grinding, and hand-sanding wood, including the speeds at which wood-sanding machinery should be run, the pressures best for various industrial sanding jobs, the performance of various types of abrasives on certain kinds of woods, the physical nature and cutting power of various natural and artificial minerals used to make sandpaper, and comparisons of the performance of 3M and competitive abrasives. Many graphs interpreting the technical material for laboratory workers and the sales department were included in the manual.

After setting the laboratory on the right course, Carlton gradually began coordinating the activities of research, engineering, and manufacturing, and directing the technical development of new ideas from the dream stage to commercial success.

McKnight readily recognized Carlton's qualities of leadership and, in 1928, promoted him to assistant general manager in charge of factory administration, and, in 1929, to director in charge of manufacturing. He also was elected vice-president in 1929 when Edgar Ober resigned and McKnight moved into the president's chair.

The job of director of manufacturing, which Carlton held for twenty years, was a multifaceted one requiring a variety of talents. In order to coordinate the activities of research, engineering, and manufacturing successfully, the director had to blend the talents of many men, mediate their differences, supervise their work, and inspire them to succeed. He had to be an organizer, a researcher by nature, and an adept trouble shooter. Carlton fortunately possessed these abilities in high degree. Another valuable asset was his flair for smoothing out the natural differences between the nontechnical men, who were rich in experience, and the young college-trained men, who had sound backgrounds of technical training but little practical experience.

As director, Carlton had to know far more than textbook rules for running a plant, for primarily his job was one of human relations. He had to blend the talents of the nontechnical, the college-trained, and the "idea" men, and coax the best possible performance from each. It was often a thankless job, but one which had to be done. Fortunately, it was the work Carlton liked best. Like McKnight and Bush, he could be found working evening after evening. After hours he experimented with new ideas in the laboratory, helped his men with problems, and laid out plans for the next day.

No matter what his title, Carlton never directed his men from behind a desk. Paper work was his Nemesis, and whenever possible, he personally assisted his men in conducting experiments and working out new theories. When trouble appeared, he had a sixth sense for finding a solution. Often his ideas seemed ridiculous to coworkers, and at first they told him so. Then they gradually learned that Carlton's "ridiculous" ideas generally worked, and they argued no more.

It was in the development of product ideas that Carlton made some of his most important contributions to the company. Not only was he an inventor himself, but he had the ability to generate creative thinking in others, to draw out men's ideas and nurture them to maturity. No one knew better than he that in a sympathetic atmosphere one idea fosters another, and he constantly kept his men thinking in terms of improvements for old products and suggestions for new. Through casual conversations at a laboratory bench or a machine and through impromptu meetings with his men he kept interest in product development at a high level. While talking to a man about his idea, Carlton often would jot down a suggested program for developing it and hand it to him at the end of the conversation. Through such informal guidance and close personal contact, Carlton built a manufacturing organization which cooperatively worked toward the common goal of improved quality and new products.

Almost any idea—whether wildly imaginative or soberly sensible—gained audience with management during those early years. Usually it reached Carlton first, and he had the choice of rejecting it or persuading the rest of management to back it. Fortunately, he usually took the latter course. McKnight and Bush also were receptive to new ideas, and in this sympathetic atmosphere, new product ideas budded in profusion, especially in the '20s and '30s when 3M was still small enough for suggestions to reach the top quickly.

The notable successes in product development within the company as a whole were, of course, pressure-sensitive tapes, roofing granules, adhesives, and WETORDRY sandpaper. But for every major product idea that was developed, there were several minor but important ideas in quality improvement and engineering. And there were scores of ideas which never got beyond the talk stage, but which were thoroughly considered. Carlton thought of making an eraser out of rubber and a fine grit of abrasive material. Drew had an idea for synthetic fireplace logs made from special sandpaper. Another idea was for a waterproof tubing for packaging.

Many new ideas were developed on an experimental basis but eventually dropped because the profit picture didn't look promising. Drew felt WETORDRY sandpaper should be made especially for musicians to sand down clarinet and saxophone reeds, and this was tried and sold for a while. The polishes, sanding liquids, and waxes were also in this category.

Some product experiments were costly and brought no return. Seed tape was an example. The idea for seed tape was one of the most imaginative, yet potentially practical, suggestions to come up in 3M's laboratory in the early '40s. And it is a prime example of the effort, time, and money that can be spent on research with no return.

In the early 1940s, a 3M researcher conceived the idea of coating tape with garden seeds to facilitate planting and germination. The inventor reasoned that ordinary methods wasted seeds and labor. He felt that seed tape, which could be planted in strips, would be more convenient and economical than the haphazard dropping of seeds into the ground. The even spacing would prevent over crowding, allow better germination, and eliminate the need for costly hand-thinning later. He believed, too, that the resulting uncrowded vegetables would be of better quality.

Outside of a research laboratory, the seed tape idea might sound impractical, but to men used to thinking in terms of product research, it had definite possibilities. With management's O.K., 3M engineers designed special machinery for dropping seeds on coated tape. This was a difficult production feat because garden seeds vary in size and shape. After several trials, the engineers accomplished this, and planting experiments were begun with the assistance of several Minnesota horticulturists. Radish seed, carrots, egg plant, peppers, cauliflower, celery, lettuce, parsnips, and other vegetable seeds on tape were planted in several agricultural areas where growing conditions varied. Germination results were carefully recorded.

The seed-tape group encountered every conceivable difficulty. The machinery had to be altered over and over again. The tape had to be of a nature which would allow proper germination, and this presented major technical problems. Technicians from the abrasive laboratories assisted in every way possible. More than $40,000 was spent in research in two years (1944-1946), and still more money was needed. Then, when technical difficulties were overcome and the idea finally developed to a marketable stage, management found that merchandising to home gardeners was not economical.

Richard Carlton contributed many patentable ideas to 3M, as well as stimulated ideas in other men. Several not only brought prestige and profits, but contributed to the progress of the entire abrasive industry. One of these was an improved adhesive binder which increased the salability of WETORDRY sandpaper. Another Carlton invention was a flexible and durable disc for use in automotive and general industrial abrading. The third was an electrostatic process which materially increased the cutting power of sandpaper.

Carlton developed his new adhesive binder in the late '20s. Years before, when waterproof sandpaper was made with the Okie method of coating glue-bond sandpaper with a natural resin varnish, he had realized, as had everyone, that the product would never stay on the market unless its quality were improved. The natural resin varnishes varied in quality and often contained impurities. Furthermore, the natural resin varnish sandpaper cured by oxidation and continued oxidizing after it left the drying ovens; this caused a fire hazard during shipment and in storage. Spontaneous combustion fires broke out frequently in boxcars en route and in customers' stockrooms. The cause of these fires had greatly puzzled the nontechnical men until Carlton came to 3M and explained the technical reason.

Neither could the natural resin varnishes be cured hard enough to hold the mineral properly, and as a result, the grits receded into the soft bond and didn't abrade efficiently.

These drawbacks caused endless complaints and the laboratory frantically sought a remedy. Although Carlton was not a chemist, he experimented with new and different materials in a search for a solution. He believed a synthetic resin formula for the binder and sizing might be the answer, because synthetic resins cure by polymerization and will not cause spontaneous combustion. By 1926, he had developed a patentable waterproof sandpaper made with synthetic resin, and this helped keep it salable. Modifications and improvements of the product have been made each year since to keep its quality high, and it has remained a major source of company revenue.

Carlton saw the need, too, in the automotive industry for a more efficient method of grinding contours on metal car bodies than the traditional, inflexible grinding wheel. The answer, he believed, was a flexible, durable abrasive disc. Many unsuccessful experiments had been made in the abrasive industry with paper-backed and cloth-backed discs. The paper backings tore and the cloth-backed discs wouldn't hold their shape. Carlton developed a durable, flexible abrasive disc for use on a flexible shaft grinder, which would effectively grind curved surfaces on car bodies. Eventually this disc was used for flat grinding metal work and certain woodworking jobs as well. Discs, too, became one of 3M's highest dollar-volume products.

The third important Carlton invention was a process for electrocoating sandpaper, thus increasing its cutting power. Electrocoating was the sixth important development in the progress of the coated abrasive industry in the United States.

Since 1880, five major developments had taken place which improved the efficiency and sales of abrasive products. The first was the introduction of garnet mineral for sandpaper manufacture. This was followed by the invention of an artificial abrasive; then machinery was designed for utilizing sandpaper. (Whether sandpaper helped develop sandpaper-using machinery, or whether these machines contributed primarily to the development of sandpaper is a debatable point.) Then came the open-coat method of making coated abrasives and waterproof sandpaper. Electrocoating was the next and sixth development.

3M was not the only company in the abrasive industry responsible for the development of this faster-cutting sandpaper made with an electrocoating process. There have been several instances where two or more people were working on an invention at the same time without knowing about the others, and such seems to be the case in the invention of the electrode position of abrasive mineral.

During the early part of the depression, Carlton, in an effort to improve 3M coated abrasives, worked on the electrocoating idea in cooperation with other 3M engineers, and a sheet of electrocoated abrasives was put on the market. From available information it appears that Behr-Manning

Corporation actually introduced electrostatically coated abrasives to the trade first, however. This situation led to some serious and eventually acrimonious controversy on patents. It seemed that Behr-Manning's filing dates in the patent office were ahead of 3M's, but the date of actual conception of the idea was in the realm of conjecture. Again 3M turned to patent attorney Paul Carpenter, asking him to make a survey of the situation. After an exhaustive investigation to determine what defenses 3M would have if Behr-Manning ultimately dominated the patent situation, Carpenter found a patent issued to a man named Smyser, covering an electrodeposition process of depositing fine powder on cloth coated with wax to make a polishing cloth. He felt certain the Smyser patent antedated any application by Behr-Manning or any conception date they could establish. 3M acquired all rights under this Smyser patent other than its use with a wax binder. In the meantime, patent discussions with Behr-Manning grew more strained.

The methods used by the two companies for electrocoating sandpaper were different. In the Behr-Manning process, the mineral was projected onto the adhesive surface as the backing passed the electrical field in a vertical position. In the 3M process developed by Carlton, the mineral was projected upward from a moving conveyor onto the adhesive surface of the backing as it was passing through the electrical field in a horizontal position. This process is commonly referred to as the upside-down method and ultimately proved to be the better one and was adopted by a substantial part of the industry.

Behr-Manning argued that the Smyser patent concept could not be applied to the process of electrocoating sandpaper, and that 3M would be unsuccessful in getting it reissued, which they intended to do, to cover the electrocoated sandpaper.

"If we were unsuccessful in reissuing the Smyser patent or could not enforce it with claims already made, it was possible that we were in a very untenable position as far as Behr-Manning was concerned," explains McKnight. "The tone of the discussions indicated that their terms in a license agreement would be severe if they dominated the situation. The alternative to a license would have been a long period of litigation with all of the uncertainty attending it. Considering all phases of the situation, it seemed better for us to work out a compromise with them."

The decision to compromise resulted in an agreement whereby 3M assigned the Smyser patent to Behr-Manning, and the latter assumed all the 3M obligations to Smyser. 3M also assigned to them its patent applications covering electrodeposition sandpaper and, in turn, Behr-Manning granted 3M a license to manufacture electrocoated sandpaper on a nominal royalty basis.

The devotion on the part of Carlton to the development of a sound program of research and product development had a profound effect on the fortunes of Minnesota Mining in two ways. First, because of his success in persuading management of the value of such a program, and his skill in carrying out the plans he formulated, 3M undeniably progressed faster than it would have otherwise.

Secondly, Carlton's work with research and product development over a period of years clearly showed him to be a man with high qualities of leadership, keen business acumen, breadth in his thinking, and an invaluably analytical mind in determining what products would be profitable for his company. These qualities made him a logical candidate for fifth president when, in 1949, W.L. McKnight decided that a younger man should take his place.

RISKS AND REWARDS

FIVE THRIVING BUSINESSES might have satisfied the growth ambitions of some companies, but not 3M. Success in their varied ventures far from satisfied the desire of management to broaden the company's horizons; rather, it served as a stimulant to further growth. The only question was *how* to grow. In 1937, management gathered around the conference table to find the answer.

Critical examination of the past soon brought the directors to a unanimous conclusion: the greatest single factor contributing to past growth was 3M's program of research* which had its roots in the question asked in 1913 by young William McKnight, "How can we do this better?" This program had broadened until it embraced a network of laboratories engaged in a constant search for new products and a ceaseless quest for better quality of all 3M's merchandise.

Experience had proved, time after time, that this restless researching spirit brought increasing profits which could be reinvested in 3M to help it grow. The inestimable amount of

---

*3M scientists today are careful to point out that this early research was "product development," not "pure" or "fundamental" research in the true scientific sense of the term.

money put out for product development research since the establishment of the first small, crude laboratory had been well spent.** So the directors understandably reasoned, "More research, greater growth." Accordingly 3M launched an expanded research program in 1937 and made long-range plans for pouring millions into product development and engineering research.

This faith in research was to be more than justified in ensuing years. 3M eventually earned a reputation for "fantastic inventiveness," and recently it has been fairly accurately determined that every dollar invested for research and product development since 1926 has brought back $28 in gross sales.

In past years, 3M research had centered around the improvement of its abrasive products, and the development and perfecting of "ingenious fabrications" (a term coined by management to describe products such as WETORDRY waterproof abrasive paper, SCOTCH Brand masking and cellophane tape, and COLORQUARTZ roofing granules). Little or no pure or fundamental research had been done in the laboratories. Under the new program, not only were appropriations to divisional laboratories increased, but new laboratories were established to carry on a more purely scientific type of research and the scope of 3M research broadened accordingly.

First, in 1937, a Central Research Laboratory was established to supplement the activities of all the divisional laboratories. This move was sponsored by Vice-president Carlton who recognized the need for a separate laboratory able to explore independently scientific problems too long-

---

**The exact amount of money spent by 3M for research will never be known as separate accounting of research expenditures was not made until 1926.

range in nature to be handled by the divisional laboratories, which had to be primarily concerned with the day-to-day problems of making a product more salable.

Three years later, a New Products Department was organized to study product possibilities of new ideas. Said McKnight, in announcing the new department: "As part of company policy, we are spending a substantial and increasing amount on research each year. It would seem advisable to set up a department to cooperate with all interested parties in studying the commercial value of each research project upon which money is being spent, with the responsibility of ultimately recommending to management whether the work on any given project, from a commercial point of view, should be continued or discontinued."

In 1943, a Products Fabrication Laboratory was set up to develop methods of manufacture for new products.

In 1944 still another move was made to build an industrial research team second to none and to keep 3M growing. Management authorized enlargement of the Engineering Department so that it could handle the now complex needs of 3M in this line. When 3M was small, a few engineers and draftsmen had been able to design or procure equipment for all product departments. The design and construction of buildings and facilities was generally done by outside service organizations. As the company grew and the size and number of new projects increased, Engineering's work load became so great that often all its men were working on a single project for one particular department. This meant that others received little or no engineering service for long periods of time. When management was considering ways to broaden its research activities, it was recognized that the Engineering Department must be increased so that each product division could have engineering service whenever necessary. Bringing in outside engineering help was not in keeping with 3M policies; all phases of product development were carried out within the company if at all possible in order to protect production methods. Beginning in 1944, Engineering was gradually expanded from less than two hundred to a staff of nearly a thousand administrative, technical, security, and maintenance employees.

First, on an experimental basis, an engineer was appointed to serve the coated abrasives division. This worked so successfully that a similar appointment was made for tape, roofing granules, and other 3M divisions. More engineers were added and assigned to special jobs whenever and wherever needed. A plant protection and security department was set up under Engineering, and in 1952 an Engineering Research group was added. This group was divided into five units:

Staff Laboratory Engineering, to serve the Central Research, New Products, and Products Fabrication laboratories. Tape Development Engineering, to assist the Tape Division. Machine Development, Instrument and Control, and Chemical Engineering to serve all divisions and technical departments, in addition to assisting in product development and research.

The newly organized Engineering Department gradually assumed responsibility for design and construction of practically all 3M plants, laboratories, and administrative buildings, maintenance of these facilities, and safety and security functions. This gives all possible protection to inventions and production techniques.

This addition of Central Research, the New Products division, and the Products Fabrication Laboratory assisted by the new Engineering Department insured a continuous flow of products and aided in further growth.

New products have been steadily developed in the company laboratories. There have been so many that today even 3M employees have a hard time keeping track of the exact number of products their company is marketing. The task is made all the more difficult by the fact that the number is constantly increasing and because there are so many variations of each major product. The following list, which includes only *major* developments since expansion of the research program in 1937, gives a fair idea of the extensive scope of recent product development:

"SCOTCHLITE" Brand reflective sheeting for highway safety signs and out door advertising.

"SAFETY-WALK" non-skid, abrasive-coated sheeting for ship decks, factory floors, airplane wings, and other hazardous walking surfaces.

"SCOTCH" Brand magnetic sound-recording tape.

"THERMO-FAX" Brand duplicating process, for copying office records in a one-step operation.

Ribbons for gift packaging—"DECORETTE," "LACELON," and "SASHEEN."

"SCOTCH" Brand electrical tape.

"SCOTCH" Brand filament tape for heavy-duty packaging.

Special synthetic resins, both for 3M's own raw material needs and for sale.

Tympan papers for the graphic arts industry.

3M Brand presensitized aluminum photo-offset plates for lithographic printing.

A fluorochemical foaming agent for use in commercial chrome plating (marketed to electroplaters under the trade name of "ZERO-MIST" by the Udylite Company, Detroit). When added to a plating bath, this fluorochemical forms a layer of foam which traps acid mist and spray, which have always been a serious health and corrosion hazard in chrome plating.

These are some of the successes. To include in a history only a company's successes in product development, however, presents an incomplete picture. For every success in industrial product development, there are many failures. To tell that side of the story is equally important. The amount of talent, time, effort, and money it takes industry to develop one product as mutually valuable to both the public and the company as, for example, SCOTCH Brand cellophane tape, is staggering. Dozens of projects fail for every one that clicks.

During the same seventeen years that the above-mentioned products were profitably marketed, 3M worked on many projects which were dropped for one reason or another. An attempt was made to develop a marketable magnesia cement for use in patching concrete floors and as a substitute for concrete floors. Other projects included work on silicons, silanes, and beer bottle labels that would disintegrate when the bottle was washed, alpha cellulose, seed tape, and a porous rubber sheeting for hospital use. These are only a few.

Often, thousands of dollars were spent before it could be determined whether 3M could make a product superior enough to warrant volume production, or even whether the product could be perfected. An outstanding illustration is the amount of money spent for laboratory charges alone between 1940 and 1952 for seven relatively unsuccessful projects. In those 12 years, more than $900,000 were spent in the laboratory on magnesia cement, alpha cellulose, seed tape, porous rubber sheeting, and various paint pigments. This sum covered only laboratory supplies and salaries, and no engineering, sales, or administrative costs.

To keep such research "losses" to a minimum and insure in every way possible the development of successful products, 3M has constantly reorganized laboratory research until today, when new ideas come up, they are given part or all of the following treatment. An idea may be rejected at any of these stages:

A basic research group explores the fundamental facts pertaining to a new idea. Another, the product development group, puts these facts to work by reducing the theoretical idea to reality. At this stage, the sales department is called in for consultation as to whether the product has a potentially profitable market. Next, the experimental product group takes over, and ideas are tested in a pilot plant operation. Then the quality control division of the laboratory establishes manufacturing specifications for the product and sets up inspection standards to assure customers of uniform and high quality. Finally, the technical sales and service branch of research takes the product to the sales department outside of the laboratory and to carefully selected customers for criticism. Possible markets are surveyed and new ideas suggested for use of the product.

Such a brief description gives a rather cold, unrealistic picture of 3M's laboratory activities, however, for it makes it appear that the drama and excitement of the good old days are gone, and that nothing is left but a kind of textbook type of research which rules out error and interesting experiences. Nothing could be further from the truth. While it is true that some of the guesswork which caused the chaos of early days has been eliminated, there is no less thrill, no less drama, in modern product development than there was with waterproof sandpaper or tapes. Take, for example, the story of one of 3M's most recent products, SCOTCH Brand magnetic sound-recording tape. Behind the development of this tape is the same kind of story which has characterized all 3M's major products. It is a story of ingenuity, patient research, human error, relentless sales efforts, and cooperation among departments.

3M began research on a magnetic sound-recording tape in 1944 in a very casual manner. A few men in the tape laboratory became intensely interested in developing a magnetic tape to replace wire. They visualized many uses for it, especially in the fields of education, business, and music. Also, it looked like a product which could advantageously be marketed through the electrical tape division's sales force. Their enthusiasm eventually persuaded management that such a product had a future. Within five years, with the aid of Central Research, the tape laboratory produced a magnetic recording tape which has been given a substantial share of the credit for revolutionizing the basic sound recording techniques of the radio, phonograph record, and motion picture industries. But, as always, before success there were uncertainties, differences of opinion, many difficult technical problems, and months of research before the tape was perfect enough to be marketed. There were heavy research charges, too, before the tape finally developed into a multimillion-dollar product earning its own way.

In making magnetic sound-recording tape, the challenge to 3M scientists was to improve on one of the oldest-known methods for transcribing sound–the magnetic principle. In spite of the fact that this principle has been known for more than half a century, little commercial exploitation of it had been made in the United States until after World War II.* Until the middle '40s, sound records were made principally by cutting grooves in a wax or similar surface.

Recording sound on wire was experiencing a brief period of popularity when 3M began experiments in recording sound on paper and plastic tape coated with a magnetic medium. The military had found wire recording successful where discs failed, particularly in recording conversation in aircraft and other moving vehicles, for training purposes, and in intelligence work. A few experimental home wire-recorders had been made.** But the boom expected in wire

---

*The first magnetic recorder had been invented before the turn of the century by Valdemar Poulsen, a Dane. The machine, which recorded sound on wire, had won its inventor the Grand Prix at the 1900 Paris Exposition. Poulsen's recorder, invented almost simultaneously with the shellac phonograph record, had no way electronically to amplify the sounds being recorded; therefore the playback was faint and could be heard only through earphones.

**The first magnetic recorder ever sold commercially in the United States was the Soundmirror, first marketed in 1937. This machine recorded only one minute of sound on steel tape and was used in voice training and other experimental ways.

recording did not develop, because of the advent of magnetic tape for recording.

Tape as a medium for recording by the magnetic principle got its start in Germany in the '30s. An instrument called the Magnetophone was invented there which could produce high-fidelity recordings on magnetic plastic tape instead of wire. A United States task force of scientists investigating the German plastics industry after VE Day uncovered this major German development and later brought it to America.[1]

The Magnetophone, cooperatively developed between *Allgemeine Elekrizitäts-Gesellschaft*, Berlin, and *I.G. Farbenindustrie, A.G.*, Ludwigshafen, was not entirely unknown to United States engineers, but the machine as known before World War II had not been a perfected instrument. The Magnetophone, using tape, found in Germany after VE Day technically surpassed any development with wire in the United States. Although the human ear can hear 15,000 cycles, wire recorders had a maximum frequency response of only 5,000 cycles per second, the best prewar phonograph records about 8,000, and many home radios and recorders less than 5,000. Tape recordings produced by the Magnetophone recorded 10,000 cycles (later stepped up to 15,000) with low distortion, uniform signal strength, and little "wow" or "flutter."* While experimental wire recorders had been developed in the United States with a frequency response equal to that of the Magnetophone, tape surpassed wire for recording in one respect. Plastic tape wouldn't tangle and could be edited simply by cutting out pieces with scissors, and taping it back together with transparent tape. U.S. scientists learned that even syllables of words or a single note of music could be clipped out.

---

*"Wow" and "flutter" are sound-recording terminology for the wavering in a sustained note caused by fluctuating speed of the phonograph turntable or other playing device.

The U.S. task force learned, too, that the Magnetophone had been in general use for some time. Among those using it were the German radio networks and the German military. The latter used it for fixed-station recording of propaganda, orders, and news; for mobile communication from jolting vehicles and ships where disc recordings fail; and in haversack-size units for front line listening posts. The Germans had experimented with plastic tapes as early as 1932 and had developed a practical tape by 1939 which supplanted steel tapes at the beginning of the war.

While in Germany between May and September, 1945, the U.S. scientists studied the performance and principles of the Magnetophone, and brought back samples of the equipment and tape. Some members of the team were so enthusiastic about the machine and tape that they instigated the development of American versions. All patents on the machine and its plastic tape were held by the U.S. Alien Property Custodian and relevant U.S. patents were available for licensing. Any company wishing to copy the Magnetophone consequently was able to do so. Among others, 3M studied the construction of the German tape through various scientific reports and felt they could produce a superior tape. This confidence proved to be well-based and 3M is given credit for being the first United States firm to master the production of high quality magnetic sound-recording tape.

All of the common production problems of tape manufacture came up on the new project, and a few additional ones peculiar to magnetic sound-recording tape. The three most challenging were to find the best magnetic iron oxide, to develop a method of dispersing the iron oxide which would assure uniform high fidelity and low noise level, and to work out a coating technique which would lay the dispersed oxide down on the backing to the necessary rigid specifications for thickness and uniformity. In coating other products, the most accurate 3M had to be was to keep the thickness down to .010" with a tolerance of plus or minus .001". For magnetic sound-recording tape, the iron oxide had to have a uniform thickness of .0005" with a tolerance of plus or minus .00001".

Too, the slitting of the tape from the original 24-inch, jumbo roll into narrow strips had to be so perfectly performed that the edges of the tape would not be damaged. If, in slitting, the oxide pattern deposited on the tape were disturbed, there would be distortion when electrical impulses were recorded and played back.

In addition, special electronic equipment had to be designed to test the recording quality of the tape while being coated in the jumbo rolls. This quality-control problem was far more complicated than any encountered with pressure-sensitive tapes. Obviously, poor quality *had* to be caught in the production stage, or there would be disaster later when a customer found the tape had failed to record an important meeting or radio show properly.

In the early years of production, 3M had a unique sales problem with magnetic tape. Until 1948, no one could decide just where sales effort should be concentrated. There was one difficulty no matter which field was chosen: No machines were available for using magnetic tape. 3M didn't want to make sound-recording machines, and many machine manufacturers were willing to proceed only if 3M guaranteed to make tape. The only course was to decide which field was most promising and then work out the venture as a whole with various machine manufacturers.

Between 1945 and 1948, 3M was in the position of the proverbial child with a penny to spend in a candy store. Several prospects looked bright and the company was uncertain which market would bring in the best return on an investment. Some of management thought effort should be concentrated on the home recording field, which wire recording had never captured. Others believed that the future for magnetic sound-recording tape was in industrial recording where high quality work is imperative, the radio and movie industries, for example. So far discs had been used for almost all professional recording work, in spite of developments with wire-recording and photographic sound tracks. There appeared to be a tremendous future, too, in the electronic computing field; scientists had already experimented with the use of magnetic tape in various machines instead of punch cards.

The horizon appeared almost limitless, provided proper machines could be developed simultaneously with the tape. Management consulted outside sound-recording and electronics authorities on the future possibilities for magnetic tape and found as many diverse opinions as within 3M. One outside scientist even predicted the day might come when a photoelectric transmitting typewriter, activated by sound-recording tape, would do away with stenographers and secretaries!

The result of 3M's uncertainty was that it developed a high quality tape before anyone got into production of the necessary recording and reproducing machinery to go with it. At this point, Vice-president Carlton wrote the laboratory, "Research is running around $23,000 a month. Isn't it time to curb research expenditures until the business end is clarified?" President McKnight agreed with Carlton and strongly recommended that a simultaneous effort be made to cooperate with machine manufacturers, to develop tape for home recorders and for professional sound-recording in the radio field, and to sell the phonograph record companies on making their masters on tape instead of discs. From this point, developments were speedy. By 1951, through the cooperative efforts of sound-recording machine manufacturers, electronics engineers, and others, 3M succeeded in developing a market in all these fields and others as well.

Industry found the tape useful for recording dictation, informal conferences and important meetings. Executives used it to improve their speaking techniques. Innumerable uses were developed in sales work. Enterprising retailers broadcasted tape-recorded sales talks to customers as they browsed through their stores. Reporters, psychiatrists, policemen, private detectives, and many others discovered tape recording a valuable tool for gathering data. Schoolteachers and music instructors found it useful for educational purposes. Tape, as predicted, was put to use for storing information in the same manner as punch cards. For example, census information has been recorded on tape and run through electronic computers. The information was first recorded on punch cards, then transferred to tape for running through the computer. Performance data on guided missiles and other aircraft can be recorded on tape by means of pulse recording. The advantage of tape for storing information is that it takes up far less space than even punch cards. In the long run, it means industry will need only filing cabinets compared to warehouses for storing recorded information.

By 1952, tape had gained popularity over wire because of its greater ease in handling. It can be edited with scissors and tape, and it does not tangle should it accidentally spin from the spool. It can be played over and over without loss of fidelity and the sound can be erased and the tape re-used.

3M's sound-recording tape division feels that Bing Crosby gave the new product its real start through his promotion of the use of tape on radio networks. After World War II, Bing decided he wanted to record his hourly dinner show. In spite of its horror of "canned" shows, the American Broadcasting Company agreed to let him do so. The first attempts to record on discs verified their fears, how ever, that transcribing the program would harm the broadcast. The results were poor because of cutting and editing difficulties with discs. Crosby, unwilling to go back to live broadcasts, looked for a better method and learned of the work being done with magnetic recording by Jack Mullin, one of the men who had been on the Quartermaster plastics team which had investigated the Magnetophone and other German developments. Mullin was working for William Palmer Company, San Francisco, prominent film-processing laboratories.

The rest is radio history. Mullin recorded Crosby's shows with the Magnetophone equipment he had brought back from Germany, and the success of his recordings for Crosby dispelled any fears that a transcribed show need be any less effective than a live broadcast.

"The success of the Crosby show opened the door for 3M into the radio industry," relates a tape executive. "Bing persuaded ABC to buy 24 Ampex machines for use in recording the time-delayed broadcasts. Ampex needed help on tape problems and called in 3M. Cooperatively, 3M, Ampex, ABC, and Crosby Enterprises developed the best-possible equipment for recording Bing's shows. ABC saved enough money over discs in a year to pay for their initial investment in the machines, and the shows were such a success that 3M magnetic sound-recording tape was 'made.' Our sales increased materially after that."

By the early '50s, uncertainty over the proper direction for research and sales efforts was over. By pushing efforts in all established fields such as radio, home recording, industry, and movies, sales were boosted from less than a half-million dollars annually to over four million in 1953.

Part of this increase in sales was also due to 3M's success in persuading the movie industry to make its primary sound-recording track with magnetic film rather than by optical recording. Magnetic film was another development of the sound-recording division. With the optical system, in which sound waves are recorded on photographic film, a delay is often experienced while the film is being developed to determine whether retakes are necessary. Magnetic film can be played back immediately, unsuitable sections cut out, and a new recording made with little delay. Today, more than 99 percent of the movie industry's primary sound takes are recorded by means of 35 mm. magnetic sound-recording film.

The advent of three-dimensional movies boosted tape sales, too, for scientists from Minnesota Mining were in on the ground floor of this development. They worked closely with the movie industry on stereophonic sound. Cinerama producers, for example, found that a single sound track was completely ineffective for the big screens. They found further that 3M's fully coated, perforated, magnetic film could be used to record up to seven sound tracks instead of the usual one, and by combining these tracks they could make the sound seem to emanate from the exact point of origin on the huge screen. Such stereophonic sound is particularly effective in scenes where there are storms, special music, or other special sound effects.

During 1953-54, the Magnetic Tape Division introduced three variations of their original sound-recording products: High output tape, extra play tape, and a partially coated, striped 35 mm. tape.

The first, the "High-output," is of the same thickness as previous tapes but has two to three times the signal output, a valuable feature for stereophonic recording and recording where low distortion is required. "Extra Play" tape was made with a 50 percent thinner coating, and 30 percent thinner backing so that twice as much tape could be wound on a given reel. For example, this gives a forty-five-minute in place of a thirty-minute reel, and allows the continuous recording of such major musical works as Beethoven's *Emperor Concerto.* Coating weight of this new "Extra Play" tape is .00038, and its tolerance is plus or minus .000005. The third variation, the striped 35 mm. not fully coated, is for use in the motion picture and television industries, where sound must be matched with picture images.

Les Paul and Mary Ford listen to one of their latest hits on "SCOTCH" Brand magnetic recording tape, the product that made their multiple-recording technique possible.

3M coated abrasives perform many tough abrading jobs in industry. Company laboratories, in close cooperation with machinery builders, have developed many new methods for utilizing abrasive belts. Shown above is an abrasive belt backstand machine operation which has replaced the conventional grinding wheel in numerous industries.

"SCOTCH" Brand sandblast stencil, a thick, pressure-sensitive, rubbery material, makes the job of lettering on granite, marble, metal, plastics, and glass easy and accurate.

In World War II, "SAFETY-WALK" Brand non-slip surfacing helped planes make a safe landing on all-metal carrier decks. This waterproof material also has many industrial uses.

When used on highway directional signs, "SCOTCHLITE" Brand reflective sheeting makes night driving safer and easier. 3M "CENTERLITE" Brand reflective compound makes the center dividing line clearly visible and helps decrease night accidents.

Reflectorized school buses add to children's safety on dark highways. A vehicle marked with "SCOTCHLITE" Brand reflective sheeting is visible to other motorists at night up to a quarter of a mile away.

Festooned coated abrasives on their way through conditioning ovens in a 3M factory. Temperature, humidity, and the speed of movement are carefully controlled to "cure" the finished product properly.

All have sold well, but the "Extra Play" tape in particular helped raise the division's sales to a new high. Successes like this make SCOTCH Brand sound-recording tape and film the kind of diversified products management likes best–those with a good sales future.

Another modern product with an eventful history and a promising future is "SCOTCHLITE" reflective sheeting which makes highway signs more visible to motorists at night than anything in the history of highway safety; the product which makes it possible for a highway speed limit sign to read "60" in daytime and "50" at night by its magiclike reflecting power. Not only does the story of SCOTCHLITE reflective sheeting illustrate perfectly the talent, time, and money it takes to develop a successful product, but it also covers an important part of the highway safety efforts America has been making ever since the automobile began showing signs of being a dangerous plaything.

SIGNS FOR SAFETY

FIFTY-ODD YEARS AGO, when America climbed into the automobile and began going places, she learned in a hurry that what was good enough for the horse and buggy wouldn't do at all for the horseless carriage.

Signposts, for example.

The rustic, arrow-shaped boards, hand-lettered and nailed to a tree or wagon wheel at the side of the road, had been adequate for directing the leisurely horse-and-buggy traveler to the next village or crossroad, but they didn't do at all for the automobile driver. As he rolled past in his Duryea, Peerless, or Locomobile at a speedy ten or fifteen miles an hour, he could hardly read the lettering in the daytime, and at night, not at all. A change was definitely needed!

Bellamy Partridge, in his entertaining history of the automobile, *Fill 'Er Up,* describes those early days:*

Knowing the way, in the early days of the automobile was important, for road signs were few and far between. The old horse and buggy signboards were almost invariably weather-beaten,

*Reprinted by permission of the publisher from *Fill 'Er Up* by Bellamy Partridge. Published by the McGraw-Hill Book Co., Inc., New York City. Copyright, 1952, by the McGraw-Hill Book Co., Inc.

and in need of repainting. If a signpost rotted and fell, or a board was knocked off by a boy with a rock, the local population was likely to take the attitude that by this time everybody knew the way, so why bother to make repairs.

The only signs that gave any indication of distance, relates Partridge, were those which told you how far it was to some specific store. "The countryfolk, with their intimate familiarity with local landmarks, paid little or no attention to their signboards and probably never missed them if they collapsed and were carried away. The city motorist, however, accustomed to a street sign on every corner, began to feel lost when he passed beyond the city limits. From the first, he had his troubles in finding his way beyond his own immediate neighborhood, and for some years, the picture of the lost and strayed tourist puzzling over unwieldy maps and scrutinizing illegible signboards with the assistance of a match had been popular subjects for jokesmiths."

In those slow-moving days of the horse and buggy, there wasn't much need for safety signs, day or night, to tell the driver to stay on his own side of the road or to warn him of a sharp curve or hill. But when the horse gave way to the high-powered motor car, the need for safety signs which could be easily seen both day and night became urgent—more and more so each year as car horsepower increased and roads were improved. The mounting injuries and death toll from car accidents were grim warning that a more adequate way must be found to warn drivers of danger, especially at night.

In the early 1900s, the problem of making the highways safer was tackled by the newly organized automobile clubs, federal and state highway engineers, and local civic groups. Experiments were made with danger and directional signs to find a way to make them readable both day and night from a moving car, resistant to weather, and economical to maintain. Gradually, the manufacturing of highway signs became an exact art requiring a corps of trained workers, instead of the work of a local artisan. Many state and county highway departments started their own sign manufacturing shops. In a short time, scientifically perfected signs took the place of old road guides; crude boards gave way to painted metal signs, and, in the early '20s, white porcelain or baked enamel signs with black lettering were found to be the most readable by day and night and the most economical investment.

Next, a federal committee to standardize highway markings was organized, and soon signs throughout the country were of uniform shape and color so motorists traveling from one state to another could immediately recognize the meaning of a sign. Octagonal signs meant a full stop; round ones gave advance warning of railroad crossings; horizontal and vertical rectangular-shaped signs contained general information, directions, and regulations. Little by little, lettering on signs was increased from a tiny two-inch to a readable twelve-inch height. Stripes were painted down the center of the road to divide driving lanes and instruct the motorist not to pass in dangerous places. The stripes were white or yellow, the two colors most visible day and night.

But all this progress didn't solve the hazards of night driving, for even the improved, standardized signs were not sufficiently visible at night to motorists traveling thirty and forty miles an hour. They could only be seen when the motorist was virtually on top of them—too late to heed the warning message. Highway safety engineers struggled daily with the problem. Legislators tried to help by passing regulations designed to curb accidents, but often these laws were hastily enacted and not too well thought out. For example, one county board forbade the use of a car after nine o'clock at night! Editors across the country tried to help curb the mounting death toll by warning drivers to be more careful and pointed out that the "white dividing line is not enough; there must also be driver courtesy."[1] In spite of all efforts, the problem became more acute.

Not until 1921 was a significant contribution made toward improving visibility of highway signs at night. In that year, a new type of sign was introduced which was several times more visible at night than a white, painted sign. On the new signs, the lettering was outlined with small, faceted glass or plastic reflector buttons which picked up the light from approaching headlights, and reflected back the message to the motorist, warning that he was approaching a dangerous curb, a slippery section, or a grade. These "cat eyes," or "road eyes" as they were called, were soon used in all types of highway signs and also in center striping, and are still in use today.

It was soon evident, however, that reflector-button signs only partially solved the problem. There were some technical drawbacks which impaired their efficiency. While the buttons definitely made the sign more visible, they reflected so *much* light that the lettering looked blurred to the motorist, and often he could not make out the message. Secondly, even though the message was more visible, the shape of the sign still was not discernible at night. Consequently, the sign lost its specific meaning for the motorist who had been trained to recognize shape as well as lettering. Thirdly, the amount of lettering which could be put on a sign with reflector buttons was limited because of their size. This type of sign was troublesome to highway maintenance engineers, too, as snowplows often knocked out the "eyes" or they were accidentally dislodged in other ways, and had to be replaced by hand.

So even though the reflector buttons were a decided improvement over plain enamel signs from a night-visibility standpoint, their disadvantages caused highway safety engineers to continue to look for a still more effective method for making night driving safer.*

*The cost of reflector button vertical highway signs was high. One STOP sign cost around $12 installed, and therefore, they were put up at only highly critical danger spots.

In the late '30s, Minnesota Mining and Manufacturing Company found such a method. 3M's expanded research program had been under way only a short time when the company joined in the search for a way to make night driving less hazardous. Its laboratory produced a dramatic new type of material which made highway signs more visible at night than ever before. The product was "SCOTCHLITE" Brand reflective sheeting, familiar now to motorists all over the world.

At first, SCOTCHLITE sheeting was used on only a few signs here and there across the country. Today, it is used on all types of highway signs, and to mark all kinds of danger spots for the night motorist: curbs, bridge abutments, road blocks, detour signs, road posts on dangerous curves. Trucks and transportation buses have reflectorized emblems on the back and side panels which increase their visibility to other motorists at night and at the same time advertise their company or product. The Great Northern Railroad has reflectorized their mountain goat emblem on freight cars. Bicycle fenders and car bumpers have been reflectorized to increase the safety of night driving. License plates in several states are now made with this 3M product. Thousands of multicolored advertising signs glowing at night along the road are made with it. Traffic policemen mark their clothing with this sheeting so they can be more easily seen. And more uses are being found every day.

The development story of SCOTCHLITE reflective sheeting is perhaps one of the most vivid examples in 3M's history of how, when an idea takes form, the embryonic product has to be shaped and reshaped to produce a marketable, profitable commodity. It is a perfect example of how the various departments within 3M cooperatively help develop an idea from the dream stage to the cash register.

By 1937, 3M's interest in product research and development was well known in its home city, and at a St. Paul

Exchange Club luncheon in June, a Ramsey County (Minnesota) highway official talked to a 3M sales executive about a market he thought the company should investigate. "There's a good business waiting for any company that can make a highway center striping which will be more visible at night than white or yellow paint," he advised. "Why couldn't the Mining coat some of that Wausau quartz with a luminous paint, or something?" He went on to tell about an experiment Ramsey County was conducting with a new kind of center striping made by sprinkling glass beads on the painted stripe. "You know the kind of beads they put on movie screens and lamp shades?" he asked. "Well, that's the kind used for this center striping. First the dividing line is painted, and while the paint is still wet, these tiny beads are sprinkled into the paint. At night motorists can see this beaded stripe about three times better than white paint because the beads reflect light from the headlights.

"With all its research facilities, the Mining ought to be able to make a brighter stripe than that," said the Ramsey County official. "It's got to be brighter, or highway departments won't be interested."

The 3M sales executive listened carefully and immediately passed the suggestion on to the roofing granules laboratory be cause of its experience with the weathering qualities of paint pigments. This laboratory was not equipped to work on a project so far afield from roofing granules, however, and did little with the idea. They pointed out that the suggestion for coating Wausau quartz with luminous paint was impractical because the paint would have insufficient weather resistance and would be scarcely more visible at night than ordinary white paint.

But the "glass beads" idea did stir the imagination of an abrasives engineer working in the laboratory next door to the roofing granules laboratory. With the center striping idea in mind, he began experimenting with making glass beads by dropping molten glass on a motor-driven paddle.

The more he thought about it, the more he felt that 3M could make a highway center striping with glass beads, just as the Ramsey County official had suggested. His enthusiasm spread to other laboratory workers.

By late summer of 1937, the engineer and his fellow laboratory workers had concocted 3M's first reflective product, a prefabricated highway center striping made by covering one side of double-coated* SCOTCH Brand cloth tape with tiny, glass beads and leaving the other tacky side free for cementing to the pavement. This first crude glass-beaded tape, an unsuccessful product, led to the development of SCOTCHLITE reflective sheeting.

Research on such products as tape had been rather quiet, though technically challenging, experiences, confined mostly to the laboratory. But experiments on the new center striping had to be made under actual operating conditions, which meant going outdoors on actual pavement to test its visibility and adhesion characteristics in all kinds of weather and under heavy traffic. Consequently when an experiment failed, everybody knew it, and there were plenty of failures.

Experiments on beaded center striping began in the spring of 1937, soon after the Exchange Club meeting. As the first step in any research project is to find out what has already been done, 3M was curious to see the experiment mentioned by the Ramsey County official. But unfortunately, for business reasons he wouldn't disclose on what street in the county the stripe had been painted. All he would say was that the beads used were from Czechoslovakia as there was no domestic source of the necessary small size (.015" in diameter). The abrasives engineer had no choice but to start hunting for the experiment. Days of cruising the streets after his regular work was done

*Tape coated with pressure-sensitive adhesive on both sides.

disclosed the stripe a few miles from the 3M plant on Edgerton Avenue. The next job was to find the domestic outlet for the glass beads. It took a letter to the Czechoslovakian consul in Washington to produce this information, and also the advice that they were hard to get because of importing difficulties.

Examination of this glass bead stripe which had been put down in 1936 revealed that it was in good condition after a Minnesota winter and after considerable traffic had passed over it. It was about three times brighter than white paint, but not as visible as reflector button center-lining from the same distance. Microscopic inspection of the stripe showed that the beads were coated quite sparsely in the paint and were so submerged in the opaque paint that only about 10 percent of each bead was exposed and could reflect light.

The 3M engineer felt certain his company could do better, and after investigation showed the market for such a material was practically untouched, began experimenting. Inasmuch as it was learned that other firms were thinking along the same lines, every effort was made to hurry this glass beads project.

As mentioned, the company's first reflective item was a center striping made by coating glass beads on double-coated cloth tape. 3M chose this method of manufacture because of its know-how on coating processes, and with the thought that the tape could be rolled down on the pavement with some sort of mechanical dispenser.

The first practical test of this tape was made November 24, 1937, on a new one-way street in St. Paul at Victoria Street and Marshall Avenue. Rectangular pieces were spaced five feet apart down the center of the pavement to direct motorists where to turn. Preliminary inspections a few days later showed that the strips reflected considerable light and were standing up under traffic. Things looked very promising and 3M was proud of its new product—at first. In the spring of 1938, plans were made to show the experiment to a customer, a supplier of sign and road materials to high way departments. A group of 3M executives took the customer to Victoria and Marshall, expecting to impress him with their prefabricated glass-beads tape. It was a most embarrassing experience. The spring thaw had loosened the strips and they were floating all over the street.

A technical lesson was learned from the experience. It was observed that the glass beads had stuck tightly to the cloth tape in spite of weather and traffic. Obviously the next step was to improve the adhesion medium for pavement. This was far from an easy task, even with the adhesive division's knowledge of cements. It was necessary to find a cement which would work in heat, cold, rain, snow, and ice, and under constant impact from traffic.

In September 1938, after studies had been made to determine proper backing, binders, and adhesives, a second major experimental installation was made. This time a three-quarter-mile strip was laid on busy Highway 61 north of 3M's plant and near St. Paul's Keller Golf course.

By now, about eight people from various departments had become interested in the glass beads project because it looked so promising. When the day came for the Highway 61 experiment, all volunteered to assist. It took all of them to do it, too, for nobody knew exactly how to go about the job. A laboratory physicist recalls that cold September day with a reminiscent smile:

"We dragged all our equipment out to the spot on Highway 61 where we were going to work, and while a 3M photographer acted as flagman to divert traffic, the rest of us acted as technicians, laborers, and consultants! This time we used a cheap asphalt for sticking the tape to the road. We had a machine to dispense the asphalt, but the trouble was, we had no way of keeping the asphalt hot enough to go through the dispenser. The same abrasives engineer who started the glass beads project volunteered to bring buckets of hot asphalt from the plant. That's when he got into trouble. To keep the asphalt from cooling off before he reached us, he had to step on the gas a bit, and about his third trip, a St. Paul policeman stopped him for speeding, but probably it's the first time anyone said they were hurrying to get hot asphalt to a highway crew. The officer thought he was crazy."

In spite of such concentrated efforts, however, this experiment was a failure. When an inspection was made three weeks later, 3M saw long strips of beaded tape waving in the breeze. Heavy traffic and frost had dislodged the tape and ruined the experiment. Discouraged, but not defeated, the volunteer crew scrambled to get another installation down before winter. This time they succeeded in laying a strip that withstood the weather. In the spring, inspection established that a beaded center striping could be satisfactory with more technical improvement. But by this time, after months of work, two facts were clear. First, a beaded center striping made with tape would be too expensive an investment for highway departments in comparison with the button-reflector type of center striping. Secondly, its brightness reflectance wasn't sufficiently greater than other methods to interest customers. Highway engineers who had seen glass bead experiments fail in the past were definitely cool to the 3M product.

Using the reflector buttons as a cost standard, the comparison in price was as follows:

Cost per mile, installed, of reflector buttons $253.00

Cost per mile, installed, of 3M beaded tape 437.00

The question now was: Should 3M continue any kind of glass bead project for highway markings? An Eastern firm was interested in cooperating with 3M on a prefabricated striping. They wished to furnish part of the raw materials and have 3M make the backing. The offer did not appeal to

Minnesota Mining as the licensing arrangement would be too complicated and unprofitable.

Vice-president Carlton, who saw possibilities in the glass beads idea and did not want to abandon it, called a conference for new suggestions. The consensus of the meeting was: Why not forget about a horizontal striping tape and work on a glass-beaded covering for vertical signs? Work on beaded center-lining was abandoned, and research begun on a reflectorized sheeting.* A few short months later, on the day Hitler invaded Poland in September 1939, the first highway signs covered with SCOTCHLITE reflective sheeting were installed to mark one of Minnesota's first cloverleaf highway intersections, and a new 3M division was on its way. Both the technical perfecting of the product and selling it were uphill jobs; it was very different from the situation with cellophane tape which the public had taken to almost immediately. But in spite of strong sales resistance and high research costs, the department grew steadily, finally earning its own way in 1947 and by 1953 grossing around $10,000,000 a year.**

SCOTCHLITE reflective sheeting is a product which has to be seen to be appreciated. It has gone through several technical refinements since 1939 to bring it to its highly perfected stage of today, but the manufacturing process has

---

*The abrasives engineer, however, never gave up on the center striping idea. Eventually, under his prodding, a reflecting compound containing glass beads was developed, and today is sold under the brand name of "CENTERLITE."

**In 1945, 3M's New Products manager, Bert S. Cross, was named general manager of the new division. Under his direction, the market for sheeting was greatly broadened and this led to the establishment on April 13, 1948 of a Reflective Products Division, with Cross as vice-president and general manager. Cross began work at 3M in 1926 as a laboratory technician, became factory manager of the Abrasives Division five years later, and New Products manager in 1942. When 3M's new division, Graphic Products, was set up in October 1952, Cross was named vice-president in charge of the division, his position today.

always remained basically the same. In nontechnical language, today's product is made by a technically tricky series of coatings: (1) A waterproof backing is covered with an opaque pigment which will reflect light. Silver will reflect the most brightly as compared to white paint; then gold, yellow, red, blue, and green, in that order. The pigment must be waterproof and must adhere to glass. (2) A coat of microscopic glass beads of high refractive index is added. The beads must be perfect spheres with no imperfections such as cracks or bubbles. The beads are about 60 percent buried in the pigment during the coating process. (3) Pigment and beads are covered with a thin coat of plastic to preserve the reflecting power of the beads and make the sheeting washable and weather resistant.

The task is to coat the pigment, beads, and plastic onto the backing in such a way that the beads will reflect the greatest amount of light back to the motorist. With SCOTCHLITE sheeting, light rays from the motorist's headlights go through the glass beads, are stopped by the pigment, and are reflected back to the driver in the form of the message on the sign and in the color of the pigment. Other types of reflecting agents either scatter the light rays or diffuse them in such a way that the message on the sign is blurred to the observer except at close range.

That first 1939 product was mediocre compared to modern SCOTCHLITE sheeting and brought little but trouble to the sales department. It was a hundred times brighter than white paint, but made only in a few colors, such as yellow, white, and silver. It was not too weather resistant. It could only be seen when light was thrown directly against it, and rain or snow cut its reflecting power considerably.

Cold weather was the worst enemy of this early product. One manufacturer put SCOTCHLITE sheeting on the side-arm stop signals for school buses so they could be seen at night and in the early morning when the driver was picking up children. Everything was fine until cold weather. When the temperature dropped, so did the reflective sheeting. It fell from the signal arms like leaves from a tree in fall. The same problem thwarted what might have been a clever safety promotion stunt sponsored by the Minnesota Safety Council. In a drive to cut down the number of car accidents, Gopher emblems made with SCOTCHLITE sheeting were distributed to car owners to symbolize the slogan, "Go For Safety." The company took a heavy ribbing on this stunt, for the emblems couldn't stand the cold weather, and became so brittle they fell off the cars. Everyone joked that the Gophers were trying to go underground to get warm.

There were other plaguing technical problems. Rain cut the visibility of a reflective sign down to only ten or fifteen times brighter than paint. This was caused by the fact that the early product had no plastic coating, and its surface of exposed beads was uneven, allowing rain to lodge between the beads and distort their reflecting power. This uneven surface caused another problem. Dirt could lodge between the tiny beads, and in a short time, the reflective sign became dirty and unsightly-looking in the daytime. Truck drivers complained that it spoiled the looks of their trucks, and so did others who bought the sheeting for advertising purposes. The dirt couldn't be washed off the sheeting once it got there.

These technical drawbacks kept the product in a semi-commercial stage until 1942. Faith in its future was so strong, however, that research and sales efforts were continued, even though there were no profits. Management gave every assistance to the new product. The little group that had sponsored its development was given laboratory space. Two salesmen were put on the road. In order to insure an adequate supply of high-quality glass beads, 3M began manufacturing its own. Central Research was responsible for the development of the high-quality bead. The manufacture of a perfect sphere, free from imperfections, in microscopic size, was a difficult technical job.

The roofing granules division contributed its knowledge on pigments so that the range of colors could be increased. The abrasive laboratory advised on coating processes. The tape and adhesives divisions contributed information on cementing agents, which were very important, because the sheeting required an especially tough adhesive to hold it to a vertical surface.

The Reflective Products Division's biggest boost and worst setback were caused by World War II. Like several other 3M products, the reflective sheeting was virtually put out of business by the war at first, but made faster progress because of the war in the long run. Supplies of two of the most important raw materials, natural rubber and resin, were cut off by the war. These losses meant that the laboratory had to start all over and develop an entirely new manufacturing method if they wanted to stay in the business. Again seeming adversity spurred the development of a superior product. The reflecting power of the sheeting was increased, and the angle at which it would pick up light rays was widened. More colors were perfected. The new type of wide-angle sheeting, now two hundred times brighter than white paint, was used extensively in America's defense program. In fact, almost all sheeting produced during the war was used by the military. During the war, through the aid of government contracts, annual gross sales of reflective sheeting earned the new group the right to become a division (1943).* After the war, efforts were resumed to increase the use of SCOTCHLITE reflective sheeting for highway safety and in the highly competitive outdoor advertising field.

In spite of its obvious value for road markings, highway departments were slow to purchase the new product for a good reason. A great deal of money was tied up in stocks of

*In 1948, SCOTCHLITE reflective sheeting was put under the new Reflective Products Division, and in 1952, reflective products, including SCOTCHLITE sheeting, were put under the new Graphic Products Division.

conventional metal signs and highway officials felt they could not afford new equipment until this supply was used up. This obstacle was partially overcome by 3M engineers who worked out arrangements for combining stock metal signs and reflective sheeting. For example, a way was devised to cement a panel saying "STOP" across the center of an octagonal metal sign. In this way the message could be seen at night, even though the shape and color of the sign were not too visible. Today, of course, entire signs are faced with SCOTCHLITE reflective sheeting and color, shape, and message are all clearly visible.

Through the medium of a subsidiary, the National Advertising Company, sales for outdoor advertising signs were increased, and the public was made aware of the product. This subsidiary was purchased in 1947.

Manufacturing problems were eased after the war by the building of a special plant south of St. Paul near Hastings, Minnesota, in 1949.

One of the biggest aids to sales was a major technical improvement in 1949, which it had taken six years of research to accomplish. To overcome the drawbacks of dirt lodging between the exposed beads and rain cutting down the reflecting power of the sheeting, a thin layer of transparent plastic was coated over the glass beads. This one step so greatly improved the product that 3M was able to get into markets they had never been able to capture. The addition of the plastic gave the sheeting a smooth, enamel-like finish which resists dirt, takes any graphic arts process of reproduction, and keeps rain and snow from cutting the reflecting power of the beads. Pictures can be printed on this new variation. It can be washed, polished, spray-coated, screen-processed, or brushed with color. In 1951, a wide-angle, smooth-surfaced sheeting was produced and ways of sticking it to surfaces were improved through the use of pressure-sensitive adhesives.

All these improvements materially speeded the trend toward reflective sheeting for both safety and outdoor advertising purposes. Other developments helped increase sales, too. Spurred by such safety campaigns as "Lite a Bike," and "Lite a Bumper" sponsored by Junior Chamber of Commerce clubs all over the nation, thousands of Americans striped the fenders of their children's bicycles and the bumpers of their own cars to make them more visible to motorists at night. Eight state legislatures have now authorized the use of reflective sheeting on license plates or license stickers: Connecticut (first, in 1947), Maine, Delaware, Rhode Island, Missouri, Washington, Oregon, and Indiana.

In the early '50s, 3M offered highway officials a solution to one of the traffic control problems that had bothered them for many years. The company suggested that its red sheeting be used on STOP signs instead of yellow. This idea was not new, but the fact that 3M had a red which could be seen at night, was new. In 1924, red had been recommended as the national standard for STOP signs, but in those days, no one could produce a red paint which would keep its color in outdoor exposure or be seen at night on a sign. As a result, yellow had to be used for STOP signs and this led to the confusion of having red mean stop at some intersections where semaphores were in operation, and yellow mean stop at other intersections where painted signs were installed. In the '40s 3M had begun work on a red material which would retain its color and give high reflectance at night, but not until the early '50s were the desired results achieved. A red was finally developed which could be seen by a driver from more than a block away under low beam headlights, and more than a quarter of a mile with high beams.

In June 1953, the Joint Committee on Uniform Traffic Control Devices proposed this red STOP sign as the national standard to its parent groups–the American Association of State Highway Officials, Institute of Traffic Engineers, and

National Conference of Street and Highway Safety. Subsequently the three groups voted in favor of adopting the sign and the Joint Committee then ordered it written into the Manual of Uniform Traffic Control Devices, which is the guidebook generally followed by the states. The use of these red signs is rapidly expanding in many states and metropolitan areas.

The future for SCOTCHLITE reflective sheeting is exceptionally promising. Millions of danger spots on highways all over the world are still inadequately marked, and while visible safety markings are not the only answer to reducing smashups, common sense dictates that a warning sign which can be seen is more effective than one which can't, and a danger spot which is marked can be avoided better than one which isn't. The greater the distance at which an object is visible to the motorist, the more time he has to act to avoid an accident.

As for the possibilities in the road advertising field, "They are limitless," says 3M, if we keep on improving our product technically and work as hard as in the past."

AFTER PEARL HARBOR

FOR 3M, as well as others, the '40s were turbulent, trying years. But despite such obstacles as war, shortages, legal complications, high taxes, and crowded working conditions, the decade was the most progressive in the company's history.

The first and greatest challenge of the '40s was World War II. Even before December 7, 1941, an ever-growing percentage of 3M's production was going into defense use. When the United States was plunged into combat, the company directed its full energy and resources towards the war effort. Primarily this called for steadily increased production of 3M's standard products rather than the manufacture of new military products; for the factories which had needed abrasives, tapes, adhesives and other 3M products to turn out civilian goods in peacetime needed these same items in increased quantity to manufacture the instruments of war.

Even though more than 2,000 3M people had gone on military leave by 1945, plant personnel, with women carrying an increasingly heavy share of the duties, kept up to very heavy production schedules. Millions of dollars' worth of standard 3M products were made in that period, and the laboratories developed and the plants manufactured additional items specifically for military use. Coated abrasives and pressure-sensitive tapes were produced for use by manufacturers of planes, ships, jeeps, and artillery. Shipbuilders used 3M sealer in laying decks. Roofing granules were produced in camouflage colors for use on the roofs and sidings of military installations.

Among the products manufactured for war was "SAFETY-WALK" Brand non-slip sheeting, a granular coated material used to make walking safe on ship decks, airplane wings, and other surfaces made hazardous by oil, water, or other substances; a special cellulose tape to bond the seams of the plastic capes issued to all servicemen in areas subject to possible enemy poisonous gas attack; and Oleum (109 percent or fuming sulfuric acid) which was manufactured at Copley, Ohio under subcontract with the Trojan Powder Company for use in the production of explosives and high octane gasoline.

Most dramatic, perhaps, were the special wartime uses made of SCOTCHLITE Brand reflective sheeting. To mention just a few, reflective strips were put on the paddles for life rafts for downed airmen to use to attract the attention of rescuers; military highway signs were reflectorized to guide drivers under semiblackout conditions; reflectorized markers were set up along unlighted airstrips so that pilots needed only to flash their lights on momentarily to make the markers visible enough to delineate the runways.

The most difficult problem for 3M to overcome during the war was the shortage of raw materials, particularly natural rubber which was needed to make adhesives for pressure-sensitive tapes, reflective sheeting, and other products. The company partially solved this shortage by purchasing the Inland Rubber Corporation of Chicago, a tire manufacturer, for its rubber quota, putting 3M in the tire business for a short time. But even with Inland's quota, the laboratories were forced to look for rubber substitutes in order to produce even defense supplies. Such items as the short roll of cellophane tape and reflective sheeting for highway signs were produced only for military use. Minnesota Mining made another important contribution to the defense effort by helping the United States increase its output of synthetic rubber during the war years. In 1942, 3M joined four other companies to form the National Synthetic Rubber Corporation for the purpose of operating a $6,000,000, government-owned synthetic rubber plant in Louisville, Kentucky. Two 3M executives served as the corporation's executive vice-president and general manager, and vice-president and treasurer, and its technical staff was drawn primarily from 3M's research organization. By utilizing experience gained through long years of peacetime research at 3M, these men helped the National Synthetic Rubber Corporation economically turn out more than sixty million pounds of high quality "Buna S" synthetic rubber a year during World War II. This was the full capacity of the Kentucky plant. 3M's part in the operation of this corporation not only gave the company another opportunity to contribute directly to the war effort, but also to acquire technical information about the manufacture and use of synthetic rubber which was to be valuable in postwar years.

As is often the case, however, the search for a substitute raw material led to better formulas for several products, including pressure-sensitive tapes, and the use of natural rubber for these items was permanently discontinued.

During these years when war production and shortages presented real challenges, another critical situation arose in the company. Early in the middle '40s, management was advised by its legal counsel that they believed a pressure-sensitive cellophane tape being sold by a Chicago manufacturer was an infringement of the basic Drew patent for SCOTCH Brand cellophane tape. The attorneys asked 3M if they wished to start suit against this concern. In the past, 3M had always avoided litigation when others had attempted infringement of various 3M patents, for McKnight's philosophy was, "Nobody wins in a law suit except the lawyers." The company hoped to avoid it in the case of International Plastic Corporation, too. President McKnight tried to work out a license agreement with the Chicago firm, but they refused to cooperate. They then warned them that a suit would be started if they did not stop infringing. When this was ignored, 3M had no alternative but to take legal action. A lawyer with a national reputation in patent litigation was retained to give an opinion. After a thorough investigation, he informed 3M, "I'd rather have your side of the case than theirs." This was enough and a patent infringement suit was started on February 16, 1944.

Minnesota Mining gambled heavily on this patent suit, for if the Drew patent were found invalid, it would be fairly simple—after 3M had pointed the way through disclosures in its patents and the example of its own manufacture—for others to duplicate its cellophane tape and actively compete for the market. On the other hand, of course, if the patent were held to be valid, International Plastic Corporation would have to stop manufacturing tape, and others would hesitate to infringe.

The case of Minnesota Mining and Manufacturing Company vs. International Plastic Corporation was heard in Chicago Federal Court from March 12 to April 10, 1945, with Judge John B. Barnes of the United States District Court, Northern District of Illinois, Eastern Division, on the bench. 3M claimed that International Plastic was infringing the Drew patent with its "Filmonize" tape, and the defendant answered that there was no invention in the manufacture of cellophane tape and further contended that Drew was not the real inventor.

Through testimony of inventor Richard Drew, and more than thirty others, 3M substantiated its claim that there was a real invention involved and that Drew was the real inventor. On May 28, 1945, Judge Barnes handed down his decision in favor of Minnesota Mining and Manufacturing Company, holding the patent valid and infringed. He issued a permanent injunction against International Plastic Corporation which restrained them from further manufacture and sale of "Filmonize" tape.

The defendant appealed the case to the United States Circuit Court of Appeals, Seventh Circuit, on July 3, 1945, and this court sustained Judge Barnes' decision as of January 9, 1947, making 3M's patent position almost invulnerable.

Meanwhile, VE and VJ Days came and management was able to turn its attention to postwar adjustments and a long-delayed expansion program.

Fortunately, conversion to peacetime production was relatively easy. Following VJ Day, there were a great many cancellations of war contracts, but on the whole, 3M had few critical adjustments in production. Almost all of the items manufactured for war also had a peacetime application. The coated abrasives, tapes, and adhesives made for defense were essentially the same as those made for normal industrial use. SAFETY-WALK non-slip products made an easy transition into industrial plants and office buildings as a safety feature as well as continuing in use on the hazardous walking surfaces of ships and airplanes. Reflective products found a vast postwar market in the highway sign and advertising fields, where it had made its start.

There were other favorable postwar developments which were the indirect result of World War II. One of the most important was the impetus given by the war to the entire coated abrasives business. Before the war, 3M engineers had designed special machinery which increased the efficiency and the cutting power of coated abrasives, but they had found it difficult to persuade industry to change over to these machines because of the need for substantial capital investment. During World War II, when the need for stepped-up production became imperative and skilled labor harder to hire, many industries adopted these machines. Many abrading departments replaced the traditional grinding and buffing wheels used to remove stock or to polish metal with a machine designed by 3M called a backstand grinder. This one change substantially promoted the use of coated abrasives on an industry-wide basis both during and after the war. In addition, industry adopted waterproof belt grinding for magnesium metal. This move eliminated the fire and explosion hazard caused by the magnesium dust created by dry abrading. Wide-belt grinders for prefinishing metal sheets before formation into parts such as car bumpers and grills found wider acceptance, and in many cases the prior method of forming the metal part and then polishing it was abandoned. Success during the war with these new abrading methods convinced industry that they should continue using them in peacetime, and this decision resulted in a substantial increase in the sale of coated abrasives after the war for 3M and other manufacturers.

The Company had really outgrown its accommodations before Pearl Harbor, and increased production for defense further in creased the need for new buildings, machinery, and office space. From 1942 through 1945 annual sales increased by more than $31,000,000, nearly doubling the 1941 volume, and with the management determined to achieve further sharp annual increases, the most immediate task facing the company was to alleviate the crowded conditions in practically all its plants, offices, and warehouses.

During the war, expansion was limited to minor additions on St. Paul abrasives buildings and Wausau roofing granules property, two new Tape buildings constructed under Certificates of Necessity, and the acquisition of one subsidiary—Mid-States Gummed Paper Company of Chicago. The latter, a manufacturer of non-pressure-sensitive, water-activated, adhesive tapes, was purchased to supplement 3M's line of pressure-sensitive tapes.

Not until 1946 was it possible to go ahead with growth plans, and in that year Minnesota Mining and Manufacturing Company undertook the largest expansion program in the firm's history. In the next four years, $30,000,000 was invested in net capital additions, exclusive of subsidiary acquisitions, with 3M's newly organized engineering department handling all major phases of the program, including the selection of sites, purchase of buildings, construction of plants, and the designing of new equipment.

In 1947, the Los Angeles adhesives and Little Rock roofing granules plants were completed, and a wartime hemp factory at Hutchinson, Minnesota was purchased from the War Assets Administration for tape-converting operations. During the next year, a large manufacturing plant in Bristol, Pennsylvania was purchased from the W.A.A. for the production of tape and adhesives. This property had been the Kaiser Cargo Fleetwings Plant No. 2. Selection of the Pennsylvania site was in keeping with 3M's desire to diversify plant locations as well as products whenever practical, and to locate in a community and state which the company felt had a tax situation favorable to corporations. Pennsylvania had no tax on individual income or on personal property, and industrial property was accorded low real estate valuations and rates.

The largest single capital addition in 1948 was a $2,000,000 plant built for the company's reflective and special products division. A block-square manufacturing building, a large warehouse, and five smaller buildings were constructed on a 250-acre tract on the Mississippi River, 17 miles southeast of downtown St. Paul and four miles northwest of Hastings, Minnesota. The equipment installed included a large furnace for making the high-quality glass needed for the tiny beads which give SCOTCHLITE sheeting its reflective power.

In 1949, work was begun on a $2,000,000 tape plant, and a former dairy building was bought to serve as a laboratory for the Products Fabrication group.

These were only the major capital additions during 1947, 1948 and 1949. During these same years a small building was built for roofing granule display, a cement house added to the Bristol property, an abrasive converting plant leased in Cumberland, Wisconsin, the Copley chemical facilities enlarged, and five advertising companies acquired. The latter included National of Westminster, Maryland, Empire of San Francisco, United Outdoor* of Long Beach, Aristocrat (Highway Displays, Inc.) of Fresno, and Lee Larson and Company of Waukesha, Wisconsin. These companies were all merged into a single subsidiary, the National Advertising Company of Waukesha.

Such tremendous expansion posed a financial dilemma for Minnesota Mining in the early postwar period. For the first time since the Baeder-Adamson purchase in 1929, the question arose as to whether expansion could be financed from within. McKnight and the board had always felt that 3M growth would be retarded if expansion were financed through repetitive sales of stocks or bonds instead of retained earnings, and before the war 3M had planned to finance its expansion of the '40s in its usual way—through investment of its surplus. With the exception of the Baeder-Adamson purchase, it had always been able to do this and still follow the policy of paying conservative dividends and maintaining a strong cash position. But even before the United States entered the war, president McKnight saw that if already-high corporation taxes were increased by war taxes, it might be necessary to borrow outside capital for postwar expansion if the payment of reasonable dividends were to be continued and the desired amount of cash kept in

*Sold on March 1, 1952 and now operating as United Outdoor Advertising Company of Long Beach, California.

the treasury. He watched the situation closely and the day after Pearl Harbor advised his staff:

"The effect of the tax liability accruing under the present Federal normal and excess profit tax law is to impair seriously our cash position."

"The possession of a large cash balance has always given us courage to make the necessary capital expenditures to develop new products and to expand to meet the requirements of a growing business. Had it been necessary in the past to borrow capital for the development of new products, it is highly probable that some of our important developments might never have been undertaken."

"Therefore, we should immediately recognize the seriousness of the situation and take whatever steps may be necessary to accumulate the most cash possible."

"Until very recently, I have felt that we should spend our money freely to build in every way for the future. I don't want to become an alarmist now, but I do believe that an alert business organization should be ready to change pace when conditions change, and I think, because of confiscatory taxation, now is the time for us to change pace."

McKnight inaugurated a twofold program for improving the cash position during the war so the company could continue to finance expansion from earnings rather than borrowing outside capital: This program included a reduction in inventories of manufactured goods and raw materials and a close control of money spent on capital account, and a reduction in operating expenses.

But in spite of such measures, the federal corporate tax structure of the '40s, which included the excess profits tax, forced 3M special stockholders' meeting. Following this, the company raised a total of $20,000,000 through the sale of $10,000,000 worth of 2¾% sinking fund debentures due in 1967, and 100,000 shares of $4 cumulative preferred stock.

This settled the financial problem, but the troubles of the '40s were not yet over. Between 1947 and 1950, two serious situations arose which required months of work to resolve. One was a need to reorganize management operations to assure the continued growth and sound health of the corporation. Another was the filing of an antitrust suit against 3M by the United States Department of Justice–the first in the company's history.

The Justice Department filed its suit on January 28, 1949, naming 3M, Behr-Manning Corporation, Carborundum Company, Armour and Company, Durex Abrasives Corporation, and the Durex Corporation as defendants. The charges were that the joint operation of Durex foreign factories restrained foreign commerce in coated abrasives. The government asked for dissolution of both Durex corporations. The legal complications created by this suit were not resolved until the early '50s after Judge Charles E. Wyzanski handed down a decision in Boston on September 14, 1950, ordering such dissolution.

REORGANIZATION

As president McKnight guided 3M through the '40s, he realized with mixed emotions that the company was developing a serious problem because of its rapidly increasing size. It was becoming more and more obvious that the system of management which had been so effective for nearly four decades was inadequate for so immense and diversified an operation. Growth was being hampered by this system of centralized authority and by company procedures which were geared to smaller operations. As the company had grown and become more diversified, those in managerial positions gradually had assumed more and more responsibility until their schedules had become far too crowded.

The latter was particularly true of president McKnight, vice-president Bush, and vice-president Carlton. McKnight's time was so absorbed by patent problems, acquisitions, foreign affairs, and the many other normal policy matters falling under a president's jurisdiction, that the hours in the day were never long enough. He seldom had time to drop into the plant or laboratories as he had done several times a week for nearly 25 years, to personally check on company progress–a habit which had contributed materially to the 3M spirit of cooperation and loyalty.

Vice-president Bush was directing not only sales but also advertising, public relations, and traffic, and he was also guiding the purchasing department. These extracurricular demands robbed him of time needed for sales management and particularly for personal contacts with his men and customers.

Vice-president Carlton had also assumed responsibilities far beyond his original sphere of activity. By the '40s, he was directing not only research, production, and engineering, but labor relations and other matters as well, and had far too little time to devote to each.

Under 3M's management system, all top executives participated directly in the development and sale of each product, with the result that responsibility for profits on each separate product was too widely divided throughout the entire organization. Gradually, each department had developed the habit of blaming someone else if profits declined. Clearly, there was a need to reorganize responsibility for profits and other operations of each separate product group.

"We had two alternatives when the time came to reorganize," explains McKnight. "We either had to continue to centralize control in a group of people in St. Paul, or to delegate authority within certain limits to a single individual in each division under a vertical type of organization. As our primary aim was to grow, we chose the latter."

"Even though we redistributed responsibilities, we would have been too big under centralized control for efficient operation and growth. Under a vertical type of organization in which divisions are given a near-autonomous status, such as our Detroit division, new divisions could be added without greatly increasing the top management load and there would be no limit to how big we could grow."

Plans for reorganization were made in the early postwar years, and the new, vertical organization was announced in April, 1948. Under the new system, executive responsibility was completely revamped. In brief, authority was redistributed as follows:

Company affairs would continue to be managed by the board of directors, working through newly created management and coordinating committees. William L. McKnight remained president, with supervision over affiliated companies. Patent counsel, the secretary and general counsel, the treasurer and controller, and the director of personnel were made directly responsible to the president.

Two executive vice-presidencies were created: (1) Executive Vice-President in Charge of Marketing and Distribution (A.G. Bush); and (2) Executive Vice-President in Charge of Production, Engineering, and Research (Richard P. Carlton). These two executive vice-presidents were given primary supervision in their respective fields of responsibility over eight product divisions newly created during 1948 under the vertical structure:

> Coated Abrasives
>
> Roofing Granules
>
> Adhesives and Coatings
>
> Central Manufacturing
>
> Color and Chemical Division
>
> Electrical Insulation and Sound-Recording Tape
>
> Pressure-Sensitive Tapes
>
> Reflective Sheeting

In setting these up, 3M drew on its experience with the Detroit Adhesives and Coatings Division which had been operating on a semi-independent basis since 1944. Each division was given its own general manager, sales force, engineering and production departments, research laboratory, and other departments necessary for unified operation. The general manager was made responsible for profits and all normal business operations of his division.

In line with long-standing policy, promotions were made from within the ranks of the company. Most of the men who were promoted had grown up with 3M, and intimately knew its early struggles and rewarding successes. Collectively, they had sold sandpaper and tape, roofing granules, adhesives, and the other products; invented products; and worked in the office or the factory. Most of them had watched and participated in the growth from a small abrasive company to a large corporation.

At the time of reorganization, president McKnight passed along to managerial employees his philosophy of management which he felt would insure the success of the new arrangement, one which he had expressed earlier to those put in charge of Detroit when it was given a large measure of independence on an experimental basis:

As our business grows, it becomes increasingly necessary for those in managerial positions to delegate responsibility and to encourage men to whom responsibility is delegated to exercise their own initiative. This requires considerable tolerance. Those men to whom we delegate authority and responsibility, if they are good men, are going to have ideas of their own and are going to want to do their jobs in their own way. It seems to me these are characteristics we want in men and [they] should be encouraged as long as their way conforms to our business policies and our general pattern of operation. Mistakes will be made, but if the man is essentially right himself, I think the mistakes he makes are not so serious in the long run as the mistakes management makes if it is dictatorial and undertakes to tell men under its authority to whom responsibility is delegated, exactly how they must do their job. If management is intolerant and destructively critical when mistakes are made I think it kills initiative and it is essential that we have many men with initiative if we are to continue to grow."

Soon after the introduction of this new system, another step was taken to enable the company to continue to grow without undue difficulty. In September, 1949, the post of chairman of the board was created, and W.L. McKnight was elected to this position. A.G. Bush was moved up from executive vice-president to chairman of the executive committee, also a new post. His committee was to be composed of the board chairman, the president, two executive vice-presidents, and the company secretary.

Then, in conformance with the principle of moving younger men up, 56-year-old Richard P. Carlton was elected 3M's fifth president. For his general staff he named two executive vice-presidents (one was in charge of sales; the other, finance and administration), and three vice-presidents in charge of research and product development, engineering and properties, and production. With the change to vertical organization, 3M was equipped to manage twenty businesses as easily as ten, which meant simply, that it could grow indefinitely.

NEW VENTURES AT HOME AND ABROAD

RICHARD CARLTON had been president less than four years when ill health made it necessary for him to resign this office on May 12, 1953. Only a few weeks later, on June 17, he died at his home in St. Paul. It was a grievous loss. During his 32 years with 3M, Carlton had built one of the outstanding industrial research teams of the United States, and in his capacity as a board member for 24 years, given invaluable counsel, particularly on product development.

Carlton's years as president were marked by a $71,000,000 increase in sales, a four-for-one stock split, and the usual steady progress in product development. But the real highlights of these four years were the ambitious expansion moves undertaken by 3M.

In rapid succession, Minnesota Mining announced: plans for a merger with Carborundum Company of Niagara Falls, New York; organization of 3M International as a means of expanding foreign sales; purchase of two more manufacturing concerns; and plans for building a $3,500,000 central research laboratory to accommodate the expansion of long-range research.

The merger with Carborundum Company, manufacturer of coated abrasives, grinding wheels, and artificial abrasives, had been under consideration many months while McKnight was president. He planned this move to give 3M better access to silicon carbide coated abrasives, grinding wheels, and artificial abrasives, as the company was purchasing more than 85 percent of the abrasive material used in the manufacture of its coated abrasives from other firms. The first disclosure of 3M's plans was made in November 1950. A joint statement was issued by 3M and Carborundum Company to the effect that a statutory merger of the two corporations was being considered, and that the merger proposal would be submitted to stockholders of both companies after approval of the plan by the respective board of directors. Stockholder meetings were tentatively set for January 1951.

Before these meetings could be held, however, new developments in the 81st Congress stopped all action. In December 1950 the Kefauver antimerger bill was passed and needed only the President's signature to become law. Counsel of both companies advised that the new bill raised a serious question as to the legality of the proposed action. They believed there was danger under the new bill that the merged operations might be interpreted as being in restraint of trade, inasmuch as both Carborundum and 3M were coated abrasive manufacturers. Immediately, merger plans were abandoned by mutual consent in view of the possible lengthy litigation which might occur.

Foreign expansion plans were more successful. After the U.S. Justice Department filed its antitrust suit against 3M and other abrasive manufacturers and ordered dissolution of all Durex operations, Minnesota Mining began the work of reestablishing and expanding foreign trade. During 1950 and 1951 the company simultaneously carried out the court's order and acquired the capital stock of the Durex English, French, and Brazilian companies and the Mexican sales company. The names of these former Durex companies were changed to Minnesota Mining & Mfg. Ltd. (England);

Minnesota de France S.A.R.L.; Minnesota Manufacturera de Mexico S.A. de C.V.; and Minnesota Manufactureira E Mercantil, Ltd. (Brazil).

Minnesota Mining also acquired the tape and adhesives and coatings assets from the Canadian company, and the tape assets of the German companies. Corporations organized in these two countries to operate these properties were called Minnesota Mining & Manufacturing Company of Canada Limited and Minnesota Mining & Manufacturing Company m.b.h. (Germany). A company was organized in Australia to manufacture tape and adhesives and coatings under the name of Minnesota Mining & Manufacturing (Australia) Pty. Limited.

Operations in all of these countries were rapidly expanded. Today, 3M's English company headquarters in Birmingham where its factory makes primarily coated abrasives; converts jumbo rolls of sandpaper into belts and other specialties at Tredegar, South Wales; produces tapes, adhesives and coatings, sealers, and reflective sheeting at Gorseinon, and magnetic recording tapes at Slough in Buckinghamshire. In addition to these four plants, regional sales offices are located in London, Birmingham, Manchester, and Glasgow, Scotland.

In France, Minnesota Mining sold the coated abrasive operation of the French Durex Company and its building in Gennevilliers and located on a 105-acre site at Beauchamps, where a modern plant was put up for manufacturing tape products.

In Canada, Minnesota Mining took over the tape and adhesives and coatings assets of the Canadian Durex Company, at Brantford, Ontario, and remained there until a suitable location for more extensive manufacturing could be found. A 100-acre tract in an industrial suburban area of London, Ontario was chosen, and on it, one of 3M's most modern and efficient foreign plants was erected to house manufacturing facilities for most of the parent company's major products.

In Germany, the company acquired the tape manufacturing facilities of the German Durex Company at Dusseldorf, including a modern building built by the Hitler regime during the war. This building was enlarged and facilities installed for making coated abrasives, a complete line of tapes, adhesives and coatings, and reflective sheeting.

Minnesota Mining's Brazilian acquisition from Durex consisted of a small building in Campinas where tape, adhesives and coatings had been manufactured. As these facilities were totally inadequate for growth plans in the country of Brazil, a 782-acre tract for a new plant was purchased near Campinas, on the main highway to Sao Paulo. The plant was built large enough to hold the old Durex equipment for manufacturing tape, adhesives, and coatings, as well as new facilities for making coated abrasives, and also to take care of future growth. In addition, sales offices were opened in Rio de Janeiro, Sao Paulo, and Porto Alegre.

The Durex Mexican Company at Mexico City acquired by 3M was very small. A general manager, three salesmen, and four office people worked in an old rented warehouse, and their principal activity was distribution of tapes, adhesives and coatings, and abrasives shipped from the United States. In the summer of 1952, Minnesota Mining found ideal plant facilities in a former tannery just outside of Mexico City, and production was started there in December 1952. 3M Mexico now employs seventy people and manufactures tapes, adhesives and coatings and converts jumbo rolls of coated abrasives shipped from the United States into abrasive specialties.

While taking over Durex plants and building new ones 3M organized the International Division with executive offices in St. Paul for the purpose of directing the operations of all foreign manufacturing plants and promoting sales

A.G. Bush, chairman of 3M's Executive Committee, presiding at a Service Award banquet for employees.

At 3M's 50th Anniversary party in 1952, W.L. McKnight, A.G. Bush and Guy Lombardo enjoyed a spin in a 1903 Ford. The music of Lombardo's Royal Canadians and an historical parade of automobiles were features of the evening's three-hour floor show.

3M's No. 6 Maker, the world's largest abrasives manufacturing plant, St. Paul, Minnesota, began operating in January 1955. The results of years of 3M research were incorporated into the building and machinery.

Artist's drawing of Central Research Building at 3M's new research center near St. Paul, Minn. The long-range scientific studies of this laboratory are part of the company's constant efforts to improve old products and discover new ones. The building was completed early in 1955.

Richard P. Carlton, 3M president 1949–1953.

3M uses two DC-3's to help integrate its widespread operations.

William L. McKnight, elected chairman of the board in September, 1949.

H.P. Buetow, elected 3M president in May, 1953.

through a sales office in New York, in all foreign countries where no manufacturing plants are owned.

This extensive foreign expansion was carried out in less than three years, and by the end of 1954, employees in foreign operations totaled 3,500, and foreign sales reached $35,000,000. The magnitude of accomplishment can best be measured by pointing out that it took the 3M parent company 35 years to develop a comparable volume in the United States, and that after twenty years of operation, the Durex Companies were doing a sales volume of $20,600,000 during their last full year of operations. 3M equity in those sales was 28 percent, or $5,700,000.

A great deal of the success of 3M's current foreign operations can be attributed to the fact that many former employees of Durex joined 3M International Division and contributed their years of experience to shaping up the new organization. This group included R.W. Young, who was president of the Durex Companies almost from the start, and later chairman of their board.*

While 3M was expanding abroad, it also acquired two more domestic companies. To help broaden its participation in the electronics field, the American Lava Corporation of Chattanooga, Tennessee was purchased and made a wholly owned subsidiary. The Irvington Varnish and Insulator Company of Irvington, New Jersey was made part of the Electrical Products Division.

American Lava Corporation manufactures an extensive line of electrical insulating materials. Located in

---

*Much credit is also due 3M's Vice-President in Charge of Production, C.B. Sampair. During the organization of 3M International, he served as a special consultant to the new division, and on January 29, 1952 became its president. Sampair began work at 3M on September 13, 1927 as a coated abrasives inspector, became superintendent of tape and coated abrasives in 1931, production manager of the St. Paul plant on January 5, 1942, and general production manager of the St. Paul branch, and subsidiary factories June 1, 1943. He was elected Vice President in Charge of Production on April 14, 1946, and today holds both this position and The Presidency of 3M International. Mr. Sampair became a director on Feb. 4, 1955.

Chattanooga, Tennessee, it is the largest plant in America devoted exclusively to the custom manufacture of technical ceramics.

Irvington Varnish and Insulator division is best known for its wide lines of insulating varnishes, varnished cloths and papers and extruded plastic insulations used in the electronics field. It also produces an extensive line of resins.

All of this expansion under President Carlton, combined with the tremendous growth of the '40s, acutely increased one longstanding need at 3M, that of more space for staff and divisional laboratories. To meet this requirement, a 125-acre tract on St. Paul's eastern boundary was purchased to accommodate a $3,500,000 laboratory for Central Research, and additional laboratories as needed for special projects. On January 15, 1953, Minnesota Mining announced that construction of the first building for the new research center would begin in the spring, and would be completed within two years.

This was the last major development before Carlton's resignation, which was submitted at the annual meeting of Minnesota Mining in May, 1953. During the remaining weeks of his life, he continued to serve as a member of the board and as vice chairman of the executive committee.

At the time of Richard Carlton's resignation, 3M again turned to its own ranks to fill the post of president. At the 1953 annual meeting, executive vice-president Herbert Paul Buetow, 55, was elected and became Minnesota Mining and Manufacturing Company's sixth president.

His election won wide approval. During his 27 years with 3M, tall, broad-shouldered Herb Buetow had gained a reputation for fair play, sound judgment, and skill in meeting challenging assignments. In his work, he had displayed an outstanding ability to delegate authority and many other characteristics essential for the complex job of heading a large corporation in the atomic age. Particularly important was his familiarity with 3M's business policies and practices, especially in the areas of finance, budgeting, and cost control.

H.P. Buetow was born in St. Paul, Minnesota on January 25, 1898, earned his B.A. degree at the University of Minnesota in 1921, and three years later, married Luella R. Witt. His entire career has been devoted to fiscal affairs. After working as an accountant in various St. Paul offices for twelve years, he joined 3M as an auditor in 1926. Subsequently he became controller in 1935, treasurer in 1939, a director in 1940, and executive vice-president in charge of finance in 1949. After the latter date, he served on the executive and finance committees.

At the time Buetow took office, 3M had a far different status in the industrial world than when he had joined the company. Statistics issued by the U.S. Government showed that for every million dollars in goods and services produced nationally in 1933, 3M's share was about $100. In 1953 the corresponding figure was roughly $500. In other words, when Buetow became president, Minnesota Mining was getting a five times larger share of the nation's business than it was during his first years with the company.

Years ago, someone remarked that "maturity" was a fighting word at 3M. Today it is still a fighting word both to the oldster in sandpaper and the youngster in ribbon; for Minnesota Mining regards itself as a young company with its greatest achievements still ahead. Through this spirit, 3M has grown from a small mining concern to a large, diversified manufacturer and has built a strong foundation for future growth. The sales volume has been increased from around $20,000 a year in 1906, 3M's first full year of manufacturing, to $230,000,000 for 1954. The company had 50 employees in 1902; today there are 17,000. At first 3M manufactured only sand paper; today the company markets 40 separate product lines and more than a thousand items within these lines. New uses and new markets for its older products are being worked out continually, and many of the newer products are considered to be still in their sales infancy.

3M's confidence in its own position in this changing world stems from an unwavering faith in its program of research and product development which through the years has produced a steady flow of new ideas to stimulate growth. Today, as in most successful corporations in America, alert and resourceful minds are at work on many frontiers—in plastics, ceramics, electronics, and chemicals, to name just a few—and unquestionably, new and valuable contributions are going to be made. Bringing these ideas along is a never-ending test of management that has long since learned that research is but the first important step of successful development. 3M's future should be bright if it continues to provide, as it has in the past, better raw materials, better tools, and better ways to make everyday jobs easier, safer, and faster.

In the challenging new field of fluorocarbon chemistry, 3M is exploring the commercial possibilities of many promising fluorochemical compounds. In plastics, the company has recently introduced two new products—a reinforced plastic sheeting, and lightweight plastic pipe—and is experimenting with many others. In the graphic arts industry 3M's leadership is being strengthened by presensitized offset plates for lithographers, a special process for copying printed material, and scientists are working on new methods for letterpress printing. Ceramics, photography, atomic energy—these subjects, too, interest Minnesota Mining today, and its researchers are working in still other fields.

The effect of all this activity on 3M's future cannot be accurately predicted, of course, but the leaders of this company aim to grow "just as big as we can grow," and not only do they believe it, they are preparing for it. As in all outstanding growth companies, its people are exploring tomorrow's wants today with the determination to be able to serve these needs just as quickly as possible.

PRODUCT GROWTH

1946-1955

Reflective compounds
Duplicating machines and papers
Tile and construction adhesives and compounds
Marine adhesives and caulking compounds
Gift-wrap ribbons
Magnetic recording tape
Filament tape
Plastic tape
Reflective highway signs
Special abrasives
Premix-highway surfacing
Lithographic plates
Fluorochemicals
Surgical drapes
Electrical insulating materials
Electrical splicing materials
Technical ceramics
Reinforced plastics
Electrical insulating varnishes and papers
Extruded plastics

1935-1945

Industrial adhesives
Special tapes
Acetate and acetate fiber tape
Waterproof abrasive cloth
Abrasive belts
Pigments-chrome and iron oxide
Special synthetic resins
Gummed paper products
Sulfuric acid
Non-slip surfacing
Reflective sheeting
Tympan papers
Rubberized auto undercoating

1925-1934

Masking tape
Abrasive discs
Sandblast stencil
Automotive adhesives
Cellophane tape
Electrical tape
Shoe tape
Fiber packing
Roofing granules

1902-1924

Abrasive grain
Sandpaper
Waterproof sandpaper
Special varnishes
Wax and polish

Most of the Company's diversification during its first 52 years developed from within by natural steps with the Company's research in bonding materials for its coated abrasives, which led to the development of pressure sensitive tapes, adhesives and coatings, and other products. The above chart indicates the new products introduced in each period. Today 3M manufactures over 40 separate product lines.

NOTES

CHAPTER 1

1. 1954 gross sales.
2. Editorial, Duluth *News Tribune,* August 30, 1901.

CHAPTER 2

1. Company Minutes, November 14, 1902 and December 2, 1902.
2. As quoted in the Two Harbors *Iron News*, March 20, 1903.
3. As quoted in the Two Harbors *Iron News,* January 30, 1903.
4. Company Minutes, February 7, 1903.
5. Two Harbors *Iron News*, May 26, 1899.
6. William A. McGonagle, *Early Recollections of Duluth & Iron Range Railroad*, undated, unpublished manuscript on file at the Minnesota Historical Society, File H.S. MS FHE 2791.D84M2.

CHAPTER 3

1. Two Harbors *Iron News*, August 14, 1903.
2. Two Harbors *Iron News*, November 3, 1903.
3. Directors' Minutes, October 6, 1903.
4. Two Harbors *Iron News*, January 22, 1904.
5. Two Harbors *Iron News*, May 6, 1904.

CHAPTER 4

1. St. Paul *Pioneer Press*, Sunday, May 3, 1885.
   Report on Lucius Ordway's marriage to Miss Jessie Gilman on April 29, 1885.
2. Duluth *News Tribune*, May 3, 1905.
3. Two Harbors *Iron News,* May 5, 1905.

CHAPTER 5

1. Historical material on abrasives were gathered, for the most part, from an industrial trade journal, the *Abrasive Industry*, as follows:

   Vol. 2, No. 2. W.S. McConnell, *Using Garnet Paper Economically*.

   Vol. 4, No. 4. Editorial, *Development of Coated Abrasives*.

   Vol. 4, No. 4. A.J. Sidford, *Surface Abrasive Manufacturers Develop Improvements*.

   Vol. 4, No. 4. Francis D. Bowman, *Use of Coated Abrasive Products*.

   Vol. 4, No. 7. *Automobile Bodies Finished With Abrasives*.

   Vol. 5, No. 6. *Quantity Production of Chairs*.

   Vol. 5, No. 6. *Sandpaper Industry Is Reviewed*.

   Vol. 17, No. 11. *Coated Abrasive Cloth Has Many Uses*.

2. Agreement dated March 23, 1905, in company archives.

3. Directors' Minutes, March 7, 1907.

4. Report on file at First National Bank, St. Paul; used with permission.

5. Directors' Minutes, March 16, 1907.

CHAPTER 6

1. Duluth *News Tribune*, May 13, 1907.

CHAPTER 7

1. Henry A. Castle, *St. Paul and Vicinity*, Lewis Publishing Company, 1912.

2. St. Paul *Pioneer Press*, April 17, 1910.

CHAPTER 8

1. Mrs. Bush later founded the Edyth Bush Little Theater, in St. Paul, Minnesota (1940) for the purpose of giving Midwesterners interested in theater work a chance to get experience under professional conditions.

CHAPTER 11

1. Draft of a letter officially approved by the 3M officers for sending out in reply to inquiries about the affairs of the company. Copy of letter in company archives.

2. Letter in company archives.

3. Minutes from special board of directors' meeting, August 11, 1916.

CHAPTER 12

1. Figures taken from a report by Archibald S. Dean, M.D., "An Epidemic of Lead Poisoning Caused by the Sandpapering of Automobile Bodies," *Journal of Industrial Hygiene*, Vol. VI, No. 6, October, 1924, pp. 245-250.

CHAPTER 13

1. Parliamentary Debates, House of Commons, England, Vol. 174, No. 90, Friday, June 20, 1924.

2. Memorandum sent by W.L. McKnight to Carlton Corwin, 3M engineer, dated May 5, 1928.

CHAPTER 14

1. Memorandum written by W.L. McKnight to key men on profit-sharing plan. Copy in Profit Sharing file, chairman of board's office. December, 1936.

2. *Three-M-News*, January 20, 1928.

3. E.B. Ober release to press dated August 1, 1929.

4. Directors' Minutes, August 12, 1929.

CHAPTER 17

1. Excerpt from letter written by Shellmar Products Corporation, Chicago, to Minnesota Mining and Manufacturing Company on September 24, 1930.

CHAPTER 18

1. St. Paul *Dispatch*, October 24, 1932.

CHAPTER 19

1. St. Paul *Pioneer Press*, February 4, 1936.
2. St. Paul *Pioneer Press*, September 3, 1937.

CHAPTER 20

1. From records in unemployment compensation file, office of chairman of board.
2. Ibid.
3. Ibid.

CHAPTER 21

1. 3M's "NW Manual."
2. Ibid.

CHAPTER 22

1. Findings of the Quartermaster team appeared in the book *German Plastics Practice* in which composition of tapes used with the Magnetophone was revealed. This book was published with the permission of the Department of Commerce by Murray Printing Company, Cambridge, Massachusetts, in 1946.

CHAPTER 23

1. "The White Line Isn't Enough," *The Saturday Evening Post*, Vol. 210, March 26, 1938, p. 12.

GENERAL REFERENCES

Publications

Two Harbors (Minnesota) *Iron News* (1898-1910)

Duluth (Minnesota) *News Tribune* (1902-1919)

St. Paul (Minnesota) *Pioneer Press* (1910-1952)

St. Paul *Dispatch* (1926-1952)

New York *Times* (1948-1952)

Abrasive Industry, Iron Age, Journal of Industrial Hygiene, The Saturday Evening Post, Science Illustrated, The Reader's Digest, American City, Travel, Fortune, Business Week, Time.

Books and Pamphlets

William E. Culkin, *North Shore Names and Places.* Scott-Mitchell Publishing Company, St. Paul, Minnesota. Minnesota Historical Society File F552. C93.

South Dakota, Fifty Years of Progress, 1889-1939. South Dakota Golden Anniversary Book Company, Sioux Falls, South Dakota.

Dwight Lowell Dumond, *America in Our Time, 1896-1946.* Henry Holt & Co., Inc., 1947.

Mark Sullivan, *Our Times: The United States 1900-1925*, Vol. 4. Charles Scribner's Sons, 1932.

James Blaine Walker, *The Epic of American Industry.* Harper & Brothers, 1949.

William Watts Folwell, *A History of Minnesota*, Vol. IV, 1930.

Minnesota and Its People, Vol. III. Minnesota Historical

Society F606B16.

Book of Minnesotans. A. N. Marquis Company, 1907.

Two Harbors in 1910. Minnesota Historical Society F612.

Edward Goodrich Acheson, *A Pathfinder* (Memoirs). 1910.

Additional Sources

Directors' Minutes and Minutes of Annual Stockholders' Meetings, 1902-1952.

Three-M-News, 1927-1928.

3M Megaphone, 1941-1954.

Company letter files, annual reports, laboratory records, and personal interviews with 3M employees, their relatives, and North Shore residents.

Miscellaneous files of the St. Louis County Historical Society, Duluth, Minnesota, and the Minnesota Historical Society, St. Paul, Minnesota.

INDEX